The Food of a Younger Land

The Food of a Younger Land

A PORTRAIT OF AMERICAN FOOD—*before the national highway system, before chain restaurants, and before frozen food, when the nation's food was seasonal, regional, and traditional*—**FROM THE LOST WPA FILES**

Edited and illustrated by

MARK KURLANSKY

RIVERHEAD BOOKS
a member of
Penguin Group (USA) Inc.
New York
2009

RIVERHEAD BOOKS
Published by the Penguin Group
Penguin Group (USA) Inc., 375 Hudson Street, New York, New York 10014, USA • Penguin Group (Canada),
90 Eglinton Avenue East, Suite 700, Toronto, Ontario M4P 2Y3, Canada (a division of Pearson Canada Inc.)
• Penguin Books Ltd, 80 Strand, London WC2R 0RL, England • Penguin Ireland, 25 St Stephen's Green, Dublin 2,
Ireland (a division of Penguin Books Ltd) • Penguin Group (Australia), 250 Camberwell Road, Camberwell,
Victoria 3124, Australia (a division of Pearson Australia Group Pty Ltd) • Penguin Books India Pvt Ltd,
11 Community Centre, Panchsheel Park, New Delhi–110 017, India • Penguin Group (NZ), 67 Apollo Drive,
Rosedale, North Shore 0632, New Zealand (a division of Pearson New Zealand Ltd) • Penguin Books (South Africa)
(Pty) Ltd, 24 Sturdee Avenue, Rosebank, Johannesburg 2196, South Africa

Penguin Books Ltd, Registered Offices: 80 Strand, London WC2R 0RL, England

Grateful acknowledgment is made to reprint the following images from the Library of Congress, Prints
and Photographs Division, FSA/OWI Collection: LC-USZ62-135594; LC-USF34-017515-E (Dorothea Lange);
LC-USF33-12379-M1 (Russell Lee); LC-USF33-003442-M2 (Arthur Rothstein); LC-USF33-013190-M4 (Russell
Lee); LC-USF33-012964-M5 (Russell Lee); LC-USF33-011941-M4 (Russell Lee);
LC-USF33-003234-M3 (Arthur Rothstein); LC-USF34-035370-D (Russell Lee).

Library of Congress Cataloging-in-Publication Data

The food of a younger land : a portrait of American food—before the national highway system, before
chain restaurants, and before frozen food, when the nation's food was seasonal, regional, and
traditional—from the lost WPA files / edited and illustrated by Mark Kurlansky.
p.   cm.
Includes bibliographical references and index.
ISBN 978-1-59448-865-8
1. Cookery, American—History.   2. Food habits—United States—History.   3. Cookery, American.
I. Kurlansky, Mark.   II. United States. Works Progress Administration.
TX715.F685   2009   2009008100
394.1'20973—dc22

Printed in the United States of America
1   3   5   7   9   10   8   6   4   2

Book design by Chris Welch
Woodcuts by the author

To the memory of Studs Terkel, one of the last of them, who talked, listened, mixed a martini, told a story, cracked a joke, thought through an issue, and fought the good fight better than most anyone else. Studs, you left just as I began to hope you would live forever. Maybe you will.

Never play cards with a man called Doc. Never eat at a place called Mom's. Never sleep with a woman whose troubles are greater than your own.

—NELSON ALGREN, *A Walk on the Wild Side,* 1956

This book is not an attempt to produce what *America Eats* might have been if it had been edited and pieces selected. Instead, it is a sampling of the broad and rich mountain of copy that the dying Federal Writers' Project generated for this, their final effort. I made selections of the most interesting pieces—poetry, short stories, essays, interviews, and recipes—because to publish all of it would have required several volumes. The reader can experience the archaeologist's adventure that I had sifting through these unedited and unpublished manuscripts with all their blemishes, including misspellings, bad English, bad Spanish, and chaotic recipes that sometimes require a cook's imagination to make work. In the process, forgotten cuisines and a vanished world are unearthed. This is the fun of finding a seventy-year-old raw manuscript.

CONTENTS

THE SOUTH EATS

THE MIDDLE WEST EATS

THE FAR WEST EATS

THE SOUTHWEST EATS

AN INFORMAL BIBLIOGRAPHY

Introduction

When someone says to me, "I went to Chicago last week" or "I went down to Virginia this summer," a question always comes into my mind, though I often resist asking it: "What did you eat? Anything interesting?"

I would like to know what politicians eat on the campaign trail, what Picasso ate in his pink period, what Walt Whitman ate while writing the verse that defined America, what midwesterners bring to potlucks, what is served at company banquets, what is in a Sunday dinner these days, and what workers bring for lunch. What people eat is not well documented. Food writers prefer to focus on fashionable, expensive restaurants whose creative dishes reflect little of what most people are eating. We know everything about Paris restaurants but nothing about what Parisians eat. We know little about what Americans eat and less about what they ate.

A few years ago, while putting together *Choice Cuts*, an anthology of food writing, I discovered to my amazement that government bureaucrats in Washington in the late 1930s were having similar thoughts. But these were not typical bureaucrats because they worked for an agency that was unique in American history, the Works Progress Administration, or WPA. The WPA was charged with finding work for millions of unemployed Americans. It sought work in every imaginable field. For unemployed writers the WPA created the Federal Writers' Project, which was charged with conceiving books, assigning them to huge, unwieldy teams of out-of-work and want-to-be writers around the country, and editing and publishing them.

After producing hundreds of guidebooks on America in a few hurried

years, a series that met with greater success than anyone had imagined possible for such a government project, the Federal Writers' Project administrators were faced with the daunting challenge of coming up
with projects to follow their first achievements. Katherine Kellock, the
writer-turned-administrator who first conceived the idea for the guidebooks, came up with the thought of a book about the varied food and
eating traditions throughout America, an examination of what and how
Americans ate.

She wanted the book to be enriched with local food disagreements,
and it included New England arguments about the correct way to make
clam chowder, southern debate on the right way to make a mint julep,
and an absolute tirade against mashed potatoes from Oregon. It captured now nearly forgotten food traditions such as the southern New
England May breakfast, foot washings in Alabama, Coca-Cola parties in
Georgia, the chitterling strut in North Carolina, cooking for the threshers in Nebraska, a Choctaw funeral, and a Puget Sound Indian salmon
feast. It also had old traditional recipes such as Rhode Island jonny
cakes, New York City oyster stew, Georgia possum and taters, Kentucky
wilted lettuce, Virginia Brunswick stew, Louisiana tête de veau, Florida
conch, Minnesota lutefisk, Indiana persimmon pudding, Utah salmi
of wild duck, and Arizona menudo. Ethnic food was covered, including
black, Jewish, Italian, Bohemian, Basque, Chicano, Sioux, Chippewa,
and Choctaw. Local oddities, such as the Automat in New York, squirrel
Mulligan in Arkansas, Nebraska lamb fries or Oklahoma prairie oysters,
and ten-pound Puget Sound clams, were featured. Social issues were
remembered, as in the Maine chowder with only potatoes, the Washington State school lunch program, and the western Depression cake. There
was also humor to such pieces, as the description of literary teas in New
York, the poem "Nebraskans Eat the Weiners," and the essay on trendy
food in Los Angeles.

Kellock called the project *America Eats.*

If I search my childhood memories, having been born in the late
1940s, I can recall some of the lingering vestiges of the America that is
described in *America Eats.* It was an America without fast food. Even in
restaurants and at roadside stands, the prevailing style was what might

be called "home cooking." Home cooking was a mixed blessing, as it is in many homes, better than the industrialized fare along today's expressways but not as good as many of today's restaurants. The interstate highway system had not yet been built, and Americans traveled through farm country and down the main streets of towns on two-lane roads in dark-colored cars with standard transmissions, split windshields, and simple dashboards with radios that worked on occasion and clocks that never kept time.

Most people had refrigerators that older people referred to as Frigidaires, after the brand, the way some of us today still call photocopies Xeroxes. Some people still had iceboxes, but ice deliveries were becoming scarce. Frozen food was sold, but the tiny little freezers in the new modern refrigerators frosted up, did not maintain low temperatures, and, in any event, had little space. A freezer cold enough to keep food safely for long periods or to keep ice cream hard was rare. It was still best to go to the soda fountain for ice cream, and you always got a seltzer on the side.

America had few suburbs and a lot of farms and farming families, and most of the coastal towns had commercial fishing boats. Food was seasonal, and an early melon from Texas or a winter carrot from California was a noted event. I can still remember when my great-uncle Max shipped us a crate of individually wrapped grapefruits from Florida.

Food was far more regional than it is today. Being raised in New England and New York, I was struck by the differences in how people ate in other parts of the country—how breakfasts got bigger as you traveled west and hamburgers became increasingly adorned until by California they were virtually a salad sandwich. In New England you ate corn relish or cottage cheese, each served in little metal cups before the meal in the better restaurants, where popovers were often dispensed from a deep tin box, big enough to be an oven and strapped to the server's shoulders. You had to find a Jewish bakery to get a respectable rye bread. Crusty bread came from Italian bakeries. Italian food was served in tomato sauce, and though macaroni and spaghetti came in many shapes and sizes, no one called it "pasta" even though the dish before it was frequently called "antipasto." My parents liked Italian neighborhoods because there and nowhere else you could get an espresso, known as a *demitasse*.

As you left the Northeast you said good-bye to almost all traces of Jewish food, including bagels, until you reached California. I remember being struck by the fried food and the powdered sugar in the South. In Seattle we ate aplets and cotlets, the little apricot or apple sugar-dusted fruit bars of Washington state. In Albuquerque I thrilled to my first taste of Mexican food and in Pismo Beach, California, I got to eat for the first time wonderful crunchy sandwiches called tacos.

The only chain restaurants I recall were A&W Root Beer, with frothy root beer on tap, and Howard Johnson's, a New England company—my father claimed to have worked as a student for Howard himself in the first store in Quincy, Massachusetts—and I liked their ice cream and their fried clams.

America was starting to build highways, sell farms to build suburbs, and industrialize the production of food. The ways of prewar America were rapidly vanishing. The war industries that brought America out of the Depression had changed the landscape. I grew up in a blue-collar community on the edge of Hartford where people worked in factories and crowded into neighborhood housing. It in no way resembled the description of it in the 1938 WPA Guide for Connecticut, the first of the guides after which the rest were modeled. The guide characterizes the crowded, fast-growing industrial area I knew as an "attractive verdant setting."

From 1940 to 1950 the population of the United States increased from 20 million to 151 million, and Americans became far more affluent. In that same decade the gross national product of the United States nearly tripled. The average yearly expenditures of an American also nearly tripled. But despite the growth in the economy, the value of exports in 1950 was only a third of what it had been in 1940. The country was changing from an export-based economy to a consumer-based one. By 1950, the military-industrial complex that Eisenhower would warn about in his 1961 farewell address had already firmly taken root. In 1950 government military spending was seven times as much as it had been in 1940.

There were twice as many cars on the roads. America was becoming a less family-centered society, which was having an enormous impact on the way Americans ate. In 1940 there were 264 divorces for every thousand people. By 1950 the divorce rate had risen to 385 per thousand.

America was becoming much more multicultural. From 1935 to 1940, the WPA years, 308,000 immigrants were officially admitted to the United States. After the war, from 1945 to 1950, 864,000 were taken in, and in the next five years another million would be admitted.

But the most striking difference of all was that in 1940 America had rivers on both coasts teeming with salmon, abalone steak was a basic dish in San Francisco, the New England fisheries were booming with cod and halibut, maple trees covered the Northeast and syruping time was as certain as a calendar, and flying squirrels still leapt from conifer to hardwood in the uncut forests of Appalachia. All of this has changed. It is terrifying to see how much we have lost in only seventy years.

To see that prewar America was a very different country, one has only to contemplate the origin of *America Eats*. To anyone who knows and understands the United States, the fact that there was a Federal Writers' Project at all seems nothing short of miraculous. This is America, the land with no Ministry of Culture, where politicians alone are portrayed on the money. Almost unique among Western republics, the likeness of not one writer, philosopher, painter, or composer has ever graced the engraving of a U.S. bill or coin. The separation of church and state may be the great articulated legal principle, but another sacrosanct concept is the separation of state and culture. And yet there was an age when the U.S. government permanently employed painters, sculptors, playwrights, musicians, actors, and writers to produce art.

All this happened, we see in retrospect, because Franklin Delano Roosevelt was a politician of extremely rare gifts. He was one of the few U.S. presidents who understood how to use an electoral mandate, what to do in that rare moment of goodwill in the American political process when, having handily won a presidential election, there is an opportunity to accomplish politically dubious things while your party is still celebrating and the opposition can only hope that, given enough rope, the new leader will surely hang himself.

Roosevelt's mandate was derived from bringing his Democratic party back to power in 1932 while the gross national product was in precipitous decline, a third of the American labor force was out of work, and millions were facing the possibility of real starvation. It was also perhaps the only moment in history in which the United States had a large leftist intelligentsia—so large, in fact, that the Communist Party of America, besieged by membership applications, was actually rejecting some.

Roosevelt's secret weapon, his powerful political tactic, was unstoppable and unreasoning optimism. He was so exuberant, so irritatingly frothy, that he was the perfect antidote to an age known as the Great Depression.

Triumphantly, electoral mandate in hand, Roosevelt declared that the government should "quit this business of relief." It was the new president's contention that in this moment of crisis, when so large a portion of the population was unemployed, it was vital to "not only sustain these people but to preserve their self-respect, their self-reliance, and courage, and determination." His idea was to let the unemployed earn money by working for the federal government. Despite considerable controversy, by April 1935, fifteen months after Roosevelt's inauguration, the Emergency Relief Act of 1935 was passed. This law gave the president the power to decree work relief programs. A few weeks later, on May 6, Roosevelt issued an executive order creating the Works Progress Administration, the WPA.

Roosevelt was proceeding with skill and caution. The WPA was a public works program that would put blue-collar laborers to work building government projects, a program that was only slightly controversial. There was the issue of whether a country with a rapidly shrinking GNP should be spending like this. But many argued that they should, in order to stimulate the economy. The WPA, both to simplify its tasks and to draw less controversy, tended toward many small, easily launched projects rather than a few massive ones. The executive order had called for "small useful projects."

But the Emergency Relief Act had also called for "assistance to educational and clerical persons; a nation-wide program for useful employment for artists, musicians, actors, entertainers, writers . . ." By the summer of 1935 Federal Project Number 1, popularly known as Federal

One, was under way. It included the Federal Art Project, Federal Music Project, Federal Theater Project, and Federal Writers' Project, all mandated by law in that one barely noticed phrase in the Emergency Relief Act.

At its height the Federal Art Project employed 5,300 artists, including Jackson Pollock, Mark Rothko, Jacob Lawrence, and Marsden Hartley, and staffed one hundred art centers in twenty-two states. The Federal Music Project, directed by former Cleveland Symphony conductor Nikolai Sokoloff, gave 5,000 performances. The Federal Theatre Project employed 12,700 people, including Orson Welles, John Houseman, Burt Lancaster, Joseph Cotten, Will Geer, Virgil Thomson, Nicholas Ray, E. G. Marshall, and Sidney Lumet, produced more than 1,200 plays in four years, mostly free of charge, and introduced one hundred new playwrights.

Writers, too, were in desperate need of work. Newspapers and magazines were folding as declining advertising revenue was being increasingly diverted to radio. Book sales were decreasing every year, even for established writers. The Federal Writers' Project directed pools of writers in each of the forty-eight states. New York City had its own project in addition to the New York State Writers' Project, and California was divided into Northern and Southern. In all there were fifty local projects answering to the FWP.

The poet W. H. Auden called the Federal Writers' Project "one of the noblest and most absurd undertakings ever attempted by any state." The idea was received by the public with predictable cynicism. Subsidizing art has never been popular with Americans. Subsidizing anything in America comes under attack. The workers of the WPA were called "shovel leaners." Now the workers of the Federal Writers' Project were labeled "pencil leaners." Editorials argued that poverty and adversity, not government subsidies, produced great writing.

The writers were constantly under suspicion of boondoggling. When the New York City Writers' Project produced a translation of the biblical *Song of Songs* from the original Hebrew into Yiddish, one perennial critic of the program looked at the translation and noticed that Yiddish, a High German language, is written with Hebrew letters. He charged, as though he had at last found a smoking gun, that they were both the same language. Others denounced the FWP as an encroachment on states' rights. Congressional criticism culminated in hearings by the House Un-American Activities Committee under Texas Democrat Martin Dies in late 1938 on alleged Communist ties, which caused considerable difficulties because, in fact, many of the better-known writers in the FWP had at one time or another had Communist affiliations. But the real goal was to attempt to show a Communist underpinning to Roosevelt's New Deal, ironic since many historians today credit the New Deal with stopping the growth of Communism in the United States.

When Henry Alsberg, a native New Yorker, was appointed director of the FWP at the age of fifty-seven, he had been a newspaper journalist, off-Broadway director, and writer, but was little known outside of New York. He had graduated from Columbia Law School at the age of twenty and had worked as a foreign correspondent, covering the tumultuous early days of the Soviet Union. He had experienced numerous adventures as a correspondent and later as director of the American Joint Distribution Committee. For a long time he contemplated an autobiography but could never finish it and went to work for Roosevelt's New Deal. As director of the FWP, a chain-smoker chronically in search of something on his ash-strewn desk, he quickly earned a reputation for his inept administrative style and his high editorial standards. Alsberg was constantly at odds with the administration over the conflict between his goal of producing good books and theirs of simply providing relief work.

The first problem of the FWP was deciding who was eligible. If it was to be only writers, what was the definition of a writer? Did it have to be a published writer? In the end, in keeping with the initial intention of the WPA, almost anyone who was reasonably literate and needed a job qualified. This included secretaries who had worked on the many local newspapers that had now folded. In fact, people who could type were especially valued. Advertising copywriters qualified, as did technical writers and out-of-work teachers. So did published poets and the authors of well-received novels.

Stetson Kennedy, then an inexperienced young aspiring writer, recalled his work for the Florida Writers' Project: "To work for the FWP you had to take an oath that you had no money, no job, and no property. I was eminently qualified." He, along with Zora Neale Hurston, the only published novelist of the two hundred people hired for the Florida project, were taken on as junior interviewers for $37.50 every two weeks. "I remember going window shopping with my wife trying to decide what we would do with all the money," said Kennedy.

The wage scale varied from state to state. A New York writer received $103 a month, and Georgia and Mississippi paid $39. Cities such as New York, Boston, Chicago, and San Francisco had a concentration of talented writers. The project would have liked to move some of those writers to other states where there was a shortage, but the pay difference made these writers unwilling to move. In some of the hard-hit prairie states where there were few professional writers, employment in the Federal Writers' Project saved unqualified people and their families from literal starvation. That, too, was a goal of the WPA.

In Chicago, the Illinois Writers' Project, directed by John T. Frederick, an English professor with an eye for emerging midwestern talent, had Nelson Algren. Algren was one of the few writers on the project who already had a published novel to his credit. Other writers in Chicago included Saul Bellow, who had recently graduated from college; Jack Conroy, who was born in a mining camp and had earned praise for two novels of working-class life; and Richard Wright, who had worked in a post office until he found employment with the Writers' Project, working on guidebooks while he wrote *Native Son* in his spare time. Arna Bontemps published his third novel, *Drums at Dusk*, while working as a supervisor. Other members of the Chicago group included oral historian Studs Terkel, who wrote radio scripts for the project, and dancer, choreographer, and anthropologist Katherine Dunham.

———

Conrad Aiken and Josef Berger were among the noted writers on the Massachusetts Project. The New York City Project had Maxwell Bodenheim, Ralph Ellison, Kenneth Patchen, Philip Rahv, and Claude McKay, who in the 1920s had written the first bestseller in America by a black writer. John Cheever worked for the New York State Project. Kenneth Rexroth, the influential Beat poet, worked for the Northern California Writers' Project.

Ralph Ellison and Claude McKay were among the prominent writers who gathered material for novels while working for the FWP. In Florida Zora Neale Hurston, though kept at the lowest position, already had to her credit three books, including her best novel, *Their Eyes Were Watching God*, and was working on a second novel. It is not by chance that African-American literature—Wright, Ellison, McKay, Hurston—made such advances under the FWP. Starting in 1936, one of the major projects under folklore editor John A. Lomax was to interview the remaining blacks in America who had memories of slavery. Every WPA guidebook included a section on black history and culture at a time when this subject was almost never taken on. Several directors felt that blacks should be working on these projects. But a February 1937 report showed that of 4,500 workers on the FWP only 106 were black.

In truth, blacks often were not treated well in the southern projects. Hurston, despite her literary accomplishment, was placed on the bottom rung of Florida workers, paid even a few dollars less than the bottom salary because allegedly it would cost her so little to live in a rural black township. When she joined the Florida Writers' Project in 1938, the Florida editorial staff was called together and told, "Zora Neale Hurston, the Florida Negro novelist, has signed onto the project and will soon be paying us a visit. Zora has been feted by New York literary circles, and is given to putting on airs, including the smoking of cigarettes in the presence of white people. So we must all make allowances for Zora."

The talented writers, both veteran and promising, were rare. Yes,

Frederick worked in Chicago with Bellow, Wright, and Algren. But he also had on the staff a calligrapher who, for lack of anything else to do, produced handsome business cards for the other writers. Challenged on the competence of FWP writers, director Henry Alsberg could produce the names of only 29 established writers out of 4,500 on the project. In mid-1938 a survey of the FWP staff showed that 82 were recognized writers and another 97 had held major editorial positions. According to the report, 238 had at some time sold something to a newspaper or magazine and 161 were labeled "beginning writers of promise." This left only another 3,893 "writers" to explain.

Working with such an uneven staff limited them to projects to which everyone could contribute and then one or two "real writers" could rework. It was Katherine Kellock, a writer who worked for Roosevelt's New Deal, who came up with an idea. She said that the Federal Writers' Project ought to "put them to work writing Baedekers," the leading English-language guidebooks of the time. This was the birth of the American Guide Series.

Katherine Kellock had given up a higher-paying job to move to the FWP and work on her idea, the guidebooks. She both talked and worked at a feverish rate. There were many jokes about the verbose Mrs. Kellock. She took on the guidebooks as a personal mission, criticizing and cajoling the various state organizations in visits and letters. After she became plagued by an accusation in the Hearst newspapers that she was a Communist, Alsberg called her in from the field and gave her a job supervising from Washington. The accusation was largely based on the fact that her husband was a correspondent for the Soviet news agency, TASS.

A small woman with a giant voice, she was often abrasive, but it was widely recognized that all she wanted was to produce great guidebooks. She believed it was important for Americans to finally start examining America. She often told workers not to worry about the writing but to just send in the information. She hungered for particulars on agriculture and history and pushed the books into a richness of detail.

It was often said that Kellock developed an appreciation of the Baedeker guides while traveling through Europe, which sounds like she was on a vacation. In fact, she had been traveling through southern and central Europe with Quaker relief organizations trying to stave off starvation in areas that had been devastated by World War I.

Baedeker had done its last guidebook on the United States in 1893 and last updated it in 1909. It had been written by an Englishman for the English. There was no guide to America for or by Americans. Many, including Henry Alsberg, believed that this could be extremely important work—the first detailed study of America, its people, culture, and ways. The Depression had awakened in Americans a deep interest in the country and for the first time in its history it was becoming fashionable to examine and look for the meaning of America and what it was to be American.

This new self-searching was clearly expressed in two 1940 songs. First there was Irving Berlin's "God Bless America," which was repeatedly bellowed on the radio by the ungentle voice of Kate Smith. Finally, a twenty-eight-year-old singer named Woody Guthrie—named after Woodrow Wilson, who was elected the year he was born, 1912—could not stand hearing Kate Smith anymore, and he wrote an antidote called "This Land Is Your Land." It is a melodic song celebrating, as does the Berlin song, the diversity and natural beauty of America. Originally the last line of the chorus was "God blessed America for me," but Guthrie later changed it to "this land was made for you and me." Guthrie's song, unlike Berlin's, also asked questions about the people who were being locked out of the American dream—the hungry, the people in welfare lines—and he asked this question toward the end of the song: "Is this land made for you and me?" Today the critical final stanza is almost never heard.

These two songs reflected a growing split in American culture, and one that would continue. Two Americas emerged out of the early twentieth century, and in 1940 each got its anthem. Kellock's idea for the guidebooks was for them to be a Guthrie song, not a Berlin—really examining and not backing off from the hard social issues.

Because they pleased local chambers of commerce and tourism interests, the guidebooks were able to garner more support for the FWP than most writing projects would have yielded. Even conservative newspapers that attacked the New Deal would accept the Federal Writers' Project because it gave work to their newspapermen who had been laid off. But this meant that these local interests had leverage to exert influence on the projects. The local chamber of commerce kept a discussion of labor disputes out of the guide to Pittsburg, Kansas, removing one of the few contentious issues in the book. Local pressure eliminated all historic debate from the description of the siege of the Alamo in the San Antonio Guide. Because the FWP was a government agency, conservative congressmen also had a say, forcing the New Jersey Guide to remove a reference to tear gas being used against striking workers. And labor issues in Butte were removed from the Montana Guide.

FWP employees wrote with a wide range of skills. As long as they were able to deliver copy containing information, a handful of reliable writers could amalgamate it and turn it into books. Some copy was little more than lists of facts. Others sent in short stories and poetry. Supervisors also came with varying levels of competence. According to Jerre Mangione, who worked on the FWP, Lyle Saxon, a supervisor in the South, was sent to one southern state director, the aunt of a senator, to find out why all of Kellock's instructions were ignored and only literary attempts were being sent in. The woman ushered Saxon into a stately pillared mansion to a room where her staff was at work and said, "Have you ever seen such an inspiring sight? Seventeen poets, all in one room, writing poetry seven hours a day."

Experienced professionals such as Lyle Saxon gathered the material and wrote the books. The Massachusetts book was largely written by Merle Colby, from an old New England family, who wrote about the history of New Englanders. Idaho was written by Vardis Fisher, who was thought to be one of the most promising western writers, often compared to his close friend Thomas Wolfe and to Faulkner and Hemingway. While his reputation has not endured, largely because he put aside the writing of successful novels for failed tomes of ancient history, he did write thirty-six books by the time of his death in 1968. Today Fisher's books remain in print and still have a following in Idaho, where he is also remembered for having commissioned for his home Idaho's only Frank Lloyd Wright building.

———————

By 1939 Katherine Kellock could see the guidebooks coming to an end. Guides had been done or were in progress for each of the forty-eight states, Puerto Rico, Alaska, and Washington, D.C. Guides to about thirty cities plus regions and even small towns had been published. They were an unexpected success. Some of the guidebooks are in print today and remain useful and enjoyable. Alfred Kazin, writing about 1930s literature in 1942, credited the guidebooks with considerable literary merit and wrote that they "set the tone of the period." But now the FWP was in need of a new idea, new ways of examining America. It turned to ethnic themes such as *Armenians in Massachusetts* and *Italians in New York* and the New York City Writers' Project planned one on Jews and Italians in New York with the working subtitle *From Shofar to Swing*. But Kellock had the idea for a nationwide examination of how America eats.

America Eats was to be put together very much like the guidebooks, with many contributions amalgamated into a few essays by the handful of competent writers. It came out of the ethnic books, which in turn came out of the "Negro" sections of the guidebooks. It was to be a book on eating traditions and foods in the various parts of the United States. Like most of the FWP work, it would have a strong social and anthropological component. It would show varying ethnic traditions as well as the regional and local customs.

With the Depression waning and war looming, it was clear that America and its customs would soon be changing. By the 1930s frozen food was appearing. Industrial food from the beginning of the century, such as Jell-O, factory-made bread, and cake mixes, was making huge gains in the market from new advertising vehicles such as radio. What could better spell the beginning of the end than bottled salad dressing, the manufacture of a product that was so easy to make at home? The editors of *America Eats* understood that in another ten years American food would be very different.

The Washington office sent a memo to regional editors calling for *America Eats* to be a 75,000-word book on "American cookery and the part it has played in the national life, as exemplified in the group meals that preserve not only traditional dishes but also traditional attitudes and customs. Emphasis should be divided between food and people."

According to the plan, the writing was to be "light but not tea shoppe, masculine not feminine." This odd but important statement was Kellock's effort to have food writing approached more seriously. Kellock did not want *America Eats* to be like most of the food writing of the day that generally appeared in women's magazines or in women's sections of newspapers. These items, almost always written by women and for women, followed the belief that women were not interested in politics and social problems. The style was bright and cheerful and all issues and social observations were avoided.

The memo went on to say, "In describing group meals tell how they are organized, who supplies and cooks the food, what the traditional dishes are, what local opinion is on heretical variations in the recipe, and what the group mores are in connection with the meal. (Virginia, for example, dusts shellfish lightly with flour before frying and scorns the Maryland custom of dipping the fish in batter.)"

Being a government agency, the FWP divided the country in accordance with the peculiarities of the U.S. Census Bureau. Like the census, the book was to have five regions, and it titled them "The Northeast Eats," "The South Eats," "The Middle West Eats," "The Far West Eats," and "The Southwest Eats." The South would include the old Confederacy minus Texas but with Kentucky, Maryland, West Virginia, Delaware, and Washington, D.C., added. Nevada and Utah were put in the Far West rather than the Southwest, and the FWP had its own invention of dividing California into Los Angeles–based Southern California in the Southwest and San Francisco–based Northern California in the Far West. The result was that the amount of copy from each region was determined not by the variety of foods, the size of the area, or the population, but rather by the number of separate Writers' Projects in each region. The South generated the most copy, because fifteen projects were reporting. The least copy came from the Southwest, with only five projects reporting. This unevenness, which is quite pronounced, probably would have been evened out in the final book. Each region was to have an essay of about one hundred pages and one, two, or three additional pieces.

The regional essays were to be produced by the Writers' Projects in whose writers Washington had particular confidence. That Louisiana was in charge of the South and Illinois with the Chicago staff was given the Middle West was predictable. But the Northeast was run by the New Jersey Project rather than New York City or Massachusetts; Arizona had the Southwest; and Montana, not Northern California with San Francisco, had the Far West. This may have reflected which projects were best holding together in the slowly evaporating FWP of 1940.

At its peak in April 1936, the Federal Writers' Project employed 6,686 people, but by the time *America Eats* was proposed in 1939 the project was down to 3,500. By November 1941 the number had dropped to 2,200. Writers didn't like working for the government and felt there was a stigma to writing for a welfare check. They also did not like writing without a byline. They left whenever they had another opportunity, and by 1940 the economy was improving. In that year alone, 2 million unemployed Americans found jobs.

Kenneth Rexroth, weary of doctoring bad writing, resigned in 1939. John Cheever, who disliked the people of Washington in their matching and predictable suits, wanted to leave, but Alsberg talked him into helping with the New York City Guide. He resigned after it came out in 1939. By 1941 Vardis Fisher had left the Idaho Writers' Project, which had few people remaining.

The New York City Writers' Project struggled to keep Richard Wright. Wright had been born in 1908 in Mississippi, the son of an illiterate sharecropper and his educated schoolteacher wife. The family moved to Memphis when he was young, and he got books from the library by presenting a signed note from a white friend stating, "Please let this niggar boy have the following books." Now, as he approached his thirties while working for the FWP, the blossoming of his career seemed an irresistible force. Most of the senior FWP editors were certain of it. He entered four short stories titled *Uncle Tom's Children* into a competition and won a

$500 prize. With that money he faded from FWP to finish *Native Son*. With Alsberg's help he won a Guggenheim grant. In 1940 *Native Son* was published and made Wright a literary star. But unlike Algren, Cheever, and many of the others, he always acknowledged a debt to the FWP for nurturing him.

Even Alsberg himself was removed, replaced by John D. Newsom, who, the reverse of his predecessor, had a reputation for getting things done but not for literary judgment.

Many of the greats and future greats were gone by the time *America Eats* copy started flowing in 1940. The writers were not eager for new projects. Stetson Kennedy recalled, "Washington kept cooking up these sidelines. *America Eats* was one of those sidelines." Nor were all the state directors enthusiastic. The Tennessee state director called Kellock's proposal "unusually uninspiring."

Lyle Saxon of New Orleans was placed in charge of the final editing of the project, something that never took place. Saxon had been considered a great catch for the FWP. As director of the Louisiana Writers' Project, he was a logical choice to be in charge of *America Eats*. He had been one of the few directors who had been able to turn in guidebooks clean enough and good enough for a final edit. His New Orleans Guide was considered the model guidebook, a local bestseller that is still read and referred to in New Orleans. In 1926 his short story "Cane River" had won an O. Henry Prize, and he was immediately hailed as the next great voice from the South. In the 1920s, while Saxon was working on the *Times-Picayune*, he hosted late-night salons with William Faulkner, Sherwood Anderson, and other celebrated literati in his French Quarter home. In 1937 his novel *Children of Strangers*, about mulattoes in northern Louisiana, was acclaimed by critics as the new great southern novel. He never fulfilled that promise, but he is still remembered in New Orleans for the New Orleans Guide, some of his Louisiana legends that are still in print, and for having been a character in the celebrated French Quarter literary scene. It is his nonfiction for which he is known today in New Orleans, and *America Eats* probably would have been one of his enduring accomplishments. Although a flagrant anti-Semite—he once wrote "a good massacre would do New York no end of good. It is

now the largest Jewish city in the world"—he considered himself a great
friend of "the Negro" and worked hard for a black presence in FWP
work.

Saxon was supposed to produce an overall essay on the South and
then the other four regional directors were to be given it as a model. In
addition, each region was to present a few "detailed descriptions of special eating occasions." The coverage of each region was to be two thirds
the essay and about one third the shorter pieces.

By 1941 several publishers, including Houghton Mifflin, which Lyle
Saxon preferred, and Harper & Brothers, had expressed interest in publishing *America Eats.*

The deadline for all copy was the end of Thanksgiving week 1941. On
December 3 a gentle reminder that the deadline had passed was sent
out. Four days later the Japanese attacked Pearl Harbor. Suddenly there
was a panic to try to complete the project before the FWP was shut down.
In the weeks following the December 7, 1941, attack, a flurry of letters
went out from Washington to the states urging them to get in their copy
before they were overrun by the war and to give progress reports on
America Eats in light of "the present emergency." One such letter to the
Massachusetts Project on December 26, 1941, said,

> This is a reminder that deadline for contributions to *America
> Eats* has long passed. Results of research already done should be
> sent at once to this office, even if in rough form and incomplete.
> It is highly important to conserve work already done, as the war
> effort may cause an abrupt change in the activities under the
> Writers' program.

In January 1942 Denis Delaney of the Massachusetts Project replied
that Massachusetts would not be able to make a major contribution to
America Eats because the state project had shrunk to the point that
most of their writers were replacements from other states who knew little of New England traditions.

Other states rushed in copy. The entire file for the state of Washington is stamped "received Dec. 17, 1941." All five regional essays were called in, and they arrived in various states of disrepair. New Jersey handed in the one for the Northeast with apologies, saying, "The whole essay boils down, I fear, to a list of foods, which we are aware falls short of the design of the book." They pleaded that more time would be needed to do the job as it should be done. Joseph Miller, the Arizona supervisor, sent in the Southwestern essay with apologies. "It's a shame, such an interesting subject, that more time couldn't have been taken to think the thing through." He then suggested that Saxon might be able to fix it. "He's a good writer." Some editors started talking about changing the book to place greater emphasis on the ability of the early pioneers to deal with privation, as more suitable to a book coming out in wartime.

On May 1, 1942, the Federal Writers' Project officially became the Writers' Unit of the War Services subdivision of the WPA, which went on to produce sixty-four Servicemen's Recreational Guides, a guide to the U.S. Naval Academy, books on military history, and books such as the *Bomb Squad Training Manual* from the Ohio Project.

On May 14 Katherine Kellock was dismissed with two weeks' notice and spent most of her remaining time making sure that every manuscript and letter she had was turned over to the Library of Congress, much of it with little cataloging or filing. On July 15 Lyle Saxon finally left the project without ever having edited *America Eats*.

By February 1943, when the WPA was finally closed down, some million words had been published about America by the Federal Writers' Project. There were at least 276 books and hundreds of pamphlets and brochures, in all more than one thousand publications. But *America Eats* was not one of them.

When I opened the files of *America Eats* in the U.S. Library of Congress, I felt as though I had accidentally stumbled back into prewar America. The manuscripts were all typed. Most of them were blurry duplicates, reproduced with carbon paper on that thin translucent paper that they used to call onionskin. The *America Eats* project often took articles from magazines or newspapers or earlier WPA publications and put them in their files with the intention of using them in the new book. These, too, were typed with duplicates in carbon paper because there were no copying machines. Within these gray cardboard boxes it was prewar America again.

What remained of *America Eats* is mostly to be found in these five boxes filled with onionskin carbon copies. There are also twenty-six photographs. This cache is clearly incomplete. The New York City pieces are entirely missing, at least some of them to be found in the Municipal Archives in New York amid the papers of another unpublished WPA project, *Feeding the City.* But of the many other missing papers, it is not always possible to say if the material was not produced or just had never been sent in to the Library of Congress. The Missouri file contains only a short memo about a cookbook. In the letters among the *America Eats* papers there is a reference to an outstanding piece on Down East cooking that had been prepared for the guide to Portland, Maine, and then omitted at the last moment to make room for photographs. At the request of the Maine Project, it was returned to them. This manuscript, which the note referred to as a "very valuable essay," vanished along with most of the Maine archive in a later fire.

The paper in the boxes at the Library of Congress amounts to a stack almost two feet high of raw, unedited manuscripts, many from amateur writers. It is far more material than the 75,000 words envisioned for the book, but FWP projects averaged 10 percent of the submitted material. A surprising number of essays begin with the line "In the fall, when the air turns crisp . . ." A memo from Washington stated, "The work should be done by creative writers who will avoid effusive style and the clichés adopted by some writers on food and who have been interested in sensory perception and in their fellow-men, their customs and crochets." This ideal was not always lived up to in these manuscripts the way it probably would have been in the final crafted book. But an astonishing array of interesting culinary and cultural observations are present.

Some of the manuscripts were information intended to be incorporated in the five regional essays. A range of short stories, poems, anecdotes, and essays were apparently vying to be run as the additional material that was to accompany the five essays. The *America Eats* staff was considering running this additional material with bylines. Professional and would-be professional writers seemed to be trying to make their pieces stand out so that they would be selected among the few signed articles. But some sent in notes, others recipes, and some submitted lists of local books for the informal bibliography.

Because many of the articles were to be incorporated into larger pieces, some have no byline. Some projects, such as New Mexico and New Hampshire, as a matter of practice, never used names. In states where authors are identified it is often in WPA fashion, as the "worker." Some of these unsigned manuscripts, though probably not many, may be from unnamed literary masters. Algren's contribution has been identified because it turns up in other collections, but inevitably, since it is not signed, there are some historians who question its authenticity.

Ironically, the chaotic pile of imperfect manuscripts has left us with a better record than would the nameless, cleaned-up, smooth-reading final book that Lyle Saxon was to have turned in. A more polished version would still be an interesting book today, a record of how Americans ate and what their social gatherings were like in the early 1940s. Like the guidebooks, it would have been well written and well laid out. And it would not have had frustrating holes and omissions. But we would have had little information on the original authors. There are among these boxes a few acknowledged masters, such as Algren and Eudora Welty, some forgotten literary stars of the 1930s, and authors of mysteries, thrillers, Westerns, children's books, and food books, as well as a few notable local historians, several noted anthropologists, a few important regional writers, playwrights, an actress, a political speechwriter, a biographer, newspaper journalists, a sportswriter, university professors and deans, and a few poets. They were white and black, Jews, Italians, and Chicanos—the sons and daughters of immigrants, descendants of Pilgrims, and of American Indians. Typical of the times, there were a few Communists, a lot of Democrats, and at least two Republicans.

One thing that shines through the mountain of individual submissions is how well they reflect the original directive: "Emphasis should be divided between food and people." It is this perspective that gives this work the feeling of a time capsule, a preserved glimpse of America in the early 1940s.

With this in mind, I selected not always the best but the most interesting pieces, both unsigned and signed. The plan called for line drawings, possibly by Ross Santee, a cowboy artist and writer who for a time directed the Arizona Project, but they were never made—it was first discussed three days before the Pearl Harbor attack. I decided to make linocuts, a popular book-illustrating technique of the period, and add a few photographs from the remarkable WPA photo archive. The files make it clear that the editors had intended to borrow, wherever necessary, from other WPA projects—they included in the manuscripts several guidebook items, some previously published and others unused.

Had *America Eats* been published as planned, we would have had a well-thought-out and organized, clearly written guide to the nation's food and eating customs just before the war. The southern section was to include a smoothly written fourteen-page essay by Lyle Saxon titled "We Refresh Our Hog Meat with Corn Pone," summing up the information from the essays, and one other individual piece, "South Carolina Backwoods Barbecue" by Genevieve Wilcox Chandler. Instead, we have a chaotic and energetic assortment of reports, stories, and poems on America and its food by hundreds of different voices, including a few who became prominent writers. Together these many writers in their different voices bring to life the food and people of 1940 America in a way the single-voiced, well-edited book would not have.

It is rare to find this kind of untouched paper trail into the past. Merle Colby, the Massachusetts writer of several of the guidebooks who had stayed on to the very end to edit service manuals, wrote the final report on *America Eats* to the Library of Congress, ending with the hope that "Here and there in America some talented boy or girl will stumble on some of this material, take fire from it, and turn it to creative use."

THE
NORTHEAST EATS

NEW JERSEY—*responsible for the region*

MAINE

NEW HAMPSHIRE

VERMONT

MASSACHUSETTS

RHODE ISLAND

CONNECTICUT

NEW YORK CITY

NEW YORK STATE

PENNSYLVANIA

The Northeast

T he strange bedfellows produced by collecting states in the U.S. Census groupings can be seen in this Northeastern segment. It may make sense to those from other parts of the country, but as any New York Yankees or Boston Red Sox fan can explain, New Yorkers and New Englanders regard their cultures as completely different. It is an age-old competition that began long before baseball, originating in the seventeenth century when conservative religious colonies controlled by England were competing with a commercial colony controlled by a Dutch trading company. Even after the British took over New Amsterdam in 1664 and renamed it New York, the competition between the ports of Boston and New York continued.

It is interesting that the FWP split New York City and New York State into separate groups because it is clear from their food contributions that New York State, especially Long Island, which was settled by people from Connecticut, has more in common with New England than with New York City.

New York City, Massachusetts, and Connecticut had all been stars of the FWP. But while New York City offered imaginative contributions despite having lost its most distinguished writers, the leading New England states were contributing very little by the time of *America Eats*, and Rhode Island, Vermont, and Maine became more important.

Eating in Vermont

ROALDUS RICHMOND

Roaldus Richmond was born in Barton, Vermont, in 1910 and died in New Hampshire in 1986. Starting out as an inexperienced young man in the Vermont Writers' Project, he went on to become a supervisor and started finding work writing Western adventure stories, including "The Chopping Block Kid," which was published in Dime Sports Magazine *in 1941, and "Duel with Death" for* Five-Novels *magazine in 1947. He later worked as an editor.*

In Vermont farmhouses and village homes there are three meals a day, breakfast, dinner and supper, and dinner comes at 12 o'clock noon, which is as it should be for men who rise early and work hard. It is characteristic that Vermonters care not at all that this custom may be derided as old-fashioned, out-moded and lacking in sophistication. Many country hotels in the state also uphold the order of dinner at noon and supper at six, both full and heavy meals. A working man with a long active forenoon behind him needs more than a sandwich and a glass of milk to sustain him through the afternoon.

In the larger towns and hotels and restaurants, however, the noontime meal is lunch, and dinner comes in the evening, which is quite proper for office workers and professional people, who do not toil with their hands and their muscles.

The following story is said to illustrate a certain type of Vermont character. Homer Field has been spending his usual forenoon on the steps of the general store, sunning himself, talking and whittling wood.

The town clock strikes twelve and Homer checks the time with his own thick watch, stirs lazily, sighs deeply, and gets slowly to his feet. "Waal, guess I'll go home to dinner," drawls Homer. "If it ain't ready on the table I'm going to give my wife hell, and if it is ready I ain't going to eat a damn thing." But most Vermonters eat well and heartily.

As a rule Vermonters are not enthusiastic about salads or fish, favorites with the sophisticated, although Vermont gardens and Vermont lakes and streams offer a wealth of possibilities for both dishes. Fancy foods and frothy things are not popular in the state, whose people go for plain, solid, substantial foodstuffs.

Vermonters love spices and use them extensively and expertly, as indicated in their gingerbread and honey cake, ginger and caraway and cinnamon cookies, spiced pickles, fruits, cakes, pies, and puddings. Vermont housewives excel in the making of spiced tomatoes, piccalilli, celery chowder, pickled butternuts, chili sauce, catsup, vinegar, pickled pears, and innumerable other pickled and spiced preparations.

Griddle cakes and sausage constitute a typical Vermont breakfast, the cakes done to a brown turn and flooded with golden Vermont syrup. Maple sugaring, by the way, is so important in the state that business and professional men use the term "sugar off," when they refer to closing some deal or transaction. "Well, Ed, it's about time we sugar that off." Vermont flapjacks, glorified griddle cakes, are sometimes eaten as a dessert, as well as for breakfast. Paper thin and plate-sized, the golden-brown flapjacks are spread thickly with butter, poured with amber maple syrup, and served piping hot.

Pickling time is a Vermont ritual in the fall, and the varieties produced are almost infinite: pickled pears, peaches, apples, plums, raspberries, cucumbers, red and green tomatoes, beets, and mustard pickles. There are others not so well known but equally delicious.

Lemon Pickle: Pare thinly a half-dozen lemons, remove the white and the seeds, and cut the pulp into slices. Put pulp and peel into a quart (or larger) jar, and sprinkle with salt. Let stand three days. In a quart of vinegar boil two or three blades of mace, a half-dozen cloves, two shallots, and some crushed mustard seed. Pour, boiling hot, over the lemons in the jar. Allow vinegar to cool, then cover tightly with a cloth, and in a month or so strain, bottle the liquid, and use the lemon as a pickle. Both the liquid and the pickle are especially good with veal cutlets or minced veal. (Cora Moore)

Sweet Pumpkin Pickle: Pumpkin is cut into squares of about two inches and placed in a preserving kettle with ten cups of cider vinegar, six cups of sugar, a teaspoonful of allspice, and three each of cinnamon, cloves and chopped ginger root. Boil two hours, adding a sliced lemon just before boiling point is reached. Scarcely known outside of the state, this is excellent with nearly any meat. (Cora Moore)

Spiced Pickled Apples: Sweet apples are pared, cored and cut in half, then cooked in boiling vinegar along with a spice bag and six pounds of brown sugar. In the spice bag should be a tablespoonful of whole cloves and a quarter-pound of stick cinnamon broken up. (Cora Moore)

Vermont Foods

CORA A. MOORE

1. *Spiced Beef:* Eaten cold for breakfast or supper. A round of beef is salted down for a week, then washed well and black pepper and mace rubbed in, then put into a stone stewpan along with 3 or 4 onions, sliced and fried, a few cloves; covered with water and baked for 5 hours. When cold, sliced and eaten as wanted.

2. *Pickled Butternuts:* So far as can be learned this idea originated and has been exclusively used in Vermont. Recipe—Butternuts should be

gathered last week of June. Pour over them a very strong salt and water brine and let the nuts lie in it for 12 days. Drain them and pour over them cold cider vinegar which has been boiled with some mustard seed, horseradish, cloves, allspice and peppercorns. Cover tightly and keep for a year before using.

3. *Baked Indian Pudding:* Heat 4 cups of milk, add ¾ cup of dark molasses, ¼ cup of granulated sugar, teaspoon salt, ½ teaspoon each of cinnamon and nutmeg, 4 tablespoons butter, and ½ cup corn meal. Cook until the mixture thickens, pour into a baking dish, and add a cup of cold milk. Do not stir. Bake in a slow oven 3 hours without stirring. Serve while warm with butter, a hard sauce or cream.

4. *Greens:* Wash and boil until tender; drain and serve with hot vinegar and butter. Or wash and parboil for 10 minutes, then douse in cold water, drain thoroughly and chop fine. Put into a frying pan with 2 tablespoonfuls of butter, stirring constantly, add ¼ cup of broth in which a tablespoonful of flour has been smoothed with some bits of butter, and serve. Hard-boiled eggs, sliced, are used as a garnish. Vermonters are much more given to their "greens" cooked one way or another, than they are to salads. Even lettuce is perhaps oftener than not cooked as above. The greens, too, are oftentimes cooked with salt pork, a bit of bacon or a ham bone.

5. *Cider Plum Pudding:* A favorite Christmas dish but, unfortunately, will not keep very long, as it is moist and light. Two eggs are blended with ½ cup of cider; ½ cup flour, 2 teaspoons baking powder, ½ teaspoon each of soda, cinnamon, salt, and nutmeg are sifted together, then turned into a large bowl; ¼ cup each of chopped raisins, dates, figs, butternut meats, citron are mixed in; and finally, ¼ cup each of bread crumbs, brown sugar, chopped suet and chopped apple are kneaded in with the fingers. Covered in a well-greased ring-mold or other dish, the pudding is ready for the steaming process.

6. *Boiled Dinner:* Controversy over the matter of cooking the vegetables separately, or with the meat, leaves Vermont housewives just as certain

as ever that they should be cooked together, and they go right on doing so, just as their grandmothers and great grandmothers did before them. The meat is beef and the vegetables are beets, carrots, turnip, potatoes, onions and then a bag pudding are all cooked together. The bag pudding is made of Indian meal, a little flour, spiced to taste and seasoned, with a cup of milk. The mixture is turned into a cloth bag and dropped into the pot to cook. Done, it is slipped out of its bag to a serving plate, to be sliced and served with sweetened cream or maple syrup.

7. *Strawberry Shortcake:* A Vermont tradition that has been adopted by the other states. The strawberry shortcakes, first of all, are made of biscuit dough, two layers buttered and laid one atop the other to bake. When done they are separated, placed buttered sides up, but first more butter spread on the lower one, spread thickly with berries which have been slightly crushed in sugar. Then, the other layer placed above it is given the same treatment, put into the oven and eaten as soon as the cake is hot again. And, with cream. No heaping whipped cream on the cake, but cream served from a pitcher, plain cream with a little sugar in it.

8. *Sour Milk Doughnuts:* No native Vermonter goes without doughnuts for breakfast, even if mother has to get up before-hand to make them. The recipe?—2 cups of flour, ¾ teaspoon soda, 1 teaspoon of cream of tartar, ¾ teaspoon of salt, and a dash of nutmeg sifted together. Add a beaten egg, ½ cup sugar, tablespoon melted butter, and ½ cup sour milk. Knead on the board adding flour, if necessary; cut and fry in deep fat. For Sugared Doughnuts, when cool, shake in a bag with some confectioners' sugar. Blueberry griddlecakes are a Vermont Sunday morning breakfast.

9. *Apple Pan Dowdy:* Have ready a baking dish lined with pie crust. Mix a quart of sliced apples, scant ½ cup sugar, and add a dash each of nutmeg, cinnamon and salt. Fill the baking dish, add ¼ cup dark molasses, dot with 3 tablespoonfuls butter cut in pieces, and two tablespoonfuls of water, and pour into the dish; cover with a punctured crust and bake. When the crust has browned and the apples are tender, chop with a silver knife, crust and all so that it is thoroughly mixed with the apples.

Bake another hour or more. This recipe is direct from Aunt Hetty's own "receipt" book and everyone in northern Vermont knows that Aunt Hetty's pan dowdy was dee-licious. Served usually as a dinner dessert.

10. *Apples and Red Cabbage:* A small red cabbage and about 5 apples, pared and quartered in a pan with a piece of butter, salt, pepper, a clove or two, and water enough to cover, placed over a slow fire to cook until tender. Then the cabbage and apples are removed to a platter, a sauce of a tablespoonful of currant jelly and another of vinegar is poured over, and the whole served very hot. Often served as a supper dish with hot biscuits or as a vegetable for dinner. Again, in place of a salad which Vermonters have never taken to very kindly. Cabbage salad is an exception.

11. *Vegetable Hash:* A supper dish. Made with about equal quantities of leftover vegetables, a bit of butter, seasoned as desired, and served with ketchup.

12. *Baked Beans:* A typical Saturday night dish. The beans must be put to soak in cold water the night before and in the morning placed in a kettle and covered with boiling water to which ½ teaspoon of dry mustard has been added for each pint of beans. They should then cook until soft but not mushy. When nearly done, add a piece of salt pork to the kettle to cook with the beans. Next pour the beans into a "bean pot" and add 2 tablespoons of sugar or molasses according to the individual taste, as some prefer the beans a rich golden color which the molasses gives, moisten with liquid in which the beans were cooked, place pork on top of beans, cover and bake for 2 hours in a slow oven.

13. *Spiced Currants and Horseradish Relishes:* Much liked with meat. For the former, 3 lbs. currants, 2¼ [lbs.] brown sugar, and a cup of vinegar are required. A stick of cinnamon and a dozen cloves are tied in a muslin bag and all cooked for about an hour then turned into jam pots or glass jars. Well worth the trouble. The horseradish relish is made nowadays by adding a little pectin to the readymade radish and boiling for a couple of minutes.

14. *Mush & Milk:* Breakfast dish. Corn meal added to boiling salted water and stirred constantly.

15. *Apple Dumplings:* Made like apple bird's nests—a square of biscuit dough with sliced apples, the four corners of the dough brought together in the center, and cooked in a steamer or baked. Eaten with cream, maple syrup or hard sauce.

16. *Salt Salmon:* Boiled or broiled and served with cream or a cream sauce.

17. *Codfish Cakes:* A breakfast, dinner or supper dish in Vermont. Salt cod-fish that has been boiled the day before is minced and mixed with warm mashed potatoes, and a beaten egg added; made into inch-thick cakes about the size of a tea-cup top and fried in butter or other shortening.

18. *Hot Pot:* A favorite farm dish. Cut about 2 lbs. lamb chuck into 2-inch pieces, add a pound of dried beans that have been soaked over-night, cover with hot water, season with salt and pepper, and cook about 2 hours or until the meat is tender.

Rhode Island May Breakfasts

WALTER HACKETT

Walter Anthony Hackett was born in Providence, Rhode Island, in 1909. After leaving the Rhode Island Writers' Project he became a war correspondent during World War II. He continued writing freelance for newspapers with numerous food articles, including "Okay, Chowder Heads, Hear This"

and "Stalking the Perfect Martini." He also wrote travel arti-
cles and children's books, including The Swans of Ballycastle
and The Queen Who Longed for Snow, *as well as* Radio Plays
for Young People, *the guidebook* France on Your Own, *and a*
1967 book on the America's Cup Races. In 1978 he moved to
Boston and died there in 1995.

The tradition of May Breakfast, which is almost entirely
forgotten in southern New England today, was popular
enough to attract two submissions to America Eats, *the other*
by Rhoda Cameron, a retired actress from Louisiana who
wrote for the Connecticut Writers' Project.

A lthough not altogether indigenous to the state, nevertheless the May Breakfast had its greatest development in Rhode Island. As an institution it rivals the older clam bake. The credit for the local May Breakfast goes to one woman who believed that in the spring people turn to thoughts of food.

As nearly as may be ascertained, the first May Breakfast was given on May 1, 1867, by Searle's Corner Benevolent Society of the Oaklawn Baptist Church. Since then dozens of other societies have imitated the Oaklawn innovators. Mrs. Roby King Wilbur was president of Searle's Corner Benevolent Society of the Oaklawn Baptist Church. She was also familiar with English May Day customs. With scant reverence for the well-known poetical fantasy, she paraphrased it to fit her revival of the old English customs "In May a person's fancy lightly turns to thoughts of food."

The English, incidentally, got the idea from the Romans, who in elaborate fashion paid tribute to Flora, goddess of flowers, in hope of obtaining protection of the blossoms. The English, carrying on the custom, added to it by raising a May Pole and having a picnic that lasted the entire day.

When Mrs. Wilbur became head of the church society at Oaklawn, one of her immediate tasks was to raise money to either repair or build a new church. Therefore, she hit upon the idea of the May Breakfast.

Gathering around her the other girls from the local society, she immediately laid plans for the early morning spread.

The records of that first early morning spread do not speak of weather. It may be assumed that it was frosty. But the affair itself wasn't a frost. There was a big crowd. Every one stuffed himself. The society reported that it was a "financial success."

Among other things served at that first breakfast was cold boiled ham. One of the charter members had a secret formula for cooking ham. Her secret has been passed along and today the Oaklawn group cooks ham the way it was cooked by Madame X for that first breakfast in '67. Cold chicken was also a part of that first May Breakfast. When that became expensive, eggs were substituted. Other delicacies included mashed turnips (later the committee, in an economic mood, decided that turnips must go), creamed potatoes, pickles, pie (all known varieties), doughnuts, fruit, and coffee. Then for the hardy gourmet there were clam cakes.

Through the years other societies took the breakfast idea to their breasts and ran their own May Day food-stuffing contests. In 1898 a society in neighboring Meshanticut Park started serving a May Day repast; this organization gave the Oaklawn group serious competition for that one year. Thereafter its efforts were overshadowed, at least financially, by the innovator. The Meshanticut group evidently couldn't match Aunt Hannah Babcock's clam cakes or Roby Wilbur's hot biscuits or Mary Moon's hot apple pie.

However, the idea prospered, and soon it became a state-wide event. It was more than a gathering of lovers of good cooking; it was also a social gathering. Before the days of automobiles, people journeyed to the Oaklawn church afoot and in horse and buggy. Whole families arose at sunrise and set out for the church. It was *the* place for a fellow to take his girl. When the trolley cars came into the picture, the event took on added numerical strength. Unfortunately it was a cold ride, especially for the boys and girls who travelled any distance, for the street railway company at that time of year always trotted out its open cars. Any old-timer will testify that to roar and jounce through the countryside in an open car on the first day of May was a "darned cold ride." But every one got his money's worth, the celebration in those first days lasted all day, providing a chance to renew old friendships. Many a matrimonial match resulted from one of these May Day gatherings. For the past years the May Breakfast is the whole celebration. People eat, shake hands all around, jump into their cars and either return home or go to work, leaving them a saddened committee of women who gloomily look around and say, "Never again. It isn't worth all the trouble."

Note: These same women would undoubtedly rise up in arms if anyone dared suggest that they retire from the May Breakfast committee.

Dishes New York City's Hotels Gave America

ALLAN ROSS MacDOUGALL

Allan Ross MacDougall had a restless and unpredictable writing career. Among his works are a 1930 food encyclopedia, The Gourmet's Almanac; *a 1944 translation of a sixteenth-century Belgian epic by Charles de Coster,* The Glorious Adventures of Tyl Ulenspiegl; *an edited volume of the letters of Edna St. Vincent Millay; and a 1956 biography of the dancer Isadora Duncan. It is surprising that the FWP did not seek a more central role for Mac-Dougall in America Eats, since he was one of the few FWP writers with a major food writing credit to his name. MacDougall's food almanac is a wonderfully quirky, always readable, though not always helpful month-by-month food guide. On mutton he wrote, "Maybe it would be better to let the poor witless sheep live." About a third of the way through the book he abandons its premise, declaring, "By this time you will have come to see that there is no reason presiding over the choice of foods treated each month."*

This piece and one on oyster stew at Grand Central were the only contributions of this offbeat but stylish food writer.

In 1956, on the day MacDougall mailed his finished biography of Isadora Duncan to New York from Paris, he went to lunch at the Café de Flore and collapsed across the table, dead of a heart attack, a fact that seems particularly bizarre considering the dancer herself was accidentally strangled by her scarf only days after completing her own autobiography, My Life, *twenty-nine years earlier.*

MacDougall died as poor as he had been when he was part of the New York City Writers' Project, and the Isadora Duncan biography was not published until four years after his death.

In the two decades between 1840 and 1860 the population of the city of New York almost tripled in size. Larger and more elaborate hotels on the European continental model sprang up. Famous imported French chefs catered to a cosmopolitan and newly rich native clientele, and many elaborate "made" dishes replaced the simple roasts and stews. Even new cuts of beef were introduced, the Steak Delmonico, for instance. Many of the culinary innovations and creations of that period have long since been forgotten; others have passed into the common language and thence into the dictionaries and cook books of the nation.

In Webster is found, beside the Delmonico steak, Waldorf Salad, Delmonico Potatoes, Chicken à la King, and Lobster à la Newburg. Like such creations of hotels outside New York as Parkerhouse rolls and Saratoga chips, the New York dishes have become household words. But often they suffer changes which transform them radically from the original hotel creation.

Waldorf Salad

The famous Waldorf Salad, for example, is generally set forth as a mixture of chopped apples, celery, and nuts dressed with mayonnaise. It is so given in the Webster definition. The original recipe as written down by Oscar in his cook book published in 1896, about three years after the opening of the Waldorf-Astoria, reads, "Peel two raw apples and cut them in small pieces, say about half an inch square, also cut celery the same way and mix it with the apples. Be careful not to let any seeds of the apples be mixed with it. The salad must be dressed with a good mayonnaise."

Of all the eating establishments which set the tone of the gilded age, none was more famous than Delmonico's in lower New York, founded by a Swiss-Italian, Lorenzo Delmonico. It was said that Delmonico menus were copied by the small hash houses of the boom towns and mining camps of the west, places which with the best will in the world could not produce even the basic ingredients of Lobster Newburg, or Guinea Hen sous Cloche, let alone the culinary skill necessary for their preparation.

Of the hundreds of creations that came from the kitchen of Delmonico's there are three which still figure in menus throughout the country. One has an international reputation. The two still served in restaurants in this country are Steak Delmonico, a planked steak, and Delmonico Potatoes, chopped, creamed, served au gratin, with little red peppers. The third whose fame had travelled round the world is Lobster Newburg.

Lobster Newburg

Many stories have been told of the origin of this dish but the most commonly accepted one is that it was the creation not of the French chef of the establishment but of one of the gourmet patrons, Skipper Ben Wenberg.

Wenberg was the captain-owner of a fleet of passenger and fruit boats that plied between New York and Latin American ports. He was an assiduous frequenter of the various Broadway "Lobster Palaces," and a particular crony of Charles Delmonico, then head of the famous restaurant. Returning from one of his South American voyages he brought back with him a new way of dressing his favorite shellfish, which he wished to show to Delmonico and some other assembled gourmets. He called for a chafing dish and in it cooked the lobster meat, using large quantities of sweet butter. To that he added the yolk of half a dozen eggs, a pint of heavy cream and a glass of rum, making a rich sauce, which he seasoned with a dash of a special red pepper brought back from some southern port.

The dish was an instantaneous success with the select group. Delmonico decided to add it to his regular menu but before doing so he substituted the suaver accent of sherry wine for the harsher one of the Wenberg rum. On the menu the dish was listed as "Lobster à la Wenberg." A few years later, following a scandalous scene caused in the public rooms by Wenberg, Charles Delmonico blacklisted the bellicose skipper. On the menu the dish he invented thereafter appeared as "Lobster à la Newberg." Since then it has suffered many other transformations in name and nature. The original wine flavor is often left out altogether, and the mixture becomes merely another dish of creamed lobster. Some recipes substitute Madeira wine for sherry and sweet paprika for the sharp cayenne.

Crème Vichyssoise

The tremendous increase in the number of restaurants in the metropolis and the continual seeking after novelty in food by the women's magazines have produced new dishes and variations on ancient dishes too numerous to have such a wide effect as did the first appearance of Lobster à la Newburg. Yet in the past decade one soup has been created by a New York chef which has been copied more or less successfully by other eating places all over the country. This soup is Crème Vichyssoise.

Despite its name this dish, a perfect prelude to a summer meal, was created for New Yorkers by Louis Diat of the Ritz-Carlton. Most continental gourmets seeing it on a menu expect it to be a cream of carrot soup, for in gastronomic terminology the name of the French watering-place and temporary capital of unoccupied France is associated with carrots. By the same token, any dish termed Florentine always features spinach, dishes termed Clamart, green peas.

Crème Vichyssoise is really a variation of the well-known Potage Parmentier (Parmentier, the French scientist being rated in France as the discoverer and popularizer of the humble potato; dishes featuring that tuber are often termed Parmentier). The chief difference between Crème Vichyssoise and Potage Parmentier is that the New York creation is creamed and served chilled. As given by Louis Diat of the Ritz-Carlton the recipe for eight servings is as follows: Slice finely the white part of 4 leeks and 1 medium sized onion. Lightly brown in 2 ounces of sweet butter, then add 5 medium sized potatoes, also sliced finely. Moisten with about 1 quart water and add a little salt. (If available use chicken consomme instead of water.) Boil 35 to 40 minutes. Mash, then strain through muslin and finish by adding 2 cups of milk and 2 of medium cream. Season to taste and bring to a boil. Let the mixture cool and strain it again through muslin. Add then 1 cup of heavy cream and set aside to cool.

The soup must be served ice cold. Finely chopped chives may be added before serving.

Porterhouse Steak

The cut of beef known only in the United States as a Porterhouse steak has been said to have originated at the Porter House Hotel in North Cambridge, Massachusetts. But others maintain with certainty that this cut was first served in 1815 at a New York porterhouse kept by Martin Morrison at 327 Pearl Street, in lower Manhattan. Funk & Wagnall's gives the definition of Porterhouse as "A choice cut of beef-steak usually next to the sirloin and including part of the tenderloin; so called from a New York porterhouse whose proprietor first brought it into vogue."

New York Literary Tea

JERRY FELSHEIM

Jerry Felsheim was a New York City writer of children's books and plays, notably Ali Baba and the Forty Thieves, *with Irving Drutman.*

As a social institution, the Literary Tea has undergone profound changes in recent years. Originally identified with women's study clubs, it has been taken over by the smart world and transformed into a cocktail party with incidental literary trimmings. Its hours are from five to seven but, as with the cocktail party, no one ever appears before six fifteen and the host is fortunate if his last guests depart by nine. More than anything else, it has become an informal gathering place for intellectual sophisticates on their way to dinner.

Since the publishing world is concentrated in New York, literary teas reach their apex in that city. Their sponsors are usually connected with the business, a publisher trying to put over a new author; an editor celebrating the start of a magazine; or again, just a head hunter parading another celebrity. In Manhattan, literary teas are given upon the slightest provocation.

The locales of these parties vary from private apartments to special rooms at the smart night clubs and hotels. One condition is paramount, however; the place must always be jammed. Seemingly no literary tea is successful unless it is crowded enough to make an exchange of intellectual ideas an impossibility. The talk is usually limited to the latest publishing blurbs and reviews, Broadway gossip, and inside tips on how much this or that author is making. "Heavy" conversation is invariably frowned upon and *chichi* wit is at a premium.

Tea is a rarity at these gatherings. The conventional beverages are dry martini and Manhattan cocktails, with scotch for those who insist. In this respect, literary teas may be considered slightly more virile than their sister art shows, where tepid sherry is most often the only drink available. Food receives little attention. Usually it consists of a few uninteresting canapés passed haphazardly about, with few takers.

Literary teas are constantly in a state of flux. The uninitiate gravitates toward the author, the author toward the editor or publisher, the publisher toward the reviewer, and the reviewer, in desperation, toward another drink. Since the general rule of conduct is to seek out those who can do one the most good, magazine editors and big-name reviewers enjoy much popularity.

If the party happens to be given in honor of a new author, he is almost always completely ignored. In fact, there is a tradition among veteran literary tea-goers to put the young author in his place as soon as possible. They accomplish this by pretending vociferously not to know for whom the party is being given. The young author usually stands awkwardly in a corner, surrounded by a few dull old ladies, with his publisher frantically trying to circulate him among the "right" people.

Ephemeral as all this may be, however, the modern literary tea has its points. It enables its devotees to renew old friendships and make new ones; it gives the publisher an opportunity to tip off the trade as to which writer he is going to push; it allows the ambitious young author to make contacts with editors; and it gives a great many people entertainment, not to mention free drinks, in the hours before dinner.

The Automat

EDWARD O'BRIEN

Although the Automat was thought of as a New York City institution, its founding company, Horn & Hardart, also usually associated with New York, was based in Philadelphia. A forerunner of fast food, automats were a rapidly growing trend in the early twentieth century. The idea of dispensing cafeteria food from coin slots originated in Germany. In Times Square in the summer of 1912 Horn & Hardart opened their first New York City Automat. Originally their only fare was fish cakes, beans, buns, and coffee, each of which was on display in little compartments with windows that opened if a nickel was put in the slot. By the time of America Eats, *automats offered a wide range of food, but still each compartment opened with a nickel. They were well established in New York and became even more popular after the war, even in the 1950s, when they raised the prices of some items to a dime. But gradually fast-food restaurants eroded their following and in the 1980s Horn & Hardart closed many of their automats and replaced them with Burger King restaurants. In 1991 the last automat on 42nd Street and Third Avenue closed.*

A sight to the out-of-towner, and an honored institution among the city's millions, is the mechanical lunchroom known to fame as the Automat. This type of self-service eating place is the result of deep probing into the needs of the five-minute metropolitan center. Here, the man-in-a-hurry is worried by no middle-men; his relationship with his fodder, over which he may gloat, ruminate, or despair, is strictly private. He selects, pays, conveys, eats, and departs, leaving no tip, uttering no sound.

Two hundred and fifty thousand New Yorkers go through these silent processes daily in favorite or convenient Automats. Some are regular customers, others appear only on certain days, keeping a tryst with a favorite dish. No New York wife knows her husband until she has studied him in an Automat. And all suburban mothers have learned that on a day in town lunch at the Automat is the kids' delight.

A stranger entering these precincts is led by the crowd toward a trim marble counter, in which are several plate-like depressions. A nickel is the unit of purchase, so coins or bills are here exchanged for scintillating showers of nickels, which are miraculously never too many, never too few. With a fistful of nickels, and wearing hat, coat, carrying brief-case or handbag, the crowd moves on toward the walls of food, assembling as they go trays, silver, and napkins.

Dozens of illuminated metal cubicles, separated from the hungry by little plate-glass doors, exhibit single servings of some edible. Prices in nickels are posted beside the glass door: Chicken Pie 4 nickels; Hot Mince Pie 2 nickels. The trick is to push the required number of nickels into the right slot, whisk out the food before the door slams shut again, and juggle the dish onto the tray, without dropping bags, parcels, or other belongings.

Beverage pumps require three operations. The cup or glass is placed under the spout, a nickel into the slot, a handle is pushed down, and carefully measured liquid sluices into the container—cream and coffee simultaneously in balanced proportions that are the result of many surveys and much research into man's tastes. For orders of black coffee or tea, with or without cream or lemon, an attendant must be summoned to the cubbyhole, by ringing a bell after the nickel has been deposited.

As there are no discernible vacant places at the tables during rush hours, the title of "tray jockey" is bestowed on those skilled regulars who, through long practice in broken-field running, have become adept in the business of seat-snatching.

That Automat diners return daily to their trials is not due to love of punishment but to the fact that food here is hard to beat. The hot beef or chicken pies, baked in individual deep dishes and covered with brown and flaky crusts, are among the culinary wonders of New York—produced, as they are, in perfect and uniform thousands! And the piping-hot corned beef hash, made of honest lean beef and never too sharply flavored, is as good as any man's mother can cook.

Clam chowder, not Boston-, not New York–style, but with a flavor all its own, and English beef soup, are both so popular as to keep trade rivals sniffing around. Little pots of slow-baked beans, garnished with strips of crisp pork, rival Boston's and the door of their cell rattles like a machine gun all day long.

Thousands breakfast on the beloved cinnamon bun, a modestly named confection stuffed with raisins and covered with treacle. This, with a cup of excellent, rich-creamed coffee, inspires many a wan New Yorker to start the day with a glow. Bread, superior corn bread, bran muffins, pies, and pastries sit in the noble company of the cinnamon bun.

At the steam table the capricious may select a complete dinner, and though portions are not large, the food is better than that obtained at many cafeterias. But the nickel-in-the-slot method is still the more popular.

Quality never varies. This accounts for the loyalty of the regulars. Such achievement in mass-production cookery is credited in part to organization, in part to a staff of the most highly paid chefs in the business. And food buying is so closely gauged that there are no left-overs at the end of the day, which is 2 a.m.

New York eats in the Automat; it does not, however, smoke or converse there. Smoking, in fact, is strictly forbidden by sign and spoken warnings. But no one minds. The Automat will flourish so long as the average New Yorker remains what he is, a person who is everlastingly fond of dropping coins into slot machines, who loves good coffee, and who knows his cinnamon buns.

New York Soda-Luncheonette Slang and Jargon

A.C.	American cheese sandwich
ALL BLACK	Chocolate soda with chocolate ice cream
ANGEL'S DELIGHT	Cake with vanilla icing
ARKANSAS CHICKEN	Salt pork
ARM WAITER	Waiter who piles stacks of dishes on his arms
AXLE GREASE	Butter
A YARD OF	Dish of spaghetti
BABY	Glass of milk
BANG ONE	Order to mix a malted milk
BAY STATE BUM	Customer who demands much service and leaves no tip
BELLYWASH	Soup
BERRIES	Eggs
BLACK AND WHITE	Chocolate soda with vanilla ice cream
BLACK COW	Root beer with ice cream
BLIMP	Woman
BLIND 'EM	Two eggs fried on both sides
BLOND	Coffee with cream
BLUE HEAVEN	Bromo Seltzer
B.M.T.	Bacon and tomato sandwich with mayonnaise
BOILED LEAVES	Tea
BOOL	Soup listed on a table d'hôte menu
BOTTLE O' RED	Ketchup
BOTTLE WASHER	Assistant cook

BREAK IT AND SHAKE IT	Malted milk with egg
BRUNETTE	Black coffee
BULL'S EYES	Two fried eggs
BURN 'ER BLACK	Chocolate malted milk
BURN ONE	An order of toast
BURN ONE UP	See "Burn 'er black"
BURN THE BRITISH	Order for toasted English muffins
BURN WITH A CACKLE	See "Break it and shake it"
BUSS	To carry dirty dishes
CHEWED FINE WITH A BREATH	Order for a hamburger with onion
CHERRIES	Prunes
C.J. ON A RAFT	Cream cheese and jelly on toast
C.O. COCKTAIL	Castor oil in soda
CODFISH	See "Bay State bum"
C.O. HIGHBALL	Castor oil
COKE	Coca-Cola
COW	Milk
COW JUICE	See "Cow"; also, cream
CUP OF MUD	Cup of coffee
DEEP DOWN BLEEDING	Root beer with cherries
DEEP ONE THROUGH GEORGIA	A glass of Coca-Cola with chocolate
DRAW ONE	Order for coffee; also, water
DRAW ONE IN THE DARK	See "Brunette"
DRAW ONE ON THE SIDE	Coffee with cream served separately
DRESS ONE PIG	Ham sandwich
DYNAMITE	Baking powder
84	Four glasses of water
81	A customer
86	Supply is exhausted
82	Two glasses of hot chocolate
EMERSON HIGHBALL	See "Blue heaven"
51	Hot chocolate
FOUL BALL	Mistake
FOUNTAINEER	Soda fountain attendant
49	Look at the beautiful girl

14	See "49"
14¼	A beautiful girl, a little on the plump side
FREEZIT	Pepsi-Cola
FRY 'EM BLIND	Order to baste frying eggs
G. I.	Garbage can (general issue)
GEE	Man
GOB	See "Fountaineer"
GRAVEYARD STEW	Milk toast
GREASER	A cook
GRIT	Dishwashing powder
GUINEA FOOTBALLS	Jelly doughnuts
HEBREW ENEMIES	Pork chops
HOLD	Cancel the order
HOLSTEIN HIGHBALL	See "Baby"
HOUSEBOAT	Banana split
HUG ONE	Orange juice
ICE THE RICE	Rice pudding with ice cream
I.R.T.	Lettuce and tomato sandwich
JACK BENNY IN THE RED	Strawberry Jell-O
JEEP	Sandwich cutter and salad man
JERK, OR JERKOR	See "Fountaineer"
JERSEY COCKTAIL	See "Baby"
JIGGS	Corned beef and cabbage
JUGGLE DISHES	To wait on tables
LAKE WHITNEY	See "Draw one" (second definition)
LOVERS' DELIGHT	Chocolate éclair
MAKE TWO LOOK AT ME	See "Bull's eyes"
MARY GARDEN	Citrate of magnesia
MONEY BOWL	See "Bellywash"
MONKEY	Caramelized sugar (used in verbal directions for making gravy)
MURPHIES	Potatoes
NERVOUS PUDDING	Gelatin dessert
95	An expression describing a customer who leaves without paying

NOAH'S BOY WITH MURPHY CARRYING A WREATH	See "Jiggs"
ON A RAFT	On toast
ONE AND A HALF	Ham and American cheese sandwich
ONE LUMP	A Camel cigarette
ONE ON A PILLOW	Hamburger on a bun
ONE WITH DYNAMITE	Coca-Cola with ammonia
ONE WITHOUT THE THUMB	See "Bellywash"
PAINT IT RED	Cherry Coca-Cola
PAINT IT YELLOW	Lemon Coca-Cola
PIE BOOK	Meal ticket
POP ONE	See "Coke"
POT WALLOPER	See "Greaser"
PUT A STRETCH ON IT	Sandwich to go out
RED LEAD	See "Bottle o' red"
REPEATERS	Beans
SALVE	See "Axle grease"
SAND	Sugar
SCANDAL SOUP	See "Boiled leaves"
SHAKE A WHITE	A plain milk shake
SHEET ONE	See "Coke"
SINKERS	Doughnuts
66	See "49"
SKIN TAKER	See "Grit"
SMEAR ONE, BURN IT	Order for toasted cheese sandwich
SOP	Dish rag
SOUTHERN SWINE	Virginia ham
STACK O' BERRY	Strawberry ice cream
STACK O' WHITE	Vanilla ice cream
STARVED	An expression meaning a bad day for sales
STRETCH ONE	A large "Coke" (q.v.)
STRETCH SWEET ALICE	A large "Baby" (q.v.)
SWEET ALICE	See "Baby"
TAXI ONE	Orangeade

TAXI STRAIGHT	See "Hug one"
TEAM OF GRAYS	Sugared crullers
THE WORKS	Banana split
THIN MAN	Dime tipper
TOASTWICH	Toasted sandwich
TONIC	Soda
TURN ON THE RADIO	Light the gas stove
TWIST IT, CHOKE IT AND MAKE IT CACKLE	Chocolate malted milk with egg
TWO AND A HALF	Ham and Swiss cheese sandwich
TWO CACKLES IN OINK, IN THE SOUTHERN WAY	Ham and eggs
TWO FLOPPED	See "Blind 'em"
TWO IN THE DARK	Two pieces of rye toast
UNCLE EZRA	Alka-Seltzer
VANILLA	Nice looking girl
VERMONT	Maple syrup
WATSON, THE NEEDLE	See "Coke"
WHISTLEBERRIES	See "Repeaters"
WRECKS	Broken dishes
YESTERDAY, TODAY AND FOREVER	Hash

Drugstore Lunch

EDWARD O'BRIEN

Time was when the drug store dispensed medicines. But now, as the candid rag says with but slight exaggeration, it sells everything from pins to automobiles. Not the least of the additions to the drug store is the soda-fountain luncheonette, where anything from a "C.O. cocktail" (castor oil in soda) to "Jack Benny in the red" (strawberry Jell-O) may be had.

The stool and counter has a special attraction for the woman shopper, the office worker, and the show girl. And it has certain advantages. The drug store carries a connotation of cleanliness. One juggles no tray while stalking a seat in the noonday jam. The food, though slightly more expensive than that served in the cafeteria, is light, tasty, and briskly served. Again, the store specializes in odd knick-knacks, the delight of feminine customers who would ordinarily turn away from heavier fare. Above all, it has glorified the sandwich.

The *pièce de résistance* is the toasted "three decker" enclosing 'tween decks unusual and sometimes insidious food combinations. These may include cold meats, fish mixtures called "salads," hamburger, bacon, cheese, jelly, peanut butter, bananas, tomatoes, relish, pickles, and chopped eggs, all garnished with condiments or dressings. The popular cheese-burger is a doughty bit combining grilled hamburger and melted American cheese served on a soft bun and tasty enough to ensnare even the one-cylinder appetite.

In New York's summer heat the customer may "drink" his lunch, in which case he has a wide choice of cold drinks and ice cream. Or he may dawdle over the substantial banana split, variously known back-counter as a "house boat" or "the works," constructed of ice cream, strawberries, crushed pineapple, whipped cream, maraschino cherries, and chopped nuts, all resting heavily on the banana. Cold weather brings hot beef tea, Ovaltine, tea, coffee, chocolate, and hot milk.

Hot miniature dinners are sometimes offered: chilled fruit juice, a bowl of excellent soup, a salad, and such entrées as boiled beef tongue with raisin gravy, potato and spinach, or chow mein with rice and noodles—even leg of lamb with potato, diced carrots and mint jelly. Desserts include everything from plain pie to the hot fudge Mary Ann. All this may be had for a very reasonable fixed price.

That a drug store soda fountain can offer such a variety of food and drink with seemingly limited facilities is surprising, but these places are equipped with the latest time-saving devices and organized to separate the functions of each worker. The drip coffee is served from glass pots kept constantly in use on a five or six burner gas or electric plate, making possible the continuous brewing of fresh coffee. A small broiler and grill (the "radio," in a luncheonette gob's jargon) turns out orders of crisp bacon or ham and eggs. Each electric toaster keeps sixteen slices of bread revolving on its wheel. A small aluminum steam table holds containers of hot meats and various shining pots whence are ladled the soup, gravies, and hot vegetables. Jelly, pickle jars, and mayonnaise are handily lined up.

During rush hours the sandwich man deftly and swiftly builds "three deckers," completing each success with a shout: "Take it away!" The steam table man dishes out hot dinners. If the job is not too "hot foot," the sandwich man may handle both. The waiters serve the food, mix the drinks, and punch the checks. Used dishes are tossed into a sink under the counter where they are cleaned in a jiffy by the "bottle-washer." All is compact, tidy, stream-lined.

The stool diner does not loiter. Waiting customers may be lined up behind him three deep. Dare he rest a moment, he may be the recipient of sub-zero glares or even a little verbal "needling": . . . "He's tryin' to scrape the design off the plate—" . . . "Give 'im a couple tooth picks—" . . . "Let's try hollerin' fire!"

Italian Feed in Vermont

MARI TOMASI

Mari Tomasi was born of northern Italian parents on January 30, 1907, in Montpelier, Vermont. Her father, who had traveled in South and Central America, chose the Green Mountains because he said they reminded him of his native lake region in Italy. Her sister was a nurse and her brother and four cousins were all doctors, and it was Mari's ambition to study medicine also. But under financial pressure after her father died, she went to Trinity College in Burlington to study teaching. Soon she dropped out to write freelance newspaper and magazine articles. Although she became city editor of the Montpelier Evening Argus, *she still managed to get work from the Vermont Writers' Project interviewing quarry workers in the granite industry in Barre, Vermont, for an FWP project titled* Men Against Granite.*

In 1940 her first novel,* Deep Grow the Roots, *the story of young Italian lovers destroyed by Mussolini, was published. In 1949 she published a more successful novel,* Like Lesser Gods, *about Italian stonecutters in the quarries of Barre. She continued to live in Burlington and write until her untimely death from illness in 1965.* Like Lesser Gods *was republished in 1988 and again in 1998, and it enjoys standing as a New England Italian-American classic.*

It is striking that she lived in an America where Italian food was rare enough for her to feel the need to explain what ravioli is.

How about an Italian feed tonight?" Government official, professional, clerk, or truck driver—daily someone within a 70-mile radius of Barre makes this suggestion in gustatory anticipation.

These dinners are strictly of economic origin. Since the '80's, Barre, the largest granite center in the world, has attracted hundreds of skilled carvers from the granite and marble centers of northern Italy. Many, succumbing to occupational sickness, left young wives and growing families. A few widows turned for support to the art they knew best, cooking. They cooked at first for a neighbor, then for a neighbor's friend. Gratified palates publicized the food. Today some fifty homes in Barre make a business of providing Italian feeds.

The word *feed* no doubt calls to mind fodder, or provender for cattle; but that gourmet, the unrecorded Vermont Yankee who titled these dinners *Italian feeds*, must have been musing upon its pure derivation from the Anglo Saxon *fedan*, meaning feast. For certainly Barre's Italian feeds are feasts.

A fragrant, piquant scent excites the nostrils as you enter Maria Stefani's neat, unpretentious little house. The dining room with its piano, or perhaps a Victrola, is yours for the evening. Maria's daughter of high school age, or maybe the oldest daughter, Elena, who is a stenographer at the State Capitol six miles away, assists at the table.

Baskets of bread are the sole table adornments; long golden Italian loaves, sliced, and revealing generous centers of spongy white for those who like their bread soft; crisp rolls; and small crunchy buns shaped like starfishes, and which are best described as knobs of tender crust. These last for those who like to hear their bread crackle between their teeth.

The array of appetizers leaves the novitiate agape. Paper thin slices of *prosciutto*, a ham processed in pepper and spices. Large, red wafers of tasty *salami*. Pickled veal. Celery. Ripe olives, the dark, succulent meats falling away easily from their pits. Then there is the favorite *antipasto*, a savory achievement incorporating mushrooms, pearl onions, tuna, anchovies, broccoli—all permeated and tinctured with a tangy red sauce.

Maria Stefani beamingly assures you that you may have spaghetti or *ravioli*, or both. The platter is weighted with a mountain of white spaghetti, quivering under a dusky tomato sauce, and capped with grated Parmesan cheese. Maria scoffs at the packaged cheese already grated. "It's dry," she declares. "Its spirit is gone!" She grates her own cheese, and sprinkles it fresh, moist, and full bodied on the spaghetti. *Ravioli*, most popular of Italian dishes, are diminutive derbies of pastry, the crowns stuffed with a well-seasoned meat paste. Like the spaghetti, these are boiled, drained, and served under rich sauce and Parmesan cheese.

The food looks good; it tastes better. Geniality expands. Stomachs gorge in leisurely contentment. Belts loosen. Maria's daughter, in horror lest glutted appetites fail to appreciate the joys yet to come, hints subtly to novices, "Will you have the salad with your meat? And will you have fried chicken, or chicken *alla cacciatore?*"

Maria Stefani is not licensed to sell alcohol. But these diners are her guests, she claims; and in hospitality, as well as to whet anew their surfeiting appetites, she pours them gratis a glass of sour, ruby red wine made last fall in Angelo Boni's press down the street. Or each may sip a cup of hot coffee potently spirited with grappa, that transparent liquor distilled from Angelo Boni's grape mash.

Fried chicken is browned in spiced olive oil. A touch of the fork punctures the crisp coating; delectable juices drip from the tender inside. Chicken *alla cacciatore* (hunter's style) resembles a stew; the faint, but distinctively pert aroma of cooked wine rises from the meat, smothered though it is under a steaming sauce of tomatoes, peppers, onions and herbs.

At this stage of the feast the insalata arrives, offering a sharp and pleasant contrast to the early rich dishes. Strenuously exercised gustatory nerves carry new and delightful impulses from tongue to brain. The insalata is a light, aromatic salad of lettuce, endive, tomatoes, green peppers, onion—all tossed in chilled vinegar (usually a wine vinegar) and olive oil, and served from a bowl the sides of which have been rubbed to delicate fragrance with garlic. Contrary to common belief, the cook who prepares a true Italian feed uses that pungent bulb, garlic, with no lavish hand, but with light epicurean artistry; she allows only a delicate breath of it to imbue the food, thus teasing the appetite, and transforming a dull mouthful into a tasty smack.

Maria Stefani justifiably frowns at dessert. But, if you wish, she will serve you *spumoni*, an Italian ice cream. Then Maria nods her head towards the piano, her earrings bobbing, "Enjoy yourselves, eh? The room is yours until midnight."

Long Island Rabbit Stew: Hasenpfeffer

In the late fall of the year and early winter when game season opens on Long Island we first anticipate a rarity in food that only royalty used to enjoy. To sink one's teeth into a properly prepared snack of Hasenpfeffer is a pleasure long to be remembered and can be participated in through the winter until the end of the hunting season.

Hasenpfeffer, although generally made of rabbits, can also be made of venison. The following is the way it is prepared by that cook of cooks, Mrs. Margarite Gross, Greene Ave., Sayville, N.Y., both for her private trade and for large group gatherings, as church suppers, Hasenpfeffer dinners, etc.:

PREPARATION FOR SIX PORTIONS
Remove the pelt, head and feet of two rabbits. Draw them and quarter them, and place in brine made as follows:

    4 cups vinegar
    5 cups water
    2 teaspoons salt
    2 medium sized onions
    6 bay leaves
    25 cloves

Brine is best made in a stone crock and the pieces of rabbit should be covered with the brine. Leave in brine 3 days.

COOKING

Remove rabbits from crock and wipe dry with towel. Place rabbits in pan with hot beef drippings in it and allow the meat to brown. Then add spice and allow to simmer for about 1½ hours. Brown flour and make gravy. Serve hot, with Kartoffel Klösze.

KARTOFFEL KLÖSZE

Boil 15 large potatoes in jackets. When done peel and rice them, letting them cool about 5 minutes, then add 2 eggs, 1½ cups of flour, 1 teaspoon salt and roll into balls and roll balls in flour. Have a pot of boiling water on the fire, place the dumplings in the water that has been salted and boil for 10 minutes, remove and serve.

Hasenpfeffer and Kartoffel Klösze are generally served together but either can be served separate or with other food.

North Whitefield, Maine, Game Supper

DONALD McCORMICK

Each year in mid-October a public supper unusual in the state and in New England is served in the grange hall of the little town of Whitefield, Maine, some ten miles west of the Kennebec River near the town of Gardiner. Having once attended, there are several things that one remembers besides the extraordinary food. One of these is your determination to come earlier next year.

Unless you arrive well before serving is begun, you find the vicinity of the little hall lined with cars and the vestibule packed with people awaiting admittance. Over the heads of the throng you can see the crowded tables and the waitresses hurrying back and forth with laden trays, a view that is not gratifying to one who has travelled a number of miles in the brisk fall air and is ready to eat anytime.

When your turn comes, you are ushered to a seat at one of the long, portable tables and given a menu. The menu is only a conventionality, you soon learn, for the waitresses approach your table in turn and announce their wares. First comes one with squirrel pie, and you try an experimental helping. The meat is tender, something like chicken, but the small bones are a hazard. Another girl arrives with a dish of stewed partridge. You have a generous portion of this, and it is delicious. Before you actually start eating, you have an amazing assortment of wild life on your plate: squirrel, wild duck, coon, and a small, resilient segment of bear.

It is a hectic meal, what with your experimentation and with wrapping bits of whatever is at all portable in your paper napkin to try on your friends next day. The array of pies would ordinarily be intriguing: apple, pumpkin, squash, lemon, pineapple, chocolate, but your occupation with the meat dishes has made all this an anticlimax. Your mind is on the cooking processes that produce such tender game dishes.

The cooking, you learn at the dance that follows, is done by the relatives and friends of the North Whitefield Fish and Game Club, which sponsors this annual feast and produces the varieties of game. Not so many people know how to prepare game properly. It seems that one of the secrets is to get rid of the "wild" flavor. If you've ever experienced it, you know what they mean by this "taste sensation": it's difficult to describe but something like the flavor of pickled herring. One way to eliminate it is to parboil the game in soda and water. Venison is seldom served, the reason evidently being that the supper doesn't coincide with the local open season. Chicken and pork dishes are usually provided for those who don't care for the wild fare.

The supper is little publicized, but there is small need to solicit patronage. Tidings of the repast, which is unique in Maine as far as can be discerned, has spread throughout the state, and the hungry and the curious descend on North Whitefield from miles around. The usual price, by the way, is a dollar. However, with shot and shell up front on the OPM list, it's probably a dollar and a quarter from now on.

Raising Mushrooms in Pennsylvania

At the time of America Eats, Pennsylvania was the leading producer of cultivated mushrooms, the only mushrooms most Americans ate, fearing poisonous wild species.

Mushrooms are difficult to cultivate because they demand a very specific environment. The variety of cultivated mushroom known in the United States was first cultivated in France after the groundbreaking mushroom experiments of Louis XIV's agronomist Olivier de Serres, documented in his 1600 treatise, Le Théâtre d'agriculture des champs. *This work later in the century led to the cultivation of* Agaricus bisporus, *which have become the most commonly eaten mushroom in the world. Identifying where they were grown, the French have always called them* champignon de Paris. *The British exported them to the United States by the late nineteenth century, but the only place where they caught on as a commercial crop was in a few counties of Pennsylvania, especially Butler and Armstrong counties in the western part of the state, though this article is centered in Chester County, on the other side of the state near Delaware. While a great variety of mushrooms are cultivated in the United States today, many even exported to Europe, at the time of* America Eats *Pennsylvania's* champignon de Paris, *the common white button, was the only mushroom in America aside from those found in the forests by a brave or knowledgeable few.*

L ong, windowless, one-story oblong buildings dot the countryside of Chester County from Avondale to Kennett Square and West Chester. In these buildings, with their ever-present and essential manure piles, more than seventy percent of the country's mushroom crop is grown.

The mushroom possibly graced the groaning banquet board of Lucullus, for the epicures of ancient Greece and Rome considered certain fungi, of which the mushroom is a species, great delicacies. The Roman poet Juvenal tells of a lover of mushrooms who thus implored some reluctant farmer: "Keep your corn, O Libya, unyoke your ox, provided only you send us mushrooms!" Horace of the golden age of Rome, both poet and farmer, said with some finality that mushrooms that grow in the fields are the best, and one can have little faith in other kinds.

For many hundreds of years thereafter the growth of mushrooms was left to the hand of Nature. In the seventeenth century in France the directed cultivation of them was carried on in caves, but in this country it was not until the twentieth century that their gathering and sale constituted little more than a child's quest or a haphazard farm task. They were gathered in the pasture lands for the family table, or sold with the other farm produce for pin money.

In 1904 Edward Henry Jacob of West Chester, an accountant, recognized the limited supply and the ready market for mushrooms. From this came the realization of the commercial possibilities of their scientific production. Today approximately 700 growers within a ten-mile radius in Chester County have taken the "mushrooms from the fields," and within their sheds have made the raising of "snow apples," as they are known in the trade, a prosperous and thriving industry valued at $8,000,000 annually.

For successful growing, good manure is of prime importance, although within the past few years the use of manure has been displaced by the use of wheat spawn as a compost. This wheat spawn was developed in the laboratories of Pennsylvania State College by Dr. James Sinden, assistant professor of botany, and patented by him in 1931. He assigned his rights to the college, and a research corporation was formed to handle all patents. Licenses were issued to five mushroom-raising companies in Chester County, thereby assuring dominance of the industry within a limited area. The grain spawn is said to have reduced the cost of production one-third, and, at the same time, reduced the growing time of a better mushroom by the same ratio. The manure, or compost, must be fresh and from grain-fed horses bedded with straw. The nearness to the metropolitan market areas of New York and Philadelphia, together with the accessibility of manure from the stables of these two cities and from the farms throughout the countryside, made Chester County an ideal growing center. The advent of the automobile and the later mechanization of the farm caused a scarcity in compost, and the manure now used is obtained from brokers who procure much of it from the stables of police and cavalry barracks throughout the county. A large grower uses 20,000 tons a year at an average market cost of $7 a ton; after using it as a compost he sells it as fertilizer for $1.50 a ton.

In the past many a crop failure has been traced to the use of a compost of the manure of animals fed on sorghum, and alfalfa and molasses. The substitution of the cheaper sawdust and shavings in the place of wheat-straw bedding reduces the value of the manure, and requires more time and labor in the composting. The manure used commercially is now given a rigid chemical analysis and inspection to insure a high growing standard.

The fermentation of the manure is known as "composting." A manure, well-strawed and protected from extreme dampness to prevent the subsequent loss from "leaching" (the result of percolation of water through the mass), is spread on a concrete floor. The compost heap is never piled less than three feet high and never more than four feet. If it is too low it will not heat enough, if too high it will heat excessively and dry out.

During the process of fermentation the temperature reaches 140 degrees Fahrenheit, but the most satisfactory result is obtained when a temperature of 125 degrees is constantly maintained for several days. At the end of a one-week to two-week period the pile is forked over, and the outside of the old pile becomes the center of a new pile. It is then well shaken and mixed, the dry spots watered, and the whole pile spread with two inches of fine loam to prevent too rapid heating during this period of fermentation, as well as to hold the heat when the bed is made. Every five days the mixture is forked over and new loam added. In three weeks the dark brown moist compost is ready for use.

The cultivated mushroom, the *Agaricus campestris*, belongs to a group characterized by the lack of chlorophyll or green coloring matter, which together with sunlight enables higher plant life to manufacture its own food, starch. As a consequence the fungus can be grown in the absence of light, and a measure of economy is injected in the construction of the growing-shed by the lack of windows. Care must be taken, however, that the buildings be draftproof and a constant temperature of fifty-five to sixty degrees maintained. The sheds are ventilated to insure a steady supply of oxygen and the expulsion of carbonic acid gas, given off by the growing plants. Tiers of flat beds, six beds high, of compost ten inches deep and approximately two feet wide are arranged along the sides and middle of the building.

Mycelium cultures, developed from the spores of previous crops of mushrooms, are introduced into bottles containing sterilized compost. In three weeks the bottled, impregnated manure becomes hardened; the bottle is broken and the spawn scatteringly inserted in small pieces about one inch below the surface of the bed. At this time the bed is held at a temperature of sixty or seventy degrees, and maintained at that temperature for several weeks thereafter. Within ten days or two weeks, when the spawn begins to run, or the thin tendrils of the mycelium spread, a white mouldlike growth appears. Then a casing, or shallow layer of rich pasture or garden loam, is spread over the bed. Six or ten weeks after the spawn is spread, white pinheads that develop overnight into "buttons" appear upon the surface of the compost. The mushroom is known as a button when the membrane or veil extends unbroken from the edge of the cap or pileus to the stem. As the plant matures the pileus expands in an umbrellalike manner; the veil, which in the button covered the gills beneath the cap, becomes a ragged fringe around the edge of the pileus, and a ring or annulus of veil around the stem or stipe.

The average commercial bed produces for a period of eight months to a year. A compost impregnated with a good strain of spawn will yield one-and-a-half pounds of mushrooms to each square foot of bed surface. The retail price of the mushroom will average from thirty-five cents to one dollar a pound. The introduction of air conditioning has made possible a year-round growing season. Previous to this innovation the season extended only from May to November.

Scientific advancement has become a two-edged sword in the mushroom industry. On the one hand it has lengthened the growing season; on the other the automobile and farm mechanization have seriously imperiled the existence of the industry's prime requisite, manure. Mushroom growers are now hopefully turning to science's latest advance, the use of grain spawn as a compost, to perpetuate an industry which in its growing-sheds produces a crop that ranges from 11,000,000 to 15,000,000 pounds annually.

Vermont Sugaring-Off

ROALDUS RICHMOND

The American journalist turned food writer Waverley Root claimed that maple syrup may be the only food produced exclusively in North America. It is also one of the few products of which the little state of Vermont has remained a lead-

ing producer. It was at the time of America Eats and it still
is today.

Long before Europeans, who knew much of the maple tree
but nothing of the syrup produced from North American
maples, arrived in North America, the people of the Northeast, the Indians, slashed the trees so that the sap would run
in the first thaw. They then heated the sap with hot stones or
left it to freeze so that the water would separate into ice and
leave a concentrate. Vermont squirrels have a similar though
cruder process, biting the tree and waiting for the sap to run
and then freeze at night into icicles, which they lick.

The sap that is harvested at the end of winter is colorless
and flavorless until it is concentrated, giving no hint of what
it can become.

It is not by chance that the traditional terms in the maple
industry employ the word "sugar" rather than "syrup." For the
sugaring off, the sugar bush is tapped and the sap brought to
the sugar house, a process that is prolonged by a late snow-
fall, a sugar snow. The early settlers reduced the sap until
crystallization and used it as sugar because the other alternative, Caribbean cane sugar, was more expensive. Maple
sugar also took on political significance as a way of boycot-
ting the British, especially after the 1764 Sugar Act, and as
the politically correct alternative to slave-produced sugar in
nineteenth-century abolitionist New England.

But since the late nineteenth century, maple sugar has
not been competitive with other sugars because an enormous
quantity of sap is required to make a gallon of syrup to turn
into a modest loaf of sugar. But the syrup has remained in
great demand. Some remains unclassified for industrial use
and the rest is graded into Grade A and Grade B. Grade A,
which is finer, is sold to tourists, while for the most part the
native Vermonters keep their Grade B, which has a stronger
flavor. As with cheddar cheese and most local products, New
Englanders like it strong.

Maples do not produce syrup in Europe because long freezing nights and days above freezing are required. Global warming could end the maple industry in North America. Since the 1970s the winter temperature in America's sugar maple zone has risen between two and three degrees on average and the syruping season now begins five weeks earlier than it did at the time of America Eats. *The timing of New England's famous flaming fall foliage has become unpredictable. In the first half of the twentieth century 80 percent of the world maple syrup production was from the United States, but today 75 percent is Canadian. There are fewer and fewer maple trees, and scientists suspect that climate change is not the only problem. Acid rain caused by pollution is altering the chemical composition of the soil and making it less favorable to sugar maples.*

It is a keen morning in late March, the air like a knife, the sky clear and blue. There is still snow in the hollows and pockets of the brown earth, snow about the gray boulders in the fields and the bare trees of the woodlots. White mists rise from the snow-banked stream and fade in the early sun. Smoke plumes from the chimneys of farmhouses along the valley. Pine woods are black and somber on the far ridges, and the naked trees on the lower slopes have a gray brittle look. As the sun climbs the day grows warm. The snow patches soften and melt, the eaves drip, and in the sugar orchards sap tinkles into the pails. Farmers look at the weather and nod significantly. "She's going to run today, boys, she'll sure run today." It is the perfect sugaring day.

The sugarhouse sits in a grove of maples on the broad hilltop. It is built of unpainted boards, weathered and worn but sturdy enough. A metal-covered ventilating cupola centers the pitched shingle roof. Cords of wood are neatly stacked in the open lean-to shed at one end of the building. The sharp tang of woodsmoke mixes with the sweet vapors of boiling sap. Steam from the cupola is fanned away on the gusty March winds. Underfoot the bare ground is damp and soft, and from the woodlands comes the clean breath of snow. In the distance the Green Mountains are massed against the sky, their domes and peaks shining white in the sun.

Men and boys gather sap with horse-drawn sleds bearing large containers. The horses plunge and snort where the snow is deep, and the workers scramble from tree to tree, empty the buckets into the gathering tubs, hang the empties back up and plow on to the next maple. Sap must be gathered frequently because, like milk, it sours in the sun. In some of the more modern establishments sap is piped directly from the trees to the storage tank, but most farmers stick to the good old-fashioned way. Loaded, the sleds are hauled back to the sugarhouse. Voices ring above the rustle and scrape of runners, the creak of leather and wood, the jingle of bits. A barking dog scampers along beside the horses. The sap is poured into the storage tank, which occupies the cool north side of the sugarhouse.

From this tank the sap is piped to the evaporating pan resting on an arch over the fire in a long furnace of brick or iron. The evaporator is divided into compartments to facilitate the flow of sap and provide greater heating surface. Cold sap, admitted by the automatic regulator, forces the boiling sap onward. As it boils down the liquid increases in density and sweetness, passing from one compartment to another. Impurities are skimmed from the surface, and felt strainers remove the nitre, or "sugar sand." In the last compartment a thermometer indicates when the boiling syrup has reached the required 11-pound per gallon weight. After the syrup is drawn off a hydrometer may be used to measure the specific gravity and make doubly sure that the official weight is attained. Old-timers used to estimate this with remarkable accuracy by judging the drip or aproning of the syrup.

There is real heat in the sunshine today, a forerunner of spring. The icy edge of the morning is gone. Bareheaded men work in their shirt-sleeves, warmed by the sun flooding through leafless branches. There is a sense of life stirring in the ground, in the trees, and the running sap is music in the tin buckets. Laughing boys stop to tilt the pails and taste the cool, flat, faintly-sweet sap of the maples. It is colorless like water but it has a pleasant flavor.

Days like this usually come in March and April, although sometimes they arrive in February. The average four-week season is from about the middle of March to mid-April, but it has been known to start as early as February 22nd, or as late as the first week in April. Depending on the weather sugar-making may extend as long as six weeks, or last only two. Abrupt changes in temperature, cold freezing nights and warm sunny days are necessary for a good run of sap. The season begins when the ice-hard grip of winter is breaking and yielding to the first invasion of spring, and it ends when the continuous warm weather takes command.

The first task of the sugar-maker is to get all the buckets and utensils out of storage. These, with the evaporator and storage tank, are scrubbed and scalded to gleaming cleanliness. Then the trees are tapped, bit and bitstock being used to bore the holes about breast-high. Metal spouts, or spiles, small pipes with a hook underneath, are driven into the holes, and buckets are hung on the hooks. Now it is up to the weather-man to make the sap flow.

The informal beauty and grace of the maple is enough to make it seem incongruous that such a lovely tree should also be so utilitarian. But the rare quality of the product is in keeping with the appearance of the tree. There are nearly seventy varieties of the maple, the following six of which are found in Vermont: sugar (or rock) maple; black; silver; red; mountain; and box-alder (or ash-leafed) maple. The sugar and black are the best sugar trees, and Vermont is particularly adapted to the sugar maple. It is estimated that about 5,000,000, or 62%, of the available trees are tapped annually, producing some 10,000,000 pounds of sugar. The maple is a long-lived tree, seldom suitable for tapping until forty years old, and a better producer at twice that age. Some of the sugar bushes in the state were undoubtedly growing when the Pilgrims docked at Plymouth in 1620. The tree is comparatively slow-growing, but is strong and sturdy and easily-propagated.

The sugar content depends largely upon the leaf development and the amount of sunshine absorbed during the previous summer, the leaves under the sun's rays storing up starch and sugar. After the leaves flare into their dying colors and fall, the maple starts accumulating water, and by enzyme action changes starch and other insoluble carbohydrates to soluble sugars. Just before the leaves bud in the spring the roots draw up larger quantities of water from the earth, and the maple contains its greatest amount of liquid. This is the period when the sap flow is best. Tapping, when properly done, has no detrimental effects on the tree.

Sugaring-offs are traditional events. No self-respecting sugar-maker lets a season pass without inviting all-comers into the woods to enjoy his new-made sugar-on-snow, and his pride in his product is matched by the pleasure of the participants. Word passes quickly around the farms and villages. "Ed Stearns is sugaring-off tomorrow." "There's a sugaring at Old Man Hyde's Saturday." "The best sugaring-off to go to is up on Bailey's Bluff." In many cases these affairs mark the one instance of the year in which the practical-minded Yankee owners "give something away for nothing." And the curious thing is that even the most hard-shelled of them seem to actually enjoy it.

There's something about a sugaring-off party that makes people loosen up, drop the barriers, relax into jovial spirits and easy friendliness. A sugaring-off brings out the better side of folks. The brisk mountain air, smelling of fresh earth, cool snow, burning wood, boiling syrup, and pine boughs, whets the appetite to an incredible degree. The men and women and children swarming around the sugarplace share a common hunger, with the delightful means of satisfying it close at hand and free as the March breeze. The rigid winter is broken and gone, the feel of spring is in the air, and people grow mellow in the sunshine. Old feuds are forgotten for the time and good-fellowship prevails. Everything is natural, comfortable and pleasant. It is difficult to hate, or even dislike anyone at a Vermont sugaring-off.

The children romp and rollick about the woods, playing games, throwing snowballs, shouting with laughter. Perhaps they play Indians, remembering the Indian legend about the discovery of maple sugar. It was quite accidental. While Woksis, the mighty hunter, was after game, his squaw Moqua embroidered moccasins for him and boiled moose steak in the sweet water from the maple tree. She became so engrossed in fashioning a bear on the moccasins that she forgot to watch the kettle, and the water boiled away to a thick brown syrup, encrusting the meat. Moqua feared the wrath of Woksis, but it was too late to remedy her error. Woksis came back, hungry from the hunt, and after some complaining about the appearance of the meat, fell to eating it. Surprise and delight showed on his coppery face as he chewed. This new dish was a gift from the Great Spirit. Woksis boasted to his tribe that Kose-kus-beh, an emissary from the Happy Hunting Grounds, had shown his squaw how to prepare a delicious food by boiling the juice of the maple tree.

Boys and girls stroll around or bask in the sun, talking of school and parties and dances, basketball tournaments, the coming baseball season, the long summer vacation.

The men smoke their pipes and discuss the sugar season, Town Meeting, spring plowing and planting, milk prices, local and national politics, the War in Europe.

Women talk of children and families, marriages and clothes, swap gossip and recipes, and tell of the many ways maple sugar may contribute to culinary success. They use it to sweeten pickles and fruits, evolve maple cream puddings and sauces, make maple butternut candy and fudge, flavor baked beans, brown bread, gingerbread, cookies, tapioca, baked apples, fruit cobblers, and scores of other dishes. And what are corn fritters or flapjacks without hot golden Vermont maple syrup?

Inside the sugarhouse the owner supervises the final process over the "sugaring-off rig," a smaller arch and pan used to thicken the boiling syrup to the required consistency for sugar-on-snow. Other farmers and townsmen crowd in to watch this procedure and comment on improvements and innovations in the sugar-making business. Outside boys gather clean snow from hollows and ravines, packing it into pails and pans, bowls and boilers and tubs. The womenfolk busy themselves setting rough tables and benches with plates of fresh brown doughnuts and sour dill pickles. The outdoor air is electric with excitement and anticipation.

At last it is ready. The hot sugar is ladled onto the snow in fantastic patterns, quickly cooling and hardening into brittle amber pools against the white. The sugar is taken up with forks, wound about the tines, and lifted to the mouth. The taste is indescribable. It is rich and smooth and pleasing, delicate and pure. It is not sickish-sweet, yet sweet enough to need the sour bitterness of pickles to re-sharpen the appetite from time to time. The snow that clings to the sugar makes it cool and mellow. Crisp plain doughnuts help temper the sweetness, and strong hot coffee tops off the feast.

It is over all too soon. The most avaricious appetites are sated, and the people sit back to take their ease. Even the kids are too full of maple sugar to start playing immediately. Withdrawing a little from their elders, they stretch and pat their stomachs and brag about how much they consumed. The men loosen their belts and light pipes, cigars or cigarettes. The ladies sigh and lavish praises upon the sugar, the doughnuts, the pickles, the coffee.

There may be a fiddle in the crowd, and there's certain to be a harmonica or two. Music will be forthcoming as soon as the sugar is settled a bit. The music begins and voices join in, shy and hesitant at first but gradually gaining confidence and volume—"The Long Trail," "Jingle Bells," "Seeing Nellie Home," "Smile the While," "Put on Your Old Gray Bonnet," "Dinah," "There'll Be a Hot Time," "She'll Be Coming Round the Mountain," "Oh, Susanna," "Swanee River," "Working on the Railroad," "Alice Blue Gown," "When You Wore a Tulip," "Down by the Old Mill Stream," "Home Sweet Home" ... The grown-ups are wistful, remembering other sugaring-offs in the past. The youngsters are wistful, dreaming about what they'll do when they grow up.

The sun sinks toward the mountains on the western horizon, and the sky is a wilderness of purple and red, lavender and rose and gray. Dusk still comes early. The warmth fades from the air, the cutting edge comes back on the wind rustling through naked branches. Lights show in the scattered farms and a twinkling cluster marks the village at the end of the valley. It is suddenly cold as good-byes are said and people straggle homeward.

There is still work at the sugarhouse but spirits are high. It is going to be another cold night. Tomorrow, when the sun comes up to warm and brighten the March world, the sap will run again.

An Editorial Memorandum
on Clams

JAMES FRANCIS DAVIS

*James Francis Davis, or J. Frank Davis, as he was known to
the FWP, was born in the fishing port of New Bedford, Massachusetts, in 1870. In the early twentieth century he worked
in a variety of jobs for leading Boston newspapers, including
theater critic, political writer, city editor, and managing editor. In 1910 he retired as a result of an injury and moved to
San Antonio, Texas. From there he became a playwright and
had several successes, including* Gold in the Hills *and* The
Ladder, *which ran on Broadway from 1926 to 1927. He also
wrote short stories and magazine serialized stories, most of
which were set in Texas, for which he was made an honorary
Texas Ranger. He became the state supervisor for the Texas
Writers' Project. But when he heard that the state writers'
project for his home state, Massachusetts, was disintegrat-
ing and might not be contributing to* America Eats, *he sent
a memo on what he saw as the two essential New England
foods: clams and beans.*

*Davis died of a heart attack in May 1942, on the same day
that the Federal Writers' Project officially ended.*

*The one food that most defines New England and sets
it apart from the rest of North America is clams. It is the
only place on the Atlantic coast of North America where
clams are more valued than oysters. And this has been so
since long before those first Pilgrims scratched at the sand*

for bivalves because they didn't know how to fish. Most of the Indians who lived on the North Atlantic coast, not only in New England, ate clams and collected the shells of the ones New Englanders call quahogs, which they valued for their splash of purple and used to make purple-and-white beads, strung together in different lengths for different values and called "wampum." The currency was so sound that European settlers continued to trade in wampum and even produced it. In fact, clamshell wampum became easier to produce with the introduction of the European drill.

The European settlers also ate clams. William Bradford, governor of the Plymouth colony, described in his journal starving men in 1623 scratching at the sand trying to find clams to eat. One died of starvation while looking for clams.

There are two types of clams commonly eaten in New England: Mya arenaria *and* Mercenaria mercenaria. Mya arenaria, *the soft-shell clam, is by far the more important in New England, though of lesser importance most other places. It is found as far north as the Arctic and as far south as Cape Hatteras, but nowhere is it as loved as in New England, and New Englanders find it hard to believe that a good one can be found anywhere else. It is sometimes called an Ipswich clam for the bay on the northern coast of Cape Ann, which is where some of the best are found. They are frequently called steamers because steaming and then following a near ritual of rolling the black membrane off the neck, washing the individual clam in clam broth, and finally dipping it in butter, all done with a thumb and index finger, is the popular way of eating them. As popular are fried steamers, which is one of the rare traditional New England dishes involving frying. Steamers are also the traditional clam of New England clam chowder. All three dishes have remained as popular as they were in the time of* America Eats, *though frozen food and fast food companies have introduced an atrocity called the clam*

strip for fried clams. Often made of squid, the clam strip has
no belly, the soft central part of the clam, the size and plump-
ness of which is key to rating the quality of a good clam.

The Mercenaria mercenaria, *the hard-shell clam, is*
mostly eaten raw. It comes in three sizes. The smallest are
littlenecks. Long Islanders irritate New Englanders by insist-
ing that the name comes from Littleneck Bay, Long Island.
New Englanders, who tend to regard Long Island and most
of New York in much the same way that the Romans viewed
the tribes to the north, argue with logic that it is unlikely that
they would have accepted a Long Island name for one of their
traditional foods. They point out that littlenecks are found in
a part of Ipswich Bay known as "Little Neck." Middle-sized
hard-shells, also usually eaten raw, are called cherrystones
and no one seems annoyed that this may come from Cherry-
stone Creek, Virginia. The largest ones, not generally eaten
raw but thrown into chowder, are the quahogs, an authentic
name from the Narragansett, poquaûhock, *and in common*
English language usage in New England since at least the
mid-eighteenth century.

The clambake, as prepared at its best, has almost vanished; only a
few experts now make them, for private parties and at considerable expense (the last one I had, a dozen years ago, cost about $12 per
person for about a hundred guests, I was told, and doubtless would cost
more today).

The very earliest bakes contained nothing but clams, but as they
developed, especially in Rhode Island, other contents were added.
At Massachusetts shore resorts the clams are likely to be steamed;
at Rhode Island resorts they probably will come out of a bake; but even
at the Rhode Island places all the shore dinner "fixin's" except the clams
are cooked on kitchen ranges, and have been for at least fifty years—the
complete bake has never been practical for the feeding of great numbers.

In a proper Rhode Island clambake nothing comes off a stove but the clam chowder for the first course. The most elaborate one I ever ate included clams, quahogs, oysters, fish, lobsters, crabs, sweet potatoes, sweet corn, chicken, sausages, and tripe. As everything has to come out done at exactly the same moment, and as the time necessary for cooking the different contents varied very greatly, a high degree of skill and experience went into the timing of when each article was added.

Your story, I imagine, will go into the Rhode Island clambake as it used to be, and occasionally is now: The hole in the ground with stones covering the bottom; the wood fire burned on top of the stones until they are so hot that they will crackle at the sprinkling of water; the embers brushed off; a layer of wet seaweed; the clams; more wet seaweed covered with a tarpaulin or canvas spiked down all around to keep in the steam; quick openings and closings to put in other ingredients, the fish, chicken and similar contents sewed into cheesecloth so as not to be touched by seaweed or ashes, the sweet corn in its husks; the final triumphant opening with everything properly cooked and ready to serve. (The chowder—absent of course when no stove is handy—is served about ten minutes before the bake is opened. The traditional dessert is watermelon.)

When you write about clams, readers outside New England will be confused unless it is made clear that the clam in New England is not the same as the clam in, say, Maryland, where Little Necks on the half shell have helped to make Baltimore famous. The Little Neck, when grown, is still a clam south of New England, but in New England he is—and always was, even when he was called a Little Neck—a quahog. Outsiders frequently call New England clams "soft clams," and the Standard Dictionary says that the quahog is a "round clam," both of which are ridiculous to any true seaside Yankee. He will tell you, anywhere along the coast from Maine to Connecticut, that "a clam is a clam and a quahog is a quahog."

You probably will be saying something about clam chowder, and you may or may not know that there always has been a considerable difference between the—so-called—Massachusetts and Rhode Island clam chowders, with bitter debates as to their relative merits. As I was born in Massachusetts but once was press agent for a Rhode Island shore resort (where 6,000 clambake eaters each pleasant Sunday was the season's average) I take no sides. Both factions speak with equal scorn of "clam chowder, Coney Island style." (Incidentally, a lot of people think a good clam chowder is even better the second day, warmed up.)

Maine Clambake

HARRY M. FREEMAN

It is well known in New England that the clambake was an Indian tradition adopted by the early settlers. The Indians cooked clams on the beach to celebrate a fortuitous event such as a good fish catch. The settlers started doing the same and gradually the menu expanded. This may be one of the great apocryphal stories of food history, like Marco Polo carrying pasta to Italy from China. Piles of shells attest to the Indian fondness for shellfish, but there is no evidence for or against the hypothesis that the Indians had celebrations on the beach baking clams in seaweed with hot rocks.

The earliest evidence of clams taking on symbolic impor- tance was in the 1720 centennial celebrations of the Pilgrims' landing, when special attention was given to corn and clams as symbols of the first settlers. As Indians became fewer and fewer, New Englanders increasingly romanticized and ide- alized them. In the eighteenth and nineteenth centuries it became fashionable to have "Indian-style" outdoor clam feasts. The clams were cooked in pits on heated rocks with seaweed in what they imagined to be the Indian style. After more than a century of white people having such clambakes, it became established that the technique was taken from the Indians or

*even taught to the Pilgrims by the Indians. Starting in the
eighteenth century, these clambakes were called "squantums,"
named after a woman who was supposedly the last Indian to
live on Boston Harbor. By the mid-nineteenth century other
local foods such as corn or lobster were included at squantums. Today, as in the time of* America Eats, *clambakes
remain a common sight in summer dusk on New England
beaches.*

Those who are fond of seafood seldom can resist an opportunity to enjoy a shore dinner at their favorite seaside resort. Not many of the present generation, however, have had the wonderful experience or the epicurean delights of an out-door "clam-bake" way down in Maine.

Let us suppose you are already at the seashore, you will be awake at sunrise and in your old clothes.

You will need the help of others in your party in gathering numerous large rocks from the shore. These rocks will be spread out in the form of a flat pile. Then a large wood fire will be built on the rocks and allowed to burn several hours to thoroughly heat the rocks.

While the rocks are heating, put on your rubber boots and, with an old hoe, go to the flats to dig your clams. On the beach you will also gather a quantity of seaweed.

By this time the rocks will probably be heated, and you can remove most of the fire. A layer of seaweed is put on the hot rocks and then your clams, lobsters, potatoes, corn and whatnot. Finally place another layer of seaweed to cover your victuals.

Your muscles will now thoroughly ache and you will need to sit around to relax and smack your lips.

New York Indoor Clam-Bake

M. METEVIER OF FULTON, NEW YORK

S erved once a year. Tickets sell from $1.50 to $2.50, depending upon the number of courses to be served. No decorations whatsoever, every effort is put into the meal. Tables are covered with white paper. All food is served on paper plates. Cardboard containers are used for clam broth; the cover for melted butter.

Menu:

Clam Broth	Crackers
Raw Clams on Ice	In large platters, help yourself
Steamed Clams	Salted Potatoes
Clam Chowder	
Lobster (Steamed)	Shoe String Potatoes
One-half Broiler	Irish and Sweet Potatoes
Sweet Corn	Celery
Cottage Cheese	Pickles
Olives	Radishes
Rolls	Butter
Melon	Coffee

The above meal is favored at the K. C. Home. It is an annual feast. No program, nothing but eats!

Rhode Island Clam Chowder

WALTER HACKETT AND HENRY MANCHESTER

In the founding memorandum for America Eats, *Katherine Kellock specifies that regional food rivalries and differences were of particular interest. Clam chowder is an example. It is another one of those New England fetishes that still remains. Even within one small town, locals will argue about who has the best clam chowder. Everyone will agree that it certainly is not any good in New York or Long Island. In fact, the preceding recipe for "New York Indoor Clam-Bake" is a New Englander's idea of how New Yorkers get it wrong. Putting tomatoes in clam chowder probably comes from Portuguese or Italian cooks in New England, specifically Rhode Island. Massachusetts people expressed their scorn for the Rhode Island tomato and clam soup by calling it "Manhattan clam chowder," though it had nothing to do with Manhattan. Perhaps New Englanders were right about New Yorkers. At the time of* America Eats, *the two regions were competitive in clam production, but while New England has maintained its beds, Long Island clamming, largely due to pollution, has gone into decline.*

The origin of the word chowder *is uncertain. By one theory it comes from the archaic French coastal word* chaudière, *a large pot. Or it might come from a Celtic word, since chowders seem characteristic of the Bretons, Cornish, and Welsh. In Cornwall and Devonshire there was an old word for a fish peddler, a* jowter. *New England and Atlantic Canadian chowder was originally fishermen's fare at sea made of what*

was available from ships' provisions—salt pork, hardtack, or
dried sea biscuits and potatoes. Then a freshly caught fish,
usually a cod, was thrown in. Once chowder came to land,
clams, not found at sea, sometimes were used instead of fish.
The addition of milk did not come until the nineteenth cen-
tury, about the same time that "chowder parties" emerged.
Chowder parties, a craze in the second half of the nineteenth
century, were a variation on clambakes in which large groups
of family and friends went to the beach with a full retinue
of flatware and plates and additional food, and the chowder
was made on the beach.

I n his *A Key into the Language of America*, Roger Williams, founder of Rhode Island, wrote: "Sickissaug . . . This is a sweet kind of shellfish which all Indians generally over the country, Winter and Summer delight in; and at low water the women dig for them: this fish, and the natural liquor of it, they boil, and it makes their broth, their Nasaump (which is a kind of thickened broth)."

So it was that the Indians made, drank, and enjoyed their "thickened broth." But not for long. Oh, no! For with the entry of the white men into what is now Rhode Island, this picture of culinary contentment changed. What was good enough for the Indians wasn't good enough for the followers of Roger Williams, for they—meddlesome and finicky creatures that they must have been—became intent upon improving the "thickened broth." It is claimed by one school of little known and possibly inaccurate historians that the tribes became so wrought up over the shameful attempt of the Rhode Island white men to improve upon "thickened broth" that they—led by a sympathetic chieftain from the Massachusetts sector—broke out in open revolt. Hence, King Philip's War, from the Indian chief of the same name.

Now if these same white men had had an inkling of the furor that was to follow, an argument destined to become ageless, they possibly wouldn't have bothered to improve the primary Indian dish. They'd have forgotten all about chowder, and said: "O.K. So it's 'thickened broth.'"

All of which points to the main issue: Whether or not to use tomatoes in place of milk. It is also possible to raise a good rip-roaring argument on the subject of clams versus quahogs, likewise on the use of salt pork and onions.

Governor Winslow, of the Plymouth Colony, is said to have imported cows as early as 1624 (there were no cows on the *Mayflower*—just goats; cow fodder would have taken up the all-important space needed for antiques). A cow in a canoe—it is claimed—is an unhandy thing, so there is serious doubt that Roger Williams had one with him when he landed upon Rhode Island soil. However, at a slightly later date, there were plenty of cows within a few miles of the new colony, and no doubt some of them were brought to Providence. Thus we see the possibility—but no proof—that Rhode Island clam chowder had milk added to it as early as the second half of the seventeenth century.

How to dispose of the Tomato Challenge: *Rhode Island clam chowder contained no tomatoes until about 200 years after the founding of the state in 1636.* This is a reasonable statement because tomatoes, in those very early days, were considered poisonous. However, when tomatoes were added to clam chowder, much of it was due to the work of a transplanted Rhode Islander.

This brings to the fore one Michele Felice Corne. An Italian painter, he landed in Salem, Massachusetts, in 1800. Corne painted murals (it saved wall paper, he claimed) in Salem, Boston, and Providence. But business couldn't have been so good, because he turned to cultivating tomatoes. But people, thinking him mildly deranged, refused to eat his tomatoes. When he moved to Newport, Rhode Island, in 1822, he once again picked up the loose shreds of tomato-growing. By dint of hard work and much talk, Corne managed to win to his side a few converts, and then more and more until finally Rhode Island, along with other states, became tomato conscious. The rush to climb aboard the tomato bandwagon began.

By 1840, tomatoes were held to be healthful. Popular medicines of the day attracted customers by adding extract of tomatoes to their formulas. Now it is entirely possible that some convert to the rank of the tomato may, in an unpremeditated burst of enthusiasms, have dropped an innocent tomato into the clam chowder—when no one was looking.

This is the other half of the long-winded argument. Winning sympathy at every step, and all the while challenging the deeply-rooted milk chowder, the tomato clam chowder bloc gained in power. The cause of the tomato won additional strength when the resorts alongshore serving bakes, known as shore dinner places, added tomatoes to their chowder. Even Colonel Atwell of the famous Fields Point establishment was guilty of this culinary outrage. Probably people coming from outside the state, strangers to Rhode Island ways, took this concoction for real Rhode Island clam chowder.

Roger Williams's observations on clams conclude on a plaintive note: "The English Swine dig and root these Clams whensoever they come, and watch low water (as the Indian women do), therefore of all the English Cattell, the Swine as also of their filthy dispositions are most hateful to all Natives, and they call them filthy cut-throats, etc."

There was, perhaps, a point to the Indian's hatred of the white man. He didn't have a chance. Even the pigs raced him for his favorite food—the clam.

Below is the recipe for real Rhode Island clam chowder, which was, and still is, popular with in-staters from Newport to South County:

Fry four slices of mixed salt pork until brown; add two onions, sliced, and fry. Remove the pork and onions from the pork fat and add to it four cups of water, four cups of diced potatoes. Cook until the potatoes are nearly done, then add four cups of chopped clams from which all black parts have been removed. Add salt and pepper to taste. Scald three cups of rich milk, and add to first mixture. Let it all boil up at once and pour into a tureen in which four crackers have been broken, together with one-eighth pound of butter.

To allow the disciples of tomato clam (or quahog) chowder their innings, here is their pet recipe:

Cut one-quarter pound of fat salt pork in fine pieces. Chop two onions and add them to the pork. Fry this mixture until brown. Strain one can of tomatoes and add three quarts of water, a dash of salt and pepper and a pinch of maize. To this add the juice from the quahogs. Boil this mixture one-half hour over a slow fire. Chop a quart of quahogs (the juice already has been added to the tomato mixture) and add them and two quarts of medium sliced potatoes to the rest of the mixture. Boil slowly for another half-hour.

Long Island Clam Chowder

In most of the shore towns on the north and south shores of Long Island we pride ourselves on the Sea Food. One of our favorite dishes is the famous Long Island Clam Chowder, which is served as a part of a Shore Dinner and also served separately as a light lunch.

CLAM CHOWDER FOR 12 PERSONS
Open 35 raw clams, saving the clams and also the juice. DO NOT STEAM TO OPEN.

INGREDIENTS
  3 cups of chopped celery
  1 medium sized can of tomatoes
  5 medium sized onions
  15 medium sized potatoes
  3 medium sized carrots
  ½ medium sized turnip (optional)
  ½ teaspoon of chopped parsley
  6 slices bacon
  salt, pepper and thyme
  3 quarts of water

Chop the vegetables, (raw) onions, potatoes, carrots, celery, tomatoes and turnip. Cook them for about 1½ hours or until cooked, then add the clam broth and grease from the 6 strips of bacon but not the bacon (having fried the bacon while the vegetables were cooking). Season this with salt, pepper and thyme to suit taste. Add the rest of the 3 quarts of water. Put the clams through the meat chopper and then into the pot containing the vegetables, etc. Let come to a boil and set aside in a warm place. Reheat before serving. Serve with crackers and butter on the side.

Recipe by Mrs. Margarite Gross, Greene Avenue, Sayville, L.I., N.Y. A successful dispenser of seafood for over forty years.

Maine Chowders

MABEL G. HALL

The suggestion for potato chowder at the bottom of this recipe is a recognition of the poverty and suffering in Depression Maine. Mabel G. Hall was a local Maine historian.

Chowder is a staple dish—and ranks next to eggs as a make-shift meal for unexpected guests. The base is always the same: diced salt pork in the bottom of the kettle—while this is "trying out," the onions and potatoes are peeled. Then the onions are sliced or diced into the fat and cooked for at least half an hour, needing to be stirred from time to time. A small amount of water is then added and the potatoes diced or sliced into the brew, with sufficient water to cover the potatoes. A generous amount of salt is added and the chowder is left to cook for another half hour. Any of the following is added: clams, cut fish, or stewed corn; and at least a cup of milk. If none of these are available the dish is served as potato chowder. Seafood to be served in any form must be not more than six hours out of the water.

Oyster Stew Supreme at Grand Central, New York

ALLAN ROSS MacDOUGALL

The Grand Central Oyster Bar of which Allan Ross MacDou-
gall writes is one of the few restaurants mentioned in America
Eats *that is still in operation today. It was part of the original*
Grand Central Terminal opened in 1913 as the largest and
most luxurious train station in the world. Among the other
special features were ramps instead of stairs and a hair salon
in the women's waiting room. New York City had been famous
for centuries for the oyster beds of the harbor and other city
waterways. The shores of all five boroughs were covered in
oyster beds and the land was marked by ancient piles of dis-
carded shells. One has been carbon-dated to 6950 B.C. Oys-
ters were a part of the New York way of life.

Oysters had always been incredibly cheap in New York. The
Canal Street plan was all you could eat for six cents. They
were sold on street corners, in all-night downtown markets,
in basement "oyster cellars" in the slums, and in the famous
luxury restaurants. But up until Grand Central opened they
had not been sold in train stations. This was an out-of-town
tradition from western towns like St. Louis that received their
New York and Chesapeake oysters by train.

By the time the Oyster Bar opened, the beds were being
closed one by one for the typhus and cholera epidemics they
were causing as a result of centuries of dumping raw sewage

into the water. At the time of America Eats, *no local oysters were available in New York and New Yorkers had turned to what MacDougall refers to as "specially selected waters around Long Island."*

Oyster stew was a traditional New York dish, a late-night favorite at the Fulton Market, like onion soup at the Les Halles market in Paris. J. D. Newsom, in a memorandum on New England for America Eats, *wrote that oyster stew was a traditional Sunday breakfast in inland New England, too far from the coast for the more fragile clams. I remember that it was featured in the better Hartford restaurants when I was a child. But today it is too rich to be fashionable.*

To judge by the figures New York is the ostreaphilic capital of the world. Over 10,000,000 pounds of shell oysters and 1,000,000 pounds of shucked ones pass through Fulton Fish Market each year. The greater part remains within the city to be consumed in various forms.

For as long as there has been written history of the city there has been mention of oysters. Colonial records tell of the plentiful supply about the small islands of the Upper Bay. Today the oyster beds are cultivated in specially selected waters around Long Island and from these come a tremendous yearly harvest which supplies not only the neighboring cities but many inland and foreign markets.

Connoisseurs know Gardiner's Island Salts from Blue Points and can distinguish the sweet, dark-flavored meats of Oyster Bays from those, also

sweet, of Greenports. The Long Island varieties are many, some highly publicized, others known only to a few. Some are sought after for their marine flavor, others, sent to market already shucked, are thought to be more desirable for cooking in ways perfected through the years by culinary experts.

Of the many distinctly American methods, none is more satisfactory to the average man's taste than the Oyster Stew. Indeed, many who cannot abide the sight of a raw oyster admit a passionate fondness for the creamy goodness of a well-made oyster stew. Oyster-lovers who can take their favorite bivalve in any form also consider the stew the most acceptable method of cooking.

There is one place in New York where this stew is a supreme delight: the Oyster Bar of the Grand Central Terminal, known as a landmark on the American epicure's map. Well-travelled gourmets have been heard to say: "Prunier's of Paris for Lobster Thermidor; Scott's of Piccadilly for Devilled Crab; the Grand Central Oyster Bar for Oyster Stew."

In 1913 when the terminal was opened the Oyster Bar was a small counter with 3 or 4 seats, set off in a corner of the restaurant. The Oyster Stew served there soon, like the proverbial mouse-trap, brought the world in a well-beaten track to this counter. It was extended and extended again. The number of seats and specially contrived cooking bowls were both augmented. Today there are 42 seats, which never seem sufficient to accommodate the hungry crowds that in rush hours sometimes stand three deep. Commuters, snatching a hasty snack to tide them over until dinner at home, form a large portion of its regular customers.

The recipe for the Grand Central Terminal Oyster Stew has been given as follows:

GRAND CENTRAL OYSTER STEW
(Individual portion)

Melt ½ ounce of butter in double boiler; add ⅓ teaspoon of salt, ⅓ teaspoon celery salt, ⅓ teaspoon paprika, one shake of white pepper, 8 drops of Worcestershire sauce, 2 large tablespoons of oyster (or clam) liquor.

Boil briskly for a few minutes with constant stirring. As mixture bubbles high, add 8 large oysters and cook 3 minutes more, all the while turning the oysters gently. Add ½ pint of rich milk and continue to stir. When mixture begins to boil, pour out into a bowl, add a pat of butter and a shake of paprika. Serve with small round oyster crackers.

Rhode Island Jonny Cakes

HENRY MANCHESTER AND WILLIAM BAKER

There are only three things about jonny cakes that New Englanders agree on.

1. It is spelled j-o-n-n-y with no H.

2. While Rhode Islanders sneer at Connecticut jonny cakes, they are actually found along the Atlantic Coast from Newfoundland to Jamaica. But New Englanders insist they were invented in Rhode Island.

3. They must be made from flint corn, so called because it is hard as flint, otherwise known as Indian corn because it is a species developed by Indians. Unlike a lot of Indian corn, this type is not colorful and produces a fine white corn meal that is known in Rhode Island and eastern Connecticut as "jonny cake corn meal." The meal can be mixed with water or milk, and the amount depends on how absorbent the meal is. Sugar is or is not added. The batter is cooked in pork fat in an open fire, or on a stove . . .

To Rhode Islanders born within breeze-cooling distance of lower Narragansett Bay and the Atlantic, the ability to differentiate between genuine, honest-to-goodness jonny cakes and the palate-insulting commercial substitutes is a natural inheritance. Upon them has fallen the divine blessing of recognizing corn bread as corn bread, fried mush as fried mush, and the steaming, golden-brown jonny cakes as ambrosial crumbs graciously brushed from an angel's ethereal platter. Patterned by the weaving shadows of creaking vanes on the several extant windmills that still grind their corn into meal the "right way," this boon to man's stomach receives the chanted praises of the natives of old South County and of the historic Island of Rhode Island. The melody is the same but the words are at variance: the Islanders like thin cakes with crisp crust; the Mainlanders prefer more substantial matter separating the crispness.

The people of southern Rhode Island do not claim to have originated the delicacy, it being an Indian dish. But they do assert, and with seeming justness, that locally-grown corn ground between local millstones produces the finest meal obtainable. Not all of the state's meal is suitable for use, some being gray, coarse, and yellow.

Columbus was the first European to make note of jonny cake meal. When in Cuba, in 1492, he sampled the *Madis* of the natives and found it delightfully taste-tingling. Soon the Indians, like the proverbial builder of a better mousetrap, found a path being beaten to their door. Staunch jonny cake fanciers argue that the only possible reason civilized Europe flocked to primitive America was because of the irresistible magnetism of the jonny cake.

Be that as it may, in the deprivation of the red man of everything he possessed, the white man did not neglect the maize. Colonial epicures soon ascertained it took little time for a squaw to whip up a concoction of corn meal and cold water and place it before an open fire, or on a heated rock, to bake. The corn meal was always in the brave's meal bag as he took the trail on hunting or fighting expeditions, often being his only food supply. White wayfarers continued the custom, the meal, however, being baked in cake form and known as journey cake. From this appellation came jonny or johnny cake.

More fastidious than their teachers, the early settlers could not condone the stray dog hairs, wood ashes, and little crawling things that somehow managed to be found in the Indian dish—they were too hard to digest. They improved the jonny cake by using a board to cook it upon, adding salt (perhaps), by scalding the meal, using milk in the mixture, and by basting it with cream while it baked.

Between the dim recollection of a pre-colonial squaw squatting before her fire tending her maize and her streamlined current equivalent, the modern housewife, looms the imposing figure of Shepard Tom, nine-teenth century authority on the *proper* and *only* way to prepare jonny cakes. And if there ever was anyone who loved the tongue-burning tid-bits more than South County's beloved Thomas Robinson Hazard, well, written history has been delinquent.

Mr. Hazard's whimsical voice has been stilled these many years, but his directions as to the making of his favorite farinaceous food, as it was cooked in his day by Phillis, his grandfather's cook, are available to all in Jonny Cake Papers. The only drawback to following them implicitly is in the collecting of needed equipment: a red oak barrel-head and an old-fashioned flat-iron to support it, together with a quick green hard-wood fire roaring in an open fireplace.

After Shepard Tom's Phillis had sifted the meal for her jonny cake, she scalded it with boiling water, kneaded it in a wooden tray, and added new milk or water to make it of the right consistency. Then anointing it with sweet cream, she placed it on the jonny cake board and set it before the blazing fire. Phillis claimed there never was a genuine jonny cake that was not baked on a red oak board taken from the middle part of the head of a flour barrel. In her eyes, too, the value of a heart-shaped flat-iron for laundry use was secondary to its special adaptability as a support for her jonny cake board. First the flat's smooth and glistening surface would hold the board in a perpendicular position until the main portion of the cake was baked. Then its slanting side would support it while the top and bottom cooked. Lastly the flat's handle partly held the board as the ends received the heat. Sufficiently baked on one side, the process was repeated when the cake was turned.

Shepard Tom insisted upon the term "jonny cake" in preference to johnny cake. As to the spelling, he may have been right, but his dismal contention that, although a decent jonny cake could be baked on a stove, all good painstaking cooks are extinct is a decided breach of good taste.

By vowing to be "careful and painstaking," by following the generations-proven formula faithfully, by using down-state ground, white, bolted meal, along with milk, sugar, and water, a culinary mas-terpiece of satisfaction can be achieved.

In preparation, meal may or may not be scalded with hot water or hot milk in accordance to preference. After mixing meal with water or milk it is dropped on a smoking hot spider set atop a stove into cakes about 3" × 3" × ½" in size. The secret of cooking jonny cakes is to watch them closely and keep them supplied with enough sausage or bacon fat so they will become brown and crisp, and not burn. Cook slowly for half an hour, turn occasionally, and when done serve with plenty of butter; steak, sausages, or sausage meat make admirable side dishes.

It should be stressed that jonny cakes must be piping hot to be enjoyed. The distance between stove and table should not be great so as to insure this condition, and though grace be omitted before eating Rhode Island jonny cakes, there'll surely be an added note of thankfullness in the prayer when rendered after the repast.

Shepard Tom was remiss in but one detail in his self-appointed role as nineteenth century exponent and press agent of the jonny cakes. When cold, Rhode Island jonny cakes resemble in taste synthetic rubber.

Beans

JAMES FRANCIS DAVIS

New Englanders had two reasons for eating their beans. Neither is relevant anymore. Puritans liked them for the same reason Orthodox Jews do—they can be prepared in advance and do not need cooking on the Sabbath, which, in the case of Puritans, was Sunday. The second one is the same reason for New England rum, Indian pudding, and numerous other specialties—New England was awash in molasses from their cod, slave, and molasses trade with Caribbean sugar-growing islands. The beans were baked in molasses.

Today, whenever the Red Sox are playing in Boston's

Fenway Park, announcers reassert the nickname of Boston
as "Bean Town," though the concession stands prefer selling
clam chowder. Boston's claim to the bean title stems from a
famous speech in Worcester at Holy Cross College in 1910
when John Collins Bossidy said, "This is good old Boston, the
home of the bean and the cod, where the Lowells talk only to
the Cabots, and the Cabots talk only to God." But it is unlikely
that Boston was the home of the bean, the original "Bean
Town." Among those who claim this dubious distinction is the
North Shore town of Beverly, which by chance is also the real
home of the Cabots, who made their fortune from cod.

Lucy Larcom, a well-known local poet of nineteenth-century
Beverly, wrote, "In those early days, towns used to give each
other nicknames, like school boys—ours was called 'Bean
Town'. . . probably because it adhered a long time to the Puri-
tanic custom of saving Sunday-work by baking beans on Sat-
urday evening, leaving them in the oven overnight."

The navy bean was preferred in southern New England
and the kidney bean in the north. We have a choice of about
five thousand beans, though in modern times the navy bean
has been taking over. At the time of America Eats, *both Puri-*
tanism and the slave trade had been abandoned, but baked
beans remained in New England. Now with the modern quest
for lighter food, baked beans are in decline in New England,
though they still occasionally turn up in restaurants as a
side dish.

I n many New England homes, to this day, baked beans—usually
with brown bread—are a Saturday night ritual. The custom once
was, and still is in some Yankee households, to serve them for both Saturday night supper and Sunday morning breakfast, and the reason for it
was primarily religious.

All labor on Sunday was forbidden by the Puritans as Sabbath-
breaking, and among the strict disciples of the Massachusetts Bay

theocracy cooking was tabu; even the building of fires except when necessary for warmth was proscribed. What food was eaten on Sunday must
have been wholly prepared on a weekday. On Saturday, in the great ovens
built into the kitchen fireplaces, enough food was baked to last into the
following week. This almost invariably included baked beans, which lost
nothing in flavor by not being served immediately and by some are held
to be even better when warmed over, and baked beans logically became
the Saturday night and Sunday morning menu.

With the growth of relative liberalism came some slight modifica-
tion of the rules as to Sunday domestic labor, but members of all the
Evangelical churches continued, until late in the nineteenth century, to
interpret the matter of Sabbath-breaking strictly. From this developed a
system of Saturday and Sunday meals which provided satisfactory food
throughout the day of rest within the requirements of the householders'
religious scruples.

Dinner at noon on Saturday was a roast or—most commonly—a
corned beef "boiled dinner," and in either case enough vegetables were
cooked to supply two hearty meals. Saturday supper was baked beans
and brown bread—the kind that now is usually called "Boston brown
bread" outside of New England (what people of some other sections call
"Boston brown bread" is "graham bread" in Yankeeland). Indian pudding was also cooked on many Saturdays, especially in the winter when
a banked fire would be left in the kitchen range overnight, and this only
needs to be kept warm to be at its best in the morning.

Sunday breakfast was warmed over baked beans, brown bread, and
perhaps Indian pudding. Sunday dinner was more of yesterday's roast or
corned beef, cold, with the remaining vegetables heated up. Supper was
cold meat, bread and butter, cake, cookies, and preserves. For these fully
adequate and appetizing meals no cooking whatever had to be done on
Sunday. The only domestic labor was heating up food, making coffee and
tea, and washing dishes.

There are many recipes for baked beans, which have been handed
down for generations, and the judgment of most New Englanders as to
how they ought to be prepared is likely to be influenced importantly by
what kind mother used to make. A majority of families have preferred

pea beans (quite commonly called "California pea beans"), while others have used kidney beans or yellow-eyed beans—their choice in the beginning probably having been based on the kind that they found it easiest to raise. Mother's recipe, which her mother used, calls for sugar sweetening. Aunt Emily's—she is father's sister and got her rule from that side of the house—calls for molasses. Cousin Walter's wife combines both sugar and molasses. None of them would think of adding any onion flavor, but a branch of grandfather's family always buries a whole onion in the bean pot contents. Opinions also vary as to precisely what cut of salt pork should be nearly submerged at the top of the pot, its rind left clear so that it will be brown and crisp, a majority of cooks leaning toward the kind that they describe as "a streak o' lean and a streak o' fat."

As there is nothing approaching agreement among New Englanders themselves as to which of these different-tasting preparations is the best, and the individual who enthuses over one may find little to praise in any of the others, what wonder that visitors from afar, prepared to judge all baked beans by the first serving they get, gain widely divergent views as to whether the dish is what it has been cracked up to be.

In large hotels it is seldom notable; such homely fare is unlikely to have been given much attention in the training of expensive chefs. In large city restaurants the baked beans have probably come out of the five-gallon cans of national manufacturers, the restaurateur's sound argument in favor of this being that customers who like his beans will return to order them and be disappointed if they find any difference in style and taste—and that as he has to change cooks from time to time and no two cooks are sure to bake beans the same way, it is better to use a brand that will not vary.

The stranger fortunate enough to be invited to eat Saturday night beans in a household whose feminine head is a good cook will not then and there learn how all home-cooked baked beans in New England taste, but if the recipe is one that he likes, he will like it very much indeed.

Maine Baked Beans

MABEL G. HALL

Baked Beans—Beans are picked over every Friday night and set on the back of the stove to parboil. Before breakfast on Saturday morning the earthen bean pot is brought from the pantry, the beans are given a final rinse then put in the pot; a tablespoon of molasses, a teaspoon each of salt and dry mustard are added and nearly a quarter-pound of fat salt pork is partially submerged in the beans and the pot is filled with water. A hot fire is kept, water is added from time to time until 2 o'clock and after 3 the fire is allowed to die down.

Kenneth Roberts' Maine-Style Hot Buttered Rum

DONALD McCORMICK

Rum was so popular in the northeastern United States in the seventeenth and early eighteenth centuries that the word rum *was popularly used for any strong alcohol. Another product of the New England slave trade, rum is distilled from molasses.*

In New England small, local rum distilleries were established in many towns throughout the region.

Eighteenth-century Americans drank enormous quantities of rum. By the twentieth century this consumption had been considerably reduced, though it has remained the leading alcohol. This is one of many alcohol recipes offered to America Eats *in an America where drinking took on a special meaning because Prohibition, which lasted until 1933, was a recent memory.*

Though little is known of Donald McCormick from the Maine Writers' Workshop, Kenneth Roberts, mentioned in several manuscripts from Maine for America Eats, *was a leading Maine writer. Born in Kennebunk in 1885, he was known for well-researched historical novels, the most well-known of which was* Northwest Passage, *about the French and Indian War. In 1957, the year he died, he was awarded a Pulitzer Prize Special Citation for his work.*

R ural Maine has never recovered from the widespread reaction to the excessive drinking of the early days of the district and the state. The temperance movements of the latter half of the eighteenth century, the influence of New Deal and others, put liquor in disrepute. State-controlled liquor has been voted back, but this has had no effect on many residents.

As a result, there is little group or ceremonial drinking in Maine homesteads. It is often the case that the men of the household refrain from drinking at home as a wife, mother, or grandmother objects to alcohol. For traditional Maine drinks one must go back to the days when wines, liquors, and punches were part of most social affairs.

Hard cider is fairly common today. There are a dozen recipes for obtaining the best product; the introduction of raisins or beefsteak into the aging cider is advocated by some. Another time-honored practice is to place a barrel of hard cider in the barnyard and allow it to freeze; the remaining liquor that is drained off is applejack, a remarkably powerful fluid. Of course, there are legal technicalities concerning mere posses-sion of such un-taxed beverages.

Kenneth Roberts, Maine author of historical novels, has brought the Maine pioneer favorite, hot buttered rum, to some recent popularity through description in his works. His recipe is as follows:

> Pour one fair-sized drink (or jigger) of rum into an ordinary
> table tumbler: add one lump of sugar, a pat of butter the size of a
> single hotel helping, half a teaspoonful of cinnamon, fill up the
> tumbler with boiling water, stir well and sip thoughtfully. If too
> sweet, use less sugar in the next attempt. If not sweet enough,
> add more. If the cinnamon isn't wholly satisfactory, try cloves. If
> more butter seems desirable, use more.*

A good deal of beer and ale is consumed in Maine today. This is partially due to the strictness of state requirements in the licensing of cocktail rooms.

In any event, it must be admitted that no state traditions of convivial elbow-bending are sufficiently widespread today to merit mention.

---

*Roberts, Kenneth, *Trending into Maine*, Boston, 1938.

THE
SOUTH EATS

LOUISIANA—*responsible for the region and the overall project*

DELAWARE

MARYLAND

WASHINGTON, D.C.

VIRGINIA

WEST VIRGINIA

NORTH CAROLINA

SOUTH CAROLINA

GEORGIA

FLORIDA

ALABAMA

MISSISSIPPI

TENNESSEE

KENTUCKY

ARKANSAS

The South

Southerners, along with New Englanders, are the most tenacious of Americans in terms of clinging to regional traditions. Yet, while many of the food traditions have been maintained, there is no part of the country that has changed as much since the time of *America Eats* as the South, which was impoverished, segregated, and clinging to a war that was two and three generations behind them. It is significant that the South is usually defined by that war, a grouping of the states that comprised the Confederate States of America. But the U.S. Census Bureau did not see it that way, and so the FWP did not either. By a happy coincidence the Census Bureau's grouping makes perfect sense from a gastronomic point of view. By leaving off Texas, which has many southern cultural characteristics, they removed a state whose food more closely resembles the Southwest. And by including the border states, they brought in states that had sided with the Union but whose food traditions, and many other traditions, are clearly southern.

This journey by time capsule to the early 1940s is not always a pleasant one. It affords us a glimpse at the pre–civil rights South. This was true in the raw copy of the guidebooks as well. The Alabama guidebook copy referred to blacks as "darkies." It originally described the city of Florence struggling through "the terrible reconstruction, those evil days when in bitter poverty, her best and bravest of them sleep in Virginia battlefields, her civilization destroyed . . . And now when the darkest hour had struck, came a flash of light, the forerunners of dawn. It was the Ku Klux Klan . . ." The Dover, Delaware, report stated that "Negroes whistle melodiously." Ohio copy talked of their "love for pageantry and fancy dress." Such embarrassingly racist passages were usually edited out, but the *America Eats* manuscripts are unedited, so the word *darkies* remains in a Kentucky recipe for eggnog. In the southern essays from *America Eats*, whenever there is dialogue between a black and a white, it reads like an exchange between a slave and a master. There also seems to be a racist oral fixation. Black people are always sporting big "grins." A description of a Mississippi barbecue cook states, "Bluebill is what is known as a 'bluegum' Negro, and they call him the brother of the Ugly man, but personal beauty is not in the least necessary to a barbecue cook." And in the memos and correspondence there are traces of anti-Semitism, such as the suggestion that the New York writings about Jewish traditions be cut from the book because they were not truly American. That one was quickly refuted by the FWP staff.

While the racist attitudes of the old South are in evidence here, and are even more in evidence in some of the pieces that are not included, there is also an overall difference in the way southern food was regarded in the time of *America Eats* and the view today. While the old view was that African-American cooking was an interesting and colorful addition to the southern tradition, food writers today generally find that southern food *is* African American to its roots. A great many of the cooks, including some of the most influential, were black.

F. M. GAY'S ANNUAL BARBECUE GIVEN ON HIS PLANTATION
EVERY YEAR.

Mississippi Food

EUDORA WELTY

Eudora Welty was born in Jackson, Mississippi, in 1909. After two years at the Mississippi State College for Women, encouraged by her parents, she went to study English at the University of Wisconsin. After graduating in 1929 she spent a year at Columbia University, studying advertising. She returned to Mississippi to start a writing career, producing short stories on Mississippi life. Her first story, "Death of a Traveling Salesman," a touching story in which a salesman discovers the importance of family, was published in 1936, in a small magazine called Manuscript. *But when her father died suddenly, she sought advertising jobs to earn money.*

The following was a mimeographed pamphlet that she wrote for the Mississippi Advertising Commission and which they distributed. The FWP could have had little notion of Welty's future when they selected this piece, possibly Welty's only piece of food writing. At the time of the America Eats *project her career was beginning to develop, and her first collection was published in 1941. The Mississippi Writers' Project probably knew of her from her work in advertising for the WPA in Mississippi. A year later, when the project was closed, Welty would win her first O. Henry Prize and a Guggenheim Award. Welty went on to become one of America's most distinguished southern writers. Before her death in 2001, she had won six O. Henry Awards for Short Stories, a National Medal for Literature, a Pulitzer Prize, and France's highest honor, the Legion of Honor.*

*S*tark Young, in his book *Feliciana*, tells how a proud and lovely Southern lady, famous for her dinner table and for her closely-guarded recipes, temporarily forgot how a certain dish was prepared. She asked her Creole cook, whom she herself had taught, for the recipe. The cook wouldn't give it back.

Still highly revered, recipes in the South are no longer quite so literally guarded. Generosity has touched the art of cooking, and now and then, it is said, a Southern lady will give another Southern lady her favorite recipe and even include all the ingredients, down to that magical little touch that makes all the difference.

In the following recipes, gleaned from ante-bellum homes in various parts of Mississippi, nothing is held back. That is guaranteed. Yankees are welcome to make these dishes. Follow the directions and success is assured.

Port Gibson, Mississippi, which General Grant on one occasion declared was "too beautiful to burn," is the source of a group of noble old recipes. "Too beautiful to burn" by far are the jellied apples which Mrs. Herschel D. Brownlee makes and the recipe for which she parts with as follows:

JELLIED APPLES

Pare and core one dozen apples of a variety which will jell successfully. Winesap and Jonathan are both good.

To each dozen apples moisten well two and one-half cups of sugar. Allow this to boil for about five minutes. Then immerse apples in this syrup, allowing plenty of room about each apple. Add the juice of one-half lemon, cover closely, and allow to cook slowly until apples appear somewhat clear. Close watching and frequent turning is necessary to prevent them from falling apart.

Remove from stove and fill centers with a mixture of chopped raisins, pecans, and crystallized ginger, the latter adding very much to the flavor of the finished dish. Sprinkle each apple with granulated sugar and baste several times with the thickening syrup, then place in a 350-degree oven to glaze without cover on vessel. Baste several times during this last process.

Mrs. Brownlee stuffs eggs with spinach and serves with a special sauce, the effect of which is amazingly good. Here is the secret revealed:

STUFFED EGGS
  12 eggs
  1 lb. can of spinach or equal amount of fresh spinach
  1 small onion, cut fine
  salt and pepper to taste
  juice of 1 lemon or ½ cup vinegar
  ½ cup melted butter or oil
  1 large can mushroom soup

Boil eggs hard, peel, and cut lengthwise. Mash yolks fine. Add butter, seasoning, and spinach. Stuff each half egg, press together, and pour over them mushroom soup thickened with cornstarch, and chopped pimento for color.

Last of all, Mrs. Brownlee gives us this old recipe for lye hominy, which will awaken many a fond memory in the hearts of expatriate Southerners living far, far away.

LYE HOMINY
  1 gallon shelled corn
  ½ quart oak ashes
  salt to taste

Boil corn about three hours, or until the husk comes off, with oak ashes which must be tied in a bag—a small sugar sack will answer. Then wash in three waters. Cook a second time about four hours, or until tender.

—An all day job: adds Mrs. Brownlee.

One of the things Southerners do on plantations is give big barbecues. For miles around, "Alinda Gables," a plantation in the Delta near

Greenwood, is right well spoken of for its barbecued chicken and spare ribs.

Mr. and Mrs. Allen Hobbs, of "Alinda Gables," here tell you what to do with every three-pound chicken you mean to barbecue:

BARBECUE SAUCE
> 1 pint Wesson oil
> 2 pounds butter
> 5 bottles barbecue sauce (3½ ounce bottles)
> ½ pint vinegar
> 1 cup lemon juice
> 2 bottles tomato catsup (14 ounce bottles)
> 1 bottle Worcestershire sauce (10 ounce bottles)
> 1 tablespoon Tabasco sauce
> 2 buttons garlic, chopped fine
> salt and pepper to taste

This will barbecue eight chickens weighing from 2½ to 3 pounds. In barbecuing, says Mrs. Hobbs, keep a slow fire and have live coals to add during the process of cooking, which takes about two hours. The secret lies in the slow cooking and the constant mopping of the meat with the sauce. Keep the chickens wet at all times and turn often. If hotter sauce is desired, add red pepper and more Tabasco sauce.

Mrs. James Milton Acker, whose home, "The Magnolias," in north Mississippi is equally famous for barbecue parties under the magnificent magnolia trees on the lawn, gives a recipe which is simpler and equally delightful:

Heat together: 4 ounces vinegar, 14 ounces catsup, 3 ounces Worcestershire sauce, the juice of 1 lemon, 2 tablespoons salt, red and black pepper to taste, and 4 ounces butter. Baste the meat constantly while cooking.

Pass Christian, Mississippi, an ancient resort where the most brilliant society of the eighteenth century used to gather during the season, is awakened each morning by the familiar cry, "Oyster ma-an from Pass

Christi-a-an!" It would take everything the oyster man had to prepare this seafood gumbo as the chef at Inn-by-the-Sea, Pass Christian, orders it:

SEAFOOD GUMBO
    2 quarts okra, sliced
    2 large green peppers
    1 large stalk celery
    6 medium sized onions
    1 bunch parsley
    ½ quart diced ham
    2 cans #2 tomatoes
    2 cans tomato paste
    3 pounds cleaned shrimp
    2 dozen hard crabs, cleaned and broken into bits
    100 oysters and juice
    ½ cup bacon drippings
    1 cup flour
    small bundle of bay leaf and thyme
    salt and pepper to taste
    1 teaspoon Lea & Perrins Sauce
    1½ gallons chicken or ham stock

Put ham in pot and smother until done. Then add sliced okra, and also celery, peppers, onions, and parsley all ground together. Cover and cook until well done. Then add tomatoes and tomato paste.

Next put in the shrimp, crabs, crab meat and oysters. Make brown roux of bacon dripping and flour and add to the above. Add the soup stock, and throw into pot bay leaves and thyme, salt and pepper, and Lea & Perrins Sauce.

This makes three gallons of gumbo. Add one tablespoon of steamed rice to each serving.

The chef at Inn-by-the-Sea fries his chickens deliciously too. He uses pound or pound-and-a-half size fowls. Dressed and drawn, they are cut into halves and dipped into batter made of one egg slightly beaten to which one cup of sweet milk has been added, as well as salt and pepper. The halves of chicken are dipped and thoroughly wetted in the batter and then dredged well in dry, plain flour. The chef fries the chicken in deep hot fat until they are well done and a golden brown. He says be careful not to fry too fast.

Two other seafood recipes from the Mississippi Coast come out of Biloxi, that cosmopolitan city that began back in 1669, and where even today the European custom of blessing the fleet at the opening of the shrimp season is ceremoniously observed. "Fish court bouillon" is a magical name on the Coast, it is spoken in soft voice by the diner, the waiter, and the chef alike; its recipe should be accorded the highest respect; it should be made up to the letter, and without delay:

FISH COURT BOUILLON
   5 or 6 onions
   1 bunch parsley
   2 or 4 pieces celery
   4 pieces garlic
   6 small cans tomatoes
   1 or 2 bay leaves
   hot peppers to taste

Cut up fine, fry brown, and let simmer for about an hour, slowly. Prepare the fish, and put into the gravy. Do not stir. Cook until fish is done.

This will serve 8 to 10 people; for 10 or more double the ingredients.

To prepare fish, fry without cornmeal, and put in a plate or pan. Pour a portion of the gravy over it, and let it set for a while. Just before serving, pour the rest of the hot gravy over the fish.

Another valuable Coast recipe which comes from Biloxi is that for Okra Gumbo.

OKRA GUMBO
   2 or 3 onions
   ½ bunch parsley
   5 or 6 pieces celery
   1 small piece garlic
   4 cans of okra, or a dozen fresh pieces

1 can tomatoes

1 pound veal stew, or 1 slice raw ham

Cut all ingredients in small pieces and fry brown. Let simmer for a while. If shrimp are desired, pick and par-boil them and add to the ingredients the shrimp and the water in which they were boiled. If oysters or crab meat is desired, add to gumbo about twenty minutes before done.

Add as much water as desired.

Aberdeen, Mississippi, is a good Southern town to find recipes. Old plantations along the Tombigbee River centered their social life in Aberdeen as far back as the 1840's, and some of the recipes that were used in those days are still being made up in this part of the country.

Mrs. C. L. Lubb, of Aberdeen, uses this recipe for beaten biscuit.

BEATEN BISCUIT

4 cups flour, measured before sifting

¾ cup lard

1 teaspoon salt

4 teaspoons sugar

enough ice water and milk to make a stiff dough (about ½ cup)

Break 150 times until the dough pops. Roll out and cut, and prick with a fork. Bake in a 400-degree oven. When biscuits are a light brown, turn off the heat and leave them in the oven with the door open until they sink well, to make them done in the middle.

Mrs. Bicknell T. Eubanks, also of Aberdeen, prepares Spanish rice this way.

SPANISH RICE

4 tablespoons oil

1 cup rice

1 onion, sliced

1 green pepper, chopped

1 quart canned tomatoes

2 teaspoons salt

a little less than ¼ teaspoon pepper

Heat 2 tablespoons oil in large frying pan and add rice. Cook until brown, stirring constantly. Cook remaining 2 tablespoons oil with onion and green pepper until the onion is yellow and tender. Combine with rice. Add tomatoes and let it simmer until the rice is tender, stirring constantly. Add a little hot tomato juice if the rice seems dry. Add seasonings. Serves 6.

Vicksburg, in the old steamboat days Mississippi's wicked, wide-open town, lived high with all the trimmings. Perched on the bluffs overlooking the Mississippi, it is famous still for its excellent catfish. The disarmingly simple recipe for preparing it is here given:

Take a catfish weighing ½ pound. Season well with salt and pepper, and roll in cornmeal. Use a pot of deep fat with temperature of 360 degrees. Place the fish in the pot and fry until done. Serve very hot.

To go along with the fish, the Hotel Vicksburg serves a wickedly hot potato salad, prepared as follows:

1 quart sliced potatoes (cooked)

6 pieces chopped crisp bacon

3 chopped hardboiled eggs

1 minced large green pepper

2 minced pimentos

4 tablespoons mayonnaise

2 tablespoons prepared mustard

salt and pepper to taste

Mix and serve with quartered tomatoes, sliced dill pickles, mixed sweet pickles, and quartered onions.

A collection of recipes from the Old South is no more complete than the Old South itself without that magic ingredient, the mint julep. In the fine old city of Columbus, in the northeastern part of the state, hospitality for many years is said to have reached its height in "Whitehall," the home of Mr. and Mrs. T. C. Billups. "The drink is refreshing," says Mrs. Billups, needlessly enough, "and carries with it all the charm of the Old South when life was less strenuous than it is today; when brave men and beautiful women loved and laughed and danced the hours away, but in their serious moments, which were many, aspired to develop minds and souls that made them among the finest people this old world has known." The "Whitehall" recipe is as follows:

MINT JULEP

Have silver goblet thoroughly chilled.

Take half lump sugar and dissolve in tablespoon water.

Take single leaf mint and bruise it between fingers, dropping it into dissolved sugar.

Strain after stirring.

Fill the goblet with crushed ice, to capacity.

Pour in all the bourbon whiskey the goblet will hold.

Put a sprig of mint in the top of the goblet, for bouquet.

Let goblet stand until FROSTED.

Serve rapidly.

Who could ask for anything more?

Recipes from Prominent North Carolinians

KATHERINE PALMER

SALLY WHITE CAKE

1 lb. flour

1 lb. butter

1½ lbs. sugar

1 dozen eggs

2 lbs. citron (cut fine)

2 lbs. almonds (blanched and chopped fine)

2 medium coconuts (flour fruit well)

1 wine glass of brandy

1 wine glass of sherry

1 teaspoonful of cinnamon

1 teaspoonful of nutmeg

½ teaspoonful of mace

Cream butter. Add sugar and cream together thoroughly. Beat whites and yolks separately. Add yolks to butter and sugar, then sifted flour, fruit and seasoning. Fold in whites last. Bake in paper lined pan three hours or more.

From: Mrs. Thomas C. Darst, 510 Orange St., Wilmington, N.C.

POUND CAKE

Pound each of sugar, butter and one dozen eggs. Beat the egg yolks and sugar together, the white separate. With your hand cream butter and small quantities of flour until all creamed. Add yellow mixture by bits, creaming or beating all the time. Beat long. Fold in stiff whites. Bake carefully. Some wash the salt out of the butter.

From: Miss Nancy Watkins, Madison, N.C.

SWEET POTATO PONE

Grate 2 or 3 medium size potatoes

½ cup molasses, no sugar

½ cup milk

½ teaspoon ginger

½ teaspoon nutmeg

1 teaspoon cinnamon

butter size of walnut

Bake slowly about 1½ hours.

This recipe collected by Mrs. Edith S. Hibbs, 1720 Orange St., Wilmington, N.C.

OLD-TIMEY POTATO STEW

2 cups cold water in a stew pot

Generous piece of middling meat

6 medium size potatoes

1 large onion

Boil meat until about done. Peel potatoes, dice. Peel onion and slice in rings. Add 1 green sweet pepper, chopped. Put these ingredients into the pot with the meat. Season with salt, pepper, butter and 1 cup of sweet milk. Cook until potatoes are done but not mushy. Serve hot.

This recipe collected by Mrs. Travis Jordon, 808 Cleveland St., Durham, N.C.

CAPE FEAR JOHNNY-CAKE

2 cups flour

½ teaspoonful salt

Milk (or water) for a soft dough

¾ cup shortening, preferably half butter, half lard

A good pinch of baking powder is now sometimes used

Handle as little as possible for mixing. Roll out ½ inch thick; spread over biscuit pan and bake in hot oven. Split while hot, butter generously and cut in squares for serving.

This recipe collected by Mrs. Edith S. Hibbs, 1720 Orange St., Wilmington, N.C.

Recipes from Arkansas

Squirrels are rodents that live in trees. While they are found in most of the world, they are rarely eaten except in the United States, especially in the South. Most Europeans and urban Americans think of the squirrel as a tree-climbing rat, a pest that they would not eat. A rare exception, the famous nineteenth-century food writer Brillat-Savarin, offered a recipe for squirrel in Madeira wine. But he had been in exile in America and had reported being particularly impressed with American game.

Southerners regard squirrel as game, an edible woodland animal. Thomas Jefferson hunted squirrel and probably ate it. It is often cooked in Brunswick stew, a popular southern stew.

Mulligan is a term that was far better known at the time of America Eats *than it is today. It was a name originally used by hobos, homeless people who gathered in camps by railroad yards or garbage dumps. It means a stew made of cooking any available ingredients.*

Poke is the first salad of spring. According to Edna Lewis, an African-American chef from Virginia who died at the age of eighty-nine in 2006, poke was widely used by southern blacks not only as food but as an herbal remedy. She said, somewhat reassuringly, "You know it's not really poisonous, especially if you get it before the bloom unfurls."

SQUIRREL MULLIGAN

At various meetings and celebrations held in the woods squirrel mulligan, a lineal descendant of Brunswick stew, is a popular favorite. Cooked in an iron pot over an open fire, it is among the simplest of one-dish group meals. The recipe below (provided by Bert Jacobi of Pulaski County, who is often called upon to concoct the mulligan for special occasions) is based upon four squirrels; if there are more or less squirrels the other ingredients vary accordingly.

    4 squirrels
    3 large Irish potatoes
    1 medium-sized sweet potato
    1 large onion
    3 or 4 pods of okra
    1 pod of red pepper
    1 teaspoonful celery salt or 3 tablespoonfuls chopped celery
    ½ cup drippings or butter
    3 cups diced vegetables—cabbage, turnips, carrots, corn, field peas,
        bell peppers, or whatever other vegetables are available

The whole aggregation is put into the pot together, with enough water to keep it from burning, and cooked until done. If corn is used it should not be added until the other ingredients have nearly finished cooking.

HOT TAMALE PIE

Hot tamale pie is a frequent chief constituent of covered dish dinners, and can of course be used equally well to feed a family. The recipe is one found by Gertrude E. Conant, Extension Service nutritionist.

    2 cups cornmeal
    1½ quarts boiling water
    1½ teaspoonfuls salt
    1 chopped onion
    2 cups cold roast meat, chopped fine
    1½ cups canned tomatoes

Make a cornmeal mush of the meal, water, and salt, and cook for 1 hour. Meanwhile, brown the onion in hot fat, add meat and tomatoes, season with salt and chile pepper to taste, and let simmer five minutes. Put a 1-inch layer of the mush in the bottom of a greased baking dish, next a layer of the meat and sauce, then another layer of the mush, and so on until the dish is full, topping it with a layer of mush. Bake 20 minutes in a hot oven.

POKE SALLIT

Pioneer Arkansans, unable to obtain spinach or other greens, found a substitute in the tender shoots of the poke bush, gathered in the early spring. Poke "sallit" or salad is still so highly thought of by most Arkansans that many housewives spend hours gathering the leaves in fence corners and along roadsides, although other greens are readily available.

The usual method of preparing is to place the poke greens in a pot with sufficient water to cover them and parboil for about fifteen minutes, then drain off the water. Meanwhile, fat salt pork has been simmering in another pot for fifteen or twenty minutes, a quarter-pound of pork and a quart of water for every pound of the greens. The parboiled greens are put in the pot with the meat and cooked until tender. "Pot likker" from poke greens cooked in this way is particularly good with corn bread.

Many people like to season poke sallit with pepper sauce at the table. The pepper sauce is made in a vinegar cruet or a small pickle jar. Fresh-picked ripe bird peppers are placed in the cruet until it is a third full; then the container is filled with vinegar and the peppers allowed to steep for two or three days. As the sauce is used more vinegar may be added.

These recipes are supplied by Mrs. Ola M. O'Hara, a native of Des Arc, in Prairie County. Mrs. A. C. Jacobi of Pulaski County adds another way of preparing the greens:

SCRAMBLED POKE GREENS
    3 cups poke greens
    3 eggs
    ½ cup pork fat drippings

Boil the greens until tender, drain thoroughly. Place the drippings in an iron frying pan. Beat the eggs thoroughly and stir in the boiled greens. When the grease is hot, pour in the mixture and stir until the eggs are set. Serve hot.

ARKANSAS CHRISTMAS FRUIT CAKE

Persimmons, which grow on mountainsides through the Ozarks and to a considerable extent in the Ouachitas, have been called "Arkansas dates." They are best when allowed to dry on the tree, but if the fall rains threaten to spoil them they can be gathered and dried indoors. When dried, they add spice to many sorts of cakes and cookies.

The following recipe, which uses dried persimmons along with many other products of Arkansas farms and woodlots, was given to Gertrude E. Conant, Extension Service nutritionist, by Mrs. Sherrill, an old resident of Washington County.

FIRST MIXTURE

1½ cups sorghum

¾ cup butter

4 eggs

¾ cup unsweetened homemade grape or blackberry juice

SECOND MIXTURE (*mix and sift together*)

3 cups flour (take out ½ cup for dredging fruit)

1½ teaspoonfuls salt

1 teaspoonful soda

3 teaspoonfuls baking powder

1 teaspoonful cinnamon

1 teaspoonful nutmeg

THIRD MIXTURE

1½ cups dried fruit (apples, peaches, pears, cut fine)

1½ cups preserved fruit

1½ cups dried persimmons (cut fine)

2 cups nut meats (chinquapins, black walnuts, hickory nuts, hazelnuts, broken in pieces)

½ cup preserved watermelon rind (cut fine)

Soak fruit overnight, drain, and cut in pieces with scissors. Mix with nuts and dredge with flour.

Cream the butter and add sorghum slowly, add eggs one at a time and beat well, beat fruit juice into mixture. Combine with second mixture and blend well. Add third mixture (prepared fruit) and pour into a well-greased pan to bake or steam. If baked the pan should be lined with well-greased paper. Bake three hours in a moderate oven, then remove from pan and cool. When cold, wrap in heavy waxed paper and pack in a tin box or a heavy stone crock to ripen.

ASH CAKES

There are dozens of ways of making corn bread, and most of them are practiced in Arkansas. One of the oldest and probably the simplest of all is ash cakes, baked in the ashes on a hearth. L. M. Rall, a Negro woman of Little Rock, tells how her mother made them:

"She would make up ash cakes with a pinch of soda, hot water, a pinch of salt, and corn meal. The water must be hot. Make the paste just stiff enough to handle. Rake back a clean place on the hearth, then put the cake down and cover it with hot coals, or ashes. When it has cooked done enough, you can dust it off with a cloth. You can bake ash cakes in the oven, and they're just as good. Don't put any grease on them and very, very little soda."

CHERRY BOUNCE

It has been twenty years since drinks could be mixed legally in Arkansas, and few living persons remember any of the old-time formulae. From a veteran attorney, however, comes the story of cherry bounce, of plantation origin. According to our attorney, it was the custom of the Negro houseboys to gather up partly emptied bottles of whiskey belonging to their masters (after the masters were past noticing what happened to the bottles), fill them with fresh-picked cherries, and let the mixture steep until Christmas, when it afforded an additional mixture of cheer to the slave quarters. The discovery gradually spread, and soon home-distilled corn whiskey took the place of New Orleans bourbon in the cherry bounce.

When General Frederick Steele led his Federal army across eastern Arkansas and captured Little Rock in 1864 he destroyed all the stills he found, according to our informant, so that there was little whiskey in Arkansas during the last year or two of the War between the States. The making of cherry bounce thereupon stopped, and has never since been resumed.

Foods Along U.S. 1 in Virginia

EUDORA RAMSAY RICHARDSON

U.S. 1, a two- and four-lane road along the Atlantic coast, was the major thoroughfare of the Atlantic seaboard until I-95 was built in the 1960s. If that alone does not make it clear that America Eats *was about a different country than is known today, read the last paragraph of the following essay. Or imagine an article about eating along I-95.*

Eudora Ramsay Richardson, born in 1892, wrote for women's magazines in the 1920s and authored a few ghost stories, such as "The Haunting Eyes" for the April 1925 edition of Weird Tales *magazine;* Little Aleck, *a popular and sympathetic 1932 biography of the Confederate vice president, Alexander Stephens; and a 1936 handbook of public speaking for women. She was made head of the Virginia Writers' Project after it had failed to function effectively for its first year and a half. Despite an average monthly pay of $25.40, she was able to assemble a highly professional staff of writers, teachers, and librarians, and was credited with making it one of the best Writers' Projects. The project produced what seemed at the time unflinching studies of Virginia history, including black history, in books, articles, and forty-five radio programs.*

After the FWP ended, Richardson went back to an eclectic range of works, including academic articles on Virginia history and a book on how alcoholics could reform while avoiding complete abstinence.

E astern Virginia, through which U.S. 1 passes, is the home of hot rolls and flaky biscuits; of spoon bread, batter bread, dodgers, pones, muffins, and batter cakes—all made of water-ground corn meal and rich with eggs and creamy milk; of Virginia hams, with amber fat and tender dark red meat; of Brunswick stew, cooked till the component parts are deliciously blended; of turnip greens boiled with Virginia-cured bacon and collards fried in bacon drippings; herring roe scrambled with eggs or rolled into cakes and fried golden brown and crisp at the edges; of chess pies and apple fritters, thick with candied syrup.

Perhaps in other sections of the country as good hot bread is made as in Eastern Virginia, but never more of it. In the territory near U.S. 1 cold slices do not appear on tables. Three times a day two kinds of hot bread are served. Biscuits there may be or rolls or waffles or cakes made of wheat flour, but there will also be corn bread of some sort. The corn pone or dodger is still in good standing, and here and there will be found crackling bread and even the ash cake. An orthodox *corn pone* shows the imprint of the cook's fingers that moulded it into the proper elongated shape. It is made of meal, water, salt, and a bit of shortening and is cooked to a golden brown inside the oven. The *dodger* is the corn pone's closest of kin. It is fried, however, on an iron griddle. The *ash cake* is cooked in an open fire place, rolled in ashes near the smouldering coals. Sometimes it is wrapped in corn husks to save the trouble of dusting off ashes before serving. *Crackling bread* is the corn pone's richest relative, filled as it is with crisp bits of fat left from "trying out" lard. Spoon bread and batter bread rank at the very top of the social scale. The former is far too soft to be eaten with a fork. Its custard-like consistency is achieved by scalding the meal and sometimes by making it into a mush. To about one cup of the swollen meal are added two eggs, a teaspoon of baking powder, a tablespoon of shortening, and a pint of milk. *Spoon bread* is cooked in a slow oven. *Batter bread* contains less liquid, need not have the meal scalded, may be cooked more rapidly than spoon bread, and is stiff enough to be cut with a knife. By the way, no good Southerner tolerates either flour or sugar in corn bread.

Many *hams* that pass for the Virginian product, like young Lochinvar, came out of the west. The real thing is born and bred in the peanut section of Virginia, through which passes the southern part of U.S. 1. The meat is the color of Cuban mahogany, not an anemic pink, and the fat has the deep gold transparency of amber beads. Real Virginia ham is so tender that it can be cut by the dull edge of a fork. Contented hogs that have been fed on peanuts yield the delicious product. The smoking and the aging, however, are the second part of the secret. Months of exposure to the smoke of hard woods and then other months of mellowing are necessary before a Virginian ham is ready for the epicure. Only a conscienceless dealer sells customers hams that are less than a year old.

Another much misunderstood Virginian dish is *Brunswick stew*. Indeed, all that is stew is not Brunswick, and many a Virginian is thrown into a stew when he is subjected to heretical mixtures that foreigners try to pass for the real thing. The stew is a native of Brunswick County—and of course there is a story connected with its birth. Men, it is said, accustomed to bringing a variety of foods for hunting trips, left one of their number to do the cooking while they pursued game in territory nearby. The lazy fellow, whose talents were not culinary, dumped into one iron pot all the provisions, including the squirrels that had just been killed. So, a miracle was wrought.

Here is the way the ambrosian concoction is prepared. In 2 gallons of boiling water cook 9 pounds of squirrels—or chickens, if squirrels are not in season—until the meat is tender. Throw in 6 pounds of tomatoes, 2 large onions, 2 pounds of cabbage, 5 large potatoes, 1 pound of butter beans, 6 slices of bacon, a pod of red pepper, and salt. Cook for about 6 hours. Then add 8 ears of corn sliced off the cob. Stir constantly for a few minutes and serve. This is the real Brunswick stew. Accept no substitutes.

As you travel down U.S. 1 you will be fed *turnip greens*—often called turnip salad or turnip sallet—and in season *collards* will appear on the table. No one should miss the *black-eyed pea cakes* that come in July and August. Turnip greens really should be cooked with hog jowl, the sort Virginian hogs yield. Now there's a dish for a hungry man, whether he has been plowing or working in an office, turnip greens and hog jowl—a food that should not be mentioned unless it is right beside you! If the jowl is not available, other fat meat is substituted in the boiling. Collards should be boiled first and then fried, for there is something indefinable about collards that requires the double process. In regard to black-eyed peas the eternal question is whether to mash or not to mash, but along U.S. 1 in Virginia, the decision is usually rendered in favor of mashing. The peas are boiled with a bit of fat meat. Then they are converted into a paste, moulded into a loaf, covered with strips of bacon, and baked.

No continental continence that limits breakfasts to fruit juices and hard rolls or dry toast is tolerated along U.S. 1 in Virginia, for hearty folk, your hostess will tell you, should have hearty appetites early in the morning. Among all the many foods that are served for breakfast you will often find *fried herring* or *herring cakes*—whips for wayward appetites. The herring is rolled in corn meal and fried crisp. For the cakes herring flakes are mixed with eggs, and with potatoes, flour or corn meal.

Perhaps chess pie and fried apple pie will not be found in restaurants along the highway. No all-day picnic, however, is complete without them. *Chess pie* is made of butter, sugar, and eggs, poured uncooked into pastry and baked in a slow oven. *Fried apple pies* elsewhere are perhaps called tarts or fritters. Within their half-moon of very short pastry are sliced apples, mixed with sugar and spices. They are fried in deep fat.

If the tourist does not find the Virginian foods along the highway, he should knock at some farmhouse door, register his complaint against American standardization, and be served after a manner that conforms to the ancient rules of hospitality.

Mississippi African-American Recipes
(William Wheeler Talks)

The American persimmon, Diospyros virginiana, *is a subtropical fruit that grows mainly in the South. This must not always have been true, since the word* persimmon *comes from the Algonquin language, one of twenty-seven languages in a language group that spread from Canada to Delaware and west to the Rockies, but not to the South. The word, originally* putchamin, *may come from* pasiminan, *the Cree word for dried fruit. The Indians did dry the ripened fruit but also were the first to make persimmon into beer. This jack-o'-lantern orange fruit ripens late in the fall, and it used to be believed in the South that it could not be picked until the first frost. Southern blacks ground the seeds into coffee in the same way that William Wheeler talks of making coffee from huckleberries. Midwesterners have their own persimmon recipes, but beer and coffee are largely southern. These traditions have greatly diminished since* America Eats, *partly because there are fewer people in the South too poor to buy real coffee and partly because the American persimmon has been largely replaced by the more commercially viable Japanese persimmon,* D. kaki, *whose entry into the United States is attributed to Commodore Matthew C. Perry in 1855.*

The somewhat odd format of this valuable piece of anthropological investigation—the title "William Wheeler Talks," the slightly off attempt at dialect rather than simply recording the words as

*would have been done for a white person with a deep southern
accent, and the label "Negro" to explain who William Wheeler
was—comes out of the tradition of the slave and the Negro narratives that the FWP had been doing for years before* America Eats.

We used to gather huckleberries, put dem in a skillet, parch em real
brown. Den beat 'em up fine wid a hammer and use this fer coffee. We
used to drink bran coffee too. Dis wuz made by parchin' corn, takin' de
husks and making into a brew.

Other Recipes

Peppergrass washed rale clean, boiled down rale low with meat skins,
den add meal dumplins. You made dese dumplins like hoecake, shaped
de dumplins wid you hans. Dis is fine, Miss.

ASH CAKE

Make a hoecake out'n meal, salt, a little grease, and some boilin' water.
Shape wid yo hands. Pull out some live coals out of de fire place. Wrop
cakes in a collard leaf, place on dese coals coverin wid some more hot so
hot. Let dem bake about 15 minutes. Dey's sho fitten'.

PERSIMMON BEER

1 bushel of ripe persimmons. Pick out de seeds. Take ½ bushel of meal,
and ½ bushel of sweet potato peelings. Line a keg wid corn shucks, shake
dem out rale clean first, den pour in de meal, potato peelings, and persimmons which has all been mashed together rale good. Cover wid water.
Bore a hole in de keg to draw out de beer. Mash up some corn bread in a
cup and fill it up with dis beer and it is fine.

William Wheeler, Negro.

Leflore County

Miss.

Diddy-Wah-Diddy

ZORA NEALE HURSTON

*Zora Neale Hurston was born in 1891 in Notasulga, Alabama,
and grew up in the town of Eatonville in rural central Florida, which she once described as "a pure Negro town." She
attended Howard University and then transferred to Barnard
College, where she received a B.A. in anthropology in 1928. At
Columbia she did ethnographic research under the celebrated
anthropologist Franz Boas and was a fellow student with
Margaret Mead. Having published three books, including her
best novel,* Their Eyes Were Watching God, *led a dance group
on Broadway, and been one of the first to study vodun in Haiti
after winning a Guggenheim Fellowship for the project, she
was broke. Though she was a more accomplished writer than
most of the Federal Writers' Project participants, as well
as a highly qualified anthropologist, it was this penniless
state that qualified her for the Florida Writers' Project. She
had met with fellow Columbia graduate Henry Alsberg. Alsberg had intended for her to be a supervising editor in the
Florida project, but the Florida WPA found it unthinkable to
place a black woman in a supervisory position over whites.
She was taken on as a bottom-level interviewer. She traveled
rural Florida with a heavy "portable" disk recorder doing the
kind of anthropological investigations that had long fasci-
nated her.*

*Nor were the times after the FWP good for her. In 1948 she
published* Seraph on the Suwanee, *a novel about poor rural
whites in Florida. It was what Lyle Saxon had been praised*

*for in reverse. But it was not acceptable for a black to write
about white people. In the climate of the emerging civil rights
movement, Hurston's style, shaped by her anthropological
training and adopted by the FWP, of quoting blacks in dialect, was seen as racist. Politically she had broken with her
former colleagues of the Harlem Renaissance such as Richard
Wright and Langston Hughes, refuted their leftist politics,
and in 1952 actively campaigned for the conservative Republican Robert Taft for president. She became a leading black
of the political right, a group that did not have many blacks.
Worse, she was perceived as an opponent of the civil rights
movement, especially after writing a letter to the* Orlando
Sentinel *in 1954 denouncing the Supreme Court ruling on*
Brown v. Board of Education. *Her stance—that blacks did
not need the presence of whites to get a good education, and
that it was insulting to say that they did—might have reso-
nated fifteen years later in the black power movement. But in
1954 it found support only among white racists.*

*Desperately poor, Hurston was working as a cleaning
woman in a white man's home; the man realized the woman
he had just read about in a magazine article was his cleaning lady. In 1960 she died with no money and was buried in
an unmarked grave, almost completely forgotten until novelist
Alice Walker wrote about her in 1975, spurring a Zora Neale
Hurston revival that continues to this day.*

In the America Eats *files there are two references to Hurston, both with her name wrong. One says, "Please ask Zora
Thurston to contribute something on Negro foods." The other
asked the Florida Writers' Project, "Would Miss Thurston
write an account of a Negro picnic?" No such articles are
to be found in the* America Eats *files and Hurston's papers
have been scattered to numerous archives and libraries. Little
food writing has turned up, nothing on "Negro picnics," but
Pamela Bordelon, an academic in Pensacola, Florida, did
unearth the following unpublished piece written by Hurston*

*for the Florida Writers' Project about a mythical land
with good food, especially barbecue. The place was called
"Diddy-Wah-Diddy."*

This is the largest and best known of the Negro mythical places. Its geography is that it is "way off somewhere." It is reached by a road that curves so much that a mule pulling a wagonload of fodder can eat off the back of the wagon as he goes. It is a place of no work and no worry for man and beast. A very rootful place where even the curbstones are good sitting-chairs. The food is even already cooked. If a traveler gets hungry all he needs to do is to sit down on the curbstone and wait and soon he will hear something hollering "Eat me!" "Eat me!" "Eat me!" and a big baked chicken will come along with a knife and fork stuck in its sides. He can eat all he wants and let the chicken go and it will go on to the next one that needs something to eat. By that time a big deep sweet potato pie is pushing and shoving to get in front of the traveler with a knife all stuck up in the middle of it so he just cuts a piece off of the end and so on until he finishes his snack. Nobody can ever eat it all up. No matter how much you eat it grows just that much faster. It is said, "Everybody would live in Diddy-Wah-Diddy if it wasn't so hard to find and so hard to get to after you even know the way." Everything is on a huge scale there. Even the dogs can stand flat-footed and lick crumbs off heaven's tables. The biggest man there is known as Moon-Regulator because he reaches up and starts and stops it at his convenience. That is why there are some dark nights when the moon does not shine at all. He did not feel like putting it out that night.

Brown Hotel's Christmas Dinner, Louisville, Kentucky, 1940

The Brown Hotel is still open.

CHRISTMAS DINNER—1940

Baked Bluepoints, Rockefeller
Half Grapefruit DeLuxe
Cream of Celery au Crouton
Crabmeat and Avocado, Riche
Little Neck Clams
Fresh Fruit on Chartreuse
Assorted Canapés, Varie
Consommé Madrilène
Celery Hearts, Green and Ripe Olives, Salted Almonds
Whole Broiled Florida Pompano, Maître d'Hôtel, Sliced Cucumbers
Fried Frog Legs, Roadhouse Style, Sliced Cucumbers
Sirloin Steak, sautéed à la Minute, Cabaret Potatoes
Baked Suckling Pig, Baked Apple, Stuffed with Mince Meat
Breast of Chicken, Marie Christine under Glass
Baked Kentucky Ham, Burgundy Sauce, Spiced Watermelon
Roast Young Turkey, Giblet and Cranberry Sauce
Roast Prime Ribs of Beef au Jus, Yorkshire Pudding
Fresh Broccoli, Polonaise New Peas and Fresh Mushrooms in Cream
  Timbale of Spinach
Baked Idaho Potato, au Gratin Potatoes, Candied Sweet Potatoes

Sweetheart Salad, French Endive, Lorenzo Dressing

Plum Pudding, Hard and Brandy Sauce, Hot Mince Pie,
  Pumpkin Pie, Fruit Cake

Frozen Charlotte Russe, Coupe à la Noel, Assorted Nuts
  and Cluster Raisins

Coffee, Tea, Milk

After Dinner Mints

Brown Hotel—Louisville, Kentucky

*This is the Christmas dinner menu for the Brown Hotel's
English Grill in 2007.*

CHRISTMAS DINNER

Tuesday, December 25, 2007

Appetizer Buffet

Soup

Oyster Soup with Country Ham and Roasted Sweet Potatoes

Fried Croutons Persillade

Antipasto

Grilled Asparagus, Prosciutto and Capicola Ham, Roasted Peppers,
  Grilled Artichokes, Marinated Olives

Salads

Grilled Radicchio Salad with Roasted Chestnut
  Vinaigrette

Salmon Mousseline with Jicama Ginger Cider Slaw

Roasted Squash with Orzo Pasta, Feta Cheese and
  Vinaigrette

Seafood

Smoked Salmon with Traditional Garnishes, Mussel Salad,
  Seaweed Salad
Shrimp Cocktail, Crab Claws, Assorted Sushi

Assorted Breads and Domestic Cheeses

Assorted Pastries

Entrées

(Choice à la Carte)
Sautéed Yellowtail Snapper with Navy Bean Savoy Cabbage
Apple Wood Smoked Bacon, Toasted Coriander and
  Fennel Seed Butter
Veal Medallions with Sautéed Sweetbreads
Acorn Squash Creamy Polenta
Foie Gras Sauce
Braised Lamb Shank
Garlic Goat Cheese Mashed Potatoes and Roasted
  Root Vegetables
Merlot Wine Sauce

Desserts

Viennese Table, from our Pastry Chef
Yule Log, Cassis Mousse, Gâteau Saint-Honoré, Mini Savarin,
  Chocolate Sacher Torte
Mini Tiramisu, Raspberry Tartlets and Assorted Petits Fours

$55 per Person plus Tax and 20% Gratuity

Alabama Footwashing
at Lonely Dale

JACK KYTLE

Prior to America Eats, *Jack Kytle had done a great number of interviews for WPA oral history projects in Alabama.*

G randma" Susie Higgins is a saintly woman with the stars already being set in her crown, but at the annual footwashing and feast of thanks in Lonely Dale that sultry August day, "Grandma" Higgins was revealed as only a human being, after all.

Her soul was bared as human because the impish light of vanity appeared in her flashing black eyes that day, and because she unsheathed an avenging sword to fight for a little, grayish, conquered woman who had forgotten how to fight for herself.

In all the breadth and length of Alabama's green wilderness there is no better cook than "Grandma" Susie Higgins. She knows that she is good. Her yellow cakes with goodness knows how many eggs in their fluffy interiors are famous in the backwoods. Her chocolate cakes, with the creamy, milk-full fillings that cover all the golden layers have been praised by hundreds of preachers and laymen alike. But the crowning glory of "Grandma" Higgins' cooking lies in the magic of plain country ham and biscuit.

My, but she is a kitchen magician! There is that about her ham which brings the delicious satisfaction of perfect culinary accomplishment. Her biscuits are never cut from the white dough in tiny wheels that make only a mouthful. "Grandma" Higgins rolls them with her hands; huge, feathery knobs that come from the wood stove soft and brown; like golden nuggets of a Caesar.

The thick, browned slabs of seasoned country ham are laid into the broken interiors of these. And there is always just enough red gravy to lift such sandwiches to the heights of palatable grandeur.

On that sunlit day in Lonely Dale, "Grandma" was unusually diligent in spreading her famous feast beneath the towering oak that offered the coolest shade, beside a sparkling spring of cold water that pushed from the mountainside. She carefully spread a snow-white tablecloth over the rough pine slabs, placed side by side to serve as a table and lifted three feet from the ground by six two-by-four posts. She was smiling just a little as she began unwrapping her cakes and palate-tempting ham biscuits; and the smile was just a little grim.

Now and then she lifted her eyes from the task to quickly scan the faces of men-folk awaiting the welcome call to eat. They stood in groups, striving to keep a courteous distance, but plainly straining at the leash. They talked crops and politics and the raid last week on Sam Bernett's still, but always they watched "Grandma" Higgins.

True, other tables were being laid, but "Grandma's" table was the one from which all the others seemed to radiate. Gangling, bare-legged girls in vari-colored sun bonnets quietly helped their calico-clad elders. Now and then the girls cast shy glances at red-faced youths, who shuffled their unpolished brogans timidly in the white sand and tried desperately to return the glances. The preacher stood in front of the white-painted, steepled church, thirty yards from the eating ground. He looked at his big silvery watch that was latched to a silvery chain and edged three good strides toward "Grandma" Higgins' table.

She was unwrapping her third chocolate cake when Wash Hornbuckle wiped the perspiration from his bearded face with a red bandanna handkerchief and walked to the sparkling spring. "Grandma" paused just a moment to watch him, and it was then that she began revealing herself as only a plain human. There was a brighter flash in her black eyes, and she began baring the avenging sword.

Wash laid his piggy eyes upon "Grandma's" festive board and smiled a saintly smile. He took the tin dipper from a tree twig and calmly proceeded to rinse the snuff from his big mouth; and all the while "Grandma" Higgins only watched and bided her moment.

He was a big man, was Wash. His beard, brown and unkempt, reached to his barrel-like chest, and his arms were long and packed with power. Only his legs and feet were comical. Legs like match sticks supported a huge hulk, and his feet were wrapped in number twelve, hobnailed boots that turned up at the toes like a Turk's Sandals.

When the long-awaited call to eat came, Wash bounded to "Grandma's" table like a hound dog hot on an opossum's trail. He rubbed his huge hands together and smiled that desperate smile of a man who has reached the promised land "at long last." The preacher was right on his heels, but it was Wash who reached for the ham biscuit with an arm that was like the darting length of a bull snake.

"Stop!"

The word was like a whip's crack. Perhaps the crown of stars still rested upon "Grandma" Higgins' gray head, but it must have been sitting lop-sided upon her ear. Her eyes were like fiery beads and the avenging sword was flaming.

Wash paused, with his hand drooping limply over the coveted biscuit. A surprised, stricken expression swept into his deepest eyes. His smile faded like a forgotten fire.

"Why, Sister Higgins!"

His voice was pained in righteousness.

But "Grandma," looking for all the world like a terrier unleashing an attack on a St. Bernard, ran around the table to face him in short, indignant steps. She looked up into his bearded face, and the crown of stars tilted backward.

"You skunk!" she exploded into the beard, "you crawling, liverless skunk!"

The preacher fingered his silvery watch chain nervously and swallowed the mouthful of ham biscuit that he had managed to salvage from the storm. He spoke in pained surprise.

"Why, Sister Higgins!" he exclaimed, "that is an unheard of thing. You must ask forgiveness and wash Brother Hornbuckle's feet at our washing tomorrow."

She turned upon him, tiny fists clenched so that her knuckles were icy white.

"If I ever wash his feet," she snapped, "it will be at the end of a cooling board upon which he is laid out. And the only reason I would wash them then is because I know they need washing, and I wouldn't want him to face his good Lord with them looking as they do now!"

She darted a single, scornful glance down Wash Hornbuckle's full six feet, then pointed her finger toward a table several yards away. A tiny, grayish woman with the look of a stricken fawn in her eyes stood beside the table, her hands folding and unfolding nervously.

"Go over there," Grandma ordered, "put your arms around that sweet little wife you have and eat what she has to offer. Tell her it is the best food you have ever had, and that you are sorry for the thing you did yesterday."

There was only a great silence then, like the cloak of quiet that shrouds the wilderness before the storm. Then Wash lowered his buffalo head, turned slowly and walked toward the tiny grayish woman. He took the red bandanna handkerchief from his hip pocket and lifted it to his face. Tears welled suddenly into his piggy eyes and he blew his nose so that it gave off the blast of a trumpet.

"I will wager to you," Grandma Higgins said quietly to the preacher, "that he has an onion in that handkerchief."

"Why, Sister Higgins!" the preacher said again. "Brother Hornbuckle is the most Godly man!"

It was one of those feasts that tempt the feaster to linger and over-eat, finishing at last in the shade of some joint tree where sleep is undisturbed. "Grandma" righted her crown of stars, recaptured her smile and called for all to "stand and cram." The preacher and a hundred others took her at her word, so that the afternoon preaching was delayed more than an hour while the Man of the Word snored from the fullness of his stomach.

Only after the meeting was over did "Grandma" Higgins reveal that which barred her table to Wash Hornbuckle. She had learned that even while his mouse-like mate was preparing her simple cakes and sandwiches for the feast, Wash had taken a bowlful of batter from her table, deliberately placed his big feet in it one after the other, and had then proceeded to track over the spotless board she had recently scrubbed.

Come a sunlit day this next August, there will be another feast and footwashing service in Lonely Dale out there in the wilderness. "Grandma" Higgins again will bake her rich, fluffy cakes and place the thick slabs of country ham between golden, soft biscuits; she will again sound the call to "stand and cram," but she will have righted her starry crown. Wash Hornbuckle has earned the right to eat one of her ham biscuits and a crescent of her rich cake, because the mousy woman who belongs to him is happy again. And it is cruel for the neighbors to say that Wash has treated her kindly a whole year to gain the reward of standing room at "Grandma's" famous table.

Coca-Cola Parties in Georgia

A form of entertainment that has recently become very popular, particularly in the smaller towns, is the Coca-Cola party. Usually the ladies assemble between eleven and twelve in the morning at the home of the hostess. Trays of tall iced glasses filled with Coca-Cola are passed, followed by platters of crackers and small iced cakes. The dining table is decorated like any tea-table with flowers, fruit or mints, except that there are little buckets of ice so that guests may replenish their glasses as the ice melts. Other bottled drinks are usually provided for those who do not like Coca-Cola, but these are few in Georgia. This simple, inexpensive form of entertainment is particularly popular with the young matrons and young girls, who use it to honor a visitor or a bride. Occasionally the parties are held in the afternoon, but usually the afternoon is time for the more elaborate tea.

Delaware's Big Quarterly

The most enthusiastically attended Negro event in Delaware is the Big Quarterly celebration at Wilmington, which attracts members of the colored race from such distant points as Georgia, West Virginia, and New York. It is a day of intense religious fervor, mixed with feasting on foods prepared by some of the best Negro cooks in the state, and gaily taking over the streets of the city that have been roped off for the occasion.

Originally the celebration was a religious event marking the last quarterly meeting of the year, of the official board of the African Union Methodist Episcopal Church, established as the first all-Negro church in Delaware in 1805. It was the custom of slave owners in Delaware and nearby states to allow slaves to have a day of freedom quarterly to worship or do as they pleased, and many slaves were provided with carts and ox teams to make the trip to a common gathering place. The August meeting in Wilmington came at a time when weather conditions made traveling best, and throughout the years, attendance at Big Quarterly increased.

The modern trend of scoffing at old traditions exists but has affected Big Quarterly little. The celebration is more largely attended than in former years. It is now celebrated by Negro churches of all denominations, which hold special services, and make constructive effort to infuse the spiritual meaning of the celebration, without spoiling the feasting. These services are augmented by crusading missionaries, both men and women, who loudly exhort the passing throngs to Christianity from street corners.

Not the least of the attractions drawing the large crowds are the tables lining the sidewalks, where the savory aroma from sizzling dishes tantalizes the appetite. In addition to the sidewalk concessions, practically every house in the section is an "eatery" for the day. Feasting begins early in the morning, and continues throughout the day. The varied menu consists of fried chicken, chicken pot-pie, ham and cabbage, hot corn pone, greens and side meat, frank-furters, watermelon, soft drinks, pigs' feet, pork roasts, and baked ham thickly studded with cloves. There is no formality to the eating, most of the diners making their selections from the stands and feasting on the succulent morsels as they walk along the street, then stopping at the next stand that attracts the eye and palate. All the diners are not just promenaders, but many are singers, breaking forth with Negro spirituals at such times as their mouths are empty, while those who have seen the "light" of conversion are ready, between nibbles on the breast of fried chicken, to loudly proclaim their faith.

South Carolina Backwoods Barbecue

GENEVIEVE WILCOX CHANDLER

Lyle Saxon had chosen this as one of the better pieces he had received for America Eats, *and at the end of 1941 he earmarked it to be one of the "detailed description" pieces to run separately alongside the regional essay. Genevieve Wilcox Chandler, born in 1890, was known as one of the better folklorists on WPA projects, interviewing and recording music, often from her home in Murrells Inlet. She worked for John Lomax, the WPA's celebrated folklorist and musicologist, and along with Lomax's wife, Ruth, they did much to preserve the vanishing cultures of the Carolina coast. By the time she came to the South Carolina Writers' Project she had already*

had numerous stories published in Scribner's *magazine and
other national outlets.*

Chandler died in 1980.

Note: The barbecue described below occurs in a verbatim story from Horry County. This county has always had the highest ratio of white people in the coastal counties. Horry County has been largely detached from other sections because the swamps made transportation very difficult. Now-adays good roads have been built and the county is said to have more schools than any other in the state. Contrasting the Backwoods Barbecue would be the serving of food in the fall on the occasion of the Farmer's Day, when governors, senators, and other important guests are feted by the prosperous tobacco, cotton, and truck farmers of the county.

Oh, he's one 'o the low-downdest men that ever hopped up, Zack Long is! Zack was aimin on havin a barbecue like folks will do to kinda celebrate when they tobacco's done cured and graded and tied and sold. If a man ever does feel plumb rich, then's the time. And Zack he beat around askin everybody he seen at the store and post-office and them he met on the road to come to his barbecue. Bein's he seemed so anxious, peared like me and my old man thought we'd orta go.

"We hit the house round ten in the mornin. They was thunder heads makin up and everbody had one eye on 'em and the other on the table out there under them chaney-berry[1] trees. They was beginnin to spread papers and put out stacks o' plates. If them papers hadn't been weighted down we'da et on the rough planks, the wind was breezin so. Hit peared like they wanted to eat and git through before the storm broke.

"And what a mess o' food Zack put on them planks that day! They was stewed cow and barbecued; barbecued hog and great gobs o' fat boiled. Rice was cooked in the big black iron washpot over a bed of live coals. They was such a waste o' rations to pots was crowdin each other plumb off the table. Hit pure turned a creetur's stummick. Seemed like my appertite had plumb took a vacation and that was funny bein's I hadn't seen no kind o' fresh meat in a month or more. You see, hit was August. There warn't hide nor hare of a screen to Zack's shack. Jest open to the skeeters and the flies like in old times 'fore the days o' screens. And the table was sot inside the palin's under them chaney-berry trees. Good thing too, or we'da had razor backs[2] as well as hounds under foot. But the palin's didn't interfere none tall with the flies and it peared like every fly in the county come to that barbecue.

"How many folks come? There was clost on to twenty head of chillun and mighty nigh as many head o' grown-ups and pretty night ever hound in the neighborhood. Bein's there warn't no close neighbors I kept a wonderin where all them flies hatched off. Flies must sho have a terrible nose—they must! I just couldn't figger out how they knowed bout all them rations thout some fly flewed round and spread the news. But we didn't miss what they et, and you could pure see them hounds swell!

"They'd go too near a young 'un and his Ma would squall, 'Looka Sam! Aint they no way to keep the critter's nose out the young uns rations?'

"And down that plate would go. Hound knock it outa they hand. And the kid would be give another plate piled up with sufficient rice and backbone gravy to feed a common sized family! I aint to say stingy but I pure abhors to see nothing waste. But when you come down to brass tacks Zack didn't really waste nothing—not even what fell to the ground for the hounds took care o' that and he 'portioned out what was left. That storm did make up and it poured like in Nora's[3] time but that man wouldn't sleep till he'd shared all the leavins with his neighbors, black and white. And while they was filling up on his victuals that night there warn't nary one but said, 'Zack's a good sort.' They thought he was most as good as that crisp, greasy, barbecued hog—but if the truth were tell that man, to be she, must be one of the low-downdest men that ever hopped up!

"Generous? Oh yes, it did look like he was generous to a fault. Hit pears to me hits a good thing to be generous with what cost your own sweat and elbow grease but I cross my heart to die if that man didn't kill and cook Joe Patter's young guernser heifer out the public pastor and Joe one the chief ones bid to come to the barbecue! And I ain't never spotted the sow yet—be-in the head warn't round no where handy—but

I'd know them ear-marks anywhere! And as sure as men's born to die, somewheres they is a buried hog head and I'd give a pretty sum to know if that sow's ear aint got a crop in the left and a under-bit in the right! Them was the markins on the widow Jenkins's black sow and that sow made a git-away just round the time last August Zack Long give his farewell barbecue.

"It was lucky he leave so soon. And warn't it queer how he never cracked bout how he was plannin on goin back to Georgia? Jest bout ten days after the barbecue when Joe was scourin ever bay in the pastor[4] for his guernsey heifer and the widow Alford was plannin on lawin anybody who was eatin or sellin fresh[5]—why Zack jest up and pulled out bag and baggage for parts un-known! The smoke was comin out his chimbley supper time on Wednesday. Bill Hicks was a-passin and seen hit. And that was the last smoke anyone seen from that chimbley in quite a spell.

"Nobody knowed tell he was gone how the place was done sold to strangers and papers signed. Nobody knowed tell the sheriff made his raid. Oh No! Zack had done took the still and all the evidence. Reckon he planned on usin that down in Georgia.

NOTES

1. China berry tree.
2. Hogs allowed to run wild and forage for themselves.
3. Noah's time.
4. Pasture.
5. Fresh meat.

Mississippi Barbecue Sauce

Southern interviewers usually labeled the subject by race if "Negro" but occasionally also when white.

Juice of 6 lemons
3 lemons, sliced
1 pint vinegar
3 heaping tablespoons sugar
1 heaping tablespoon prepared mustard
¾ lb. Oleo
1 small bottle tomato catsup
1 small bottle Lea & Perrins Sauce
3 chopped onions
Salt, black pepper, and red pepper to taste

Make slightly salty. After adding enough water to make approximately ¾ gals. cook 30 minutes. Baste meat on every turn and turn frequently during cooking process.

Pinky Langley (white man) uses this recipe for his swabbing barbecue sauce, 230 S. State, Jackson, Mississippi.

The Possum Club of
Polk County, Arkansas

It is unacceptable in the South to begin the word opossum
*with a vowel. Possum is another southern food with a name
of Algonquin origin, meaning "white animal," though gray
would be more accurate. The American species is native to the
woods of the Southeast and Northwest but it is mostly eaten
in the South. Even in the South it was only popular in poor
rural areas mostly among black people because it is a noc-
turnal marsupial and slaves could only hunt at night. When
cornered, an opossum pretends to be dead, which is known as
"playing possum." Like poverty, opossum dishes are less common in the South today than at the time of* America Eats, *but
they remain emblematic for people recalling their black southern roots.*

The annual banquet of the Polk County Possum Club at Mena is
perhaps Arkansas' outstanding ceremonial feast, and certainly
is characteristically Arkansan in its background and color. Organized
in 1913 as the result of a jocular possum hunting contest between two
citizens of Mena, the club held its first banquet shortly afterward. Since
that time the affairs have grown larger each year, until now between
500 and 600 guests are usually present. Membership requirements are
lax; governors and senators rub elbows with Ouachita Mountain back-
woodsmen, and only seriousness is forbidden.

Preparations begin a couple of weeks before the dinner, which has
lately been held in December. Dozens of possums are captured in the

woods and boarded in show windows by Mena merchants. When the day comes some of them are hung on trees along Mena Street, where they remain docilely throughout the celebration and provide atmosphere for city visitors. The rest go to the cooks.

In conformance with tradition, the possums are "baked" in the oven, along with a flanking corps of sweet potatoes. For stomachs too finicky to stand their rich meat (which tastes a good deal like oily pork), turkey is also on the menu. And of course there are the trimmings: green beans, turnips, and other vegetables, salad, and pumpkin pie. It is a point of etiquette that all attendants eat as much as they can hold.

After the banquet comes the initiation of new members and the election of officers for the ensuing year. The initiation is naturally a secret ceremony, but indiscreet novitiates have let slip information concerning the "possum grin" and the "possum sign." The "grin" is a baring of the teeth, in imitation of a treed possum poked by a hunter's gun; the "sign" is a clenched fist with the forefinger crooked outward, which gesture remotely resembles the furry ball of a possum's body with the long prehensile tail curving away.

Elections are featured by uproariously burlesqued campaign speeches, "ringer" candidates, and wholesale charges of fraud. Despite the presence of sundry prominent citizens at the banquets, the officials chosen have been local men. The first president, who served from 1913 until his death in 1935, was B. S. Petefish, a rural station agent; the second was English Baker, an 82-year-old mountaineer who basked in a deerskin vest; and the incumbent is Rufe Miller, a Polk County farmer.

Georgia Possum and Taters

After catching the possum "before you go to bed that night, scald the possum with lye and scrape off the hair. (Or have it done, which would be altogether more pleasant all around.) Dress whole, leaving on head and tail. Rub well with salt and put in a cool place overnight. When ready to cook, put in a deep pan with one quart of water, place three or four slices of breakfast bacon reverently across his breast, and put in oven. When half done, remove from oven and stuff with a dressing made of bread crumbs, a little onion, salt and pepper and possum juice taken from the pan in which he has been reposing. Return him to the pan, and place around him some small peeled sweet potatoes, and bake all until a light brown, basting frequently with the gravy."

Exotic Florida

Swamp Salad: the raw bud of a palmetto tree (which has the taste of a green chestnut) served with salad dressing.

Swamp Cabbage: the sliced bud of a palmetto tree boiled with salt pork until tender.

Comptie: the powdered root of a wild plant in south Florida; used as flour for making cakes or bread.

Rattlesnake Snacks: meat of skinned snake cut into thin slices, salted, and smoked over hickory. Served as hors-d'oeuvres.

Rattlesnake Entrée: meat boiled and served with supreme sauce.

Fromajardis: ring-shaped baked cheese cakes with cinnamon; a cross is cut in the rim of the cake.

Sea Turtle: sliced into steaks and fried.

Florida Gopher: sliced into steaks and fried over a low fire. (In Florida a gopher is a land turtle.)

Kentucky Ham Bone Soup
(A Plantation Recipe)

1 quart fresh or canned tomatoes

¼ teaspoon black pepper

4 medium potatoes, cut in cubes

1 small head cabbage, shredded

1 ham hock or 1 pound ham scraps

3 quarts water

3 onions

salt to taste

Boil ham in water with tomatoes, pepper and 1 onion. Cook 1 hour if ham has been previously cooked, otherwise cook 2 hours. Do not add salt as ham will usually furnish enough. Add other ingredients and simmer 2 hours. Season to taste. Skim off all fat. This is an excellent way to use the undesirable pieces of ham, and makes a hearty luncheon for the laundress or for anyone who likes it. Serve with corn bread and a slice of pie to make a really traditional Southern meal.

Kentucky Burgoo

There are a lot of arguments about burgoo, including the ori-
gin of the name, which may be Arab, Turkish, or even French.
The story told is that the inventor is the Frenchman Gus Jau-
bert, who cooked a blackbird stew for the cavalry of General
John Hunt Morgan during the Civil War and later settled in
Kentucky.

J. M. Foster of Lexington, one of the noted burgoo cooks of Kentucky, makes it from the following recipe:

"A two pound foreshank soup bone, a two pound pork shank, a breast of a lamb and a fat hen; three large onions, three large potatoes, three raw carrots, four large tomatoes, or two medium sized cans, four ears of green corn, or two cans, two pods of red pepper, two green peppers, half a pint of butter beans, a small bunch of parsley. Cook meat thoroughly, remove from liquor, pour cook water over it in a pan and strip from bones. Chop your meat in an old fashioned chopping bowl. Chop up your vegetables, put meat and vegetables together with water poured over meat, back into the soup kettle and cook till mixture is thick. Four teaspoonfuls of Worcestershire sauce added ten minutes off gives the burgoo tang."

Sergeant Saunders' Virginia Brunswick Stew

J. B. COOK

Brunswick stew traditionally used squirrel, but not the nervous fluffy rodents of city parks. The tradition was to eat the little animal that glides from tree to tree in the Appalachian forests, the flying squirrel. It is interesting that the recipes collected for America Eats *of both burgoo and Brunswick stew play down the role of squirrel. The flying squirrel that lives among the vanishing hardwood trees of unlogged old-growth forests was already becoming scarce in the 1940s and is today endangered.*

Some twenty years ago, the genial Mr. John G. Saunders, City Sergeant of Richmond, Virginia, inaugurated for the benefit of the American Legion his "Sergeant Saunders' Brunswick Stews," which have since become legend in Virginia. Selling at 50 cents a quart, enough stew was sold upon this occasion to net the Legion $500.

Since then Sergeant Saunders has made his famous stews for all the churches of all denominations and all the worthy charities that have sought to benefit from his great generosity.

When called upon for some worthy cause, Sergeant Saunders furnishes all the ingredients of the stew so that the price paid by the hundreds and sometimes thousands of people who attend these community events is practically clear profit.

Some idea of what a truly colossal feat of outdoor cooking is involved in the making of one of these stews may be realized from the following description.

In 1930, a Richmond policeman was killed in line of duty. A committee of thirty-five citizens was formed to seek ways and means to materially demonstrate to his widow the appreciation of a grateful city. Sergeant Saunders responded to the call. A large vacant lot was selected for the site, and on the day of the event the great iron cauldrons were placed and the fires started.

Six hundred gallons were to be made and so into the pots Sergeant Saunders and his assistants put 240 veal shins, 12 beef shins, 780 pounds of chicken (live weight), 48 pounds of bacon, 1,800 pounds of Irish potatoes, 18 bushels of celery, 600 pounds of onions, 24 dozen bushels of carrots, 360 pounds of cabbage, 150 gallons of canned tomatoes, 72 gallons of canned corn, 48 pounds of butter, and the whole well seasoned with salt, pepper, and thyme.

For six hours the stew steams and bubbles and is constantly stirred, sending abroad its appetizing aroma that is its own advertisement for gathering the crowds that come at the appointed time to buy by the quart or gallon. It was upon this occasion that the last quart was auctioned off and bid in for $10 dollars by Dr. Bright, who at that time was Mayor of Richmond. More than $1,000 dollars was realized for the policeman's widow.

A conservative estimate indicates that at least $16,000 has been raised for good causes during the twenty odd years these sales of "Sergeant Saunders' Brunswick Stews" have been memorable events in Richmond.

Natives of Brunswick County no doubt would take exception to Sergeant Saunders' recipe, decrying the cabbage, and breathing anathema upon the substitution of bacon for squirrel, but then the little furry public pets in old Capitol Square are carefully guarded. And would it seem fitting for Richmond's beloved Sergeant to attempt to outwit the Capital Police?

North Carolina Chitterling Strut

Palmer had previously worked on North Carolina folklore for the FWP.

Mehitable Dorsey and her man Doak butchered their hogs on the creek bank last Thursday. The chill of late fall has set in, the new moon is on the rise, so there is no danger of the meat swelling. The chitlins have been soaked in salt water for two days now and ought to be just right for frying in the pan.

By word of mouth the invite has been broadcast to the Negro population of the upper Cape Fear.

"Yall goin to Mehitable's chitlin strut?"

"Iffen we lives, we is. How 'bout yall?"

"We's good as there this verisome minute."

Darkness is falling over the low-lying lands of the river bottom as the guests begin to arrive at the Dorsey cabin.

Doak stands by the door while Mehitable works feverishly in the little lean-to kitchen. Large maroon eyes bulge from Doak's narrow, long skull. A bright blue serge suit hangs loosely on his spare body.

The unmistakable odor of frying chitlins fills the cabin. Some have declared this scent to be obnoxious, but not so the chitlin lovers, and most country Negroes of the South relish their chitlins.

Doak bids his guests welcome, at the same time transacting business with each comer.

"What you mean, 'how much?' Hector Shadwick, you been comin

to this chitlin strut long as I can 'member, and you knows the price is two-bits, twenty-five cents."

"Evenin, Deacon Basswood. And you too, Miss Flossie. Yes suh, Deacon, you and Flossie, chitlins and cider and pickle and cabbage sallet for two, fo' bits, a half-a-dollar, fifty cents. Thank you, Deacon. Come right in, and make yallselfs t'home."

Doak does not insist on money payment. He has accepted a can of sorghum molasses, bags of eggs, and canned fruit in lieu of cash. Kinfolk and a few others enter free.

The cabin fills rapidly. The Negroes are wearing their Sunday go-to-meeting clothes, mostly bright of color, inexpensive, and poorly fitting. Chitlin strut is one of the gayest events of the year.

The house is lighted by kerosene lanterns, hung from the low rafters, barely clearing the heads of the guests. They are safer than lamps, which might upset after the strutting gets under way. The cabin contains two rooms besides the kitchen. Each has a fireplace and blazing hearth fire of pine knots. A table improvised by placing planks on wooden horses has been set in the larger room almost filling the space and providing places for twelve persons. A smaller table, seating six, fits snugly into the adjoining room from which bedroom fixtures have been removed. Chairs, benches, and stools of various sizes and descriptions are set around the tables. Unframed pictures, apparently taken from magazines, are tacked on the wall. There is a broken mirror with a Kodak picture of a young Negro woman stuck between the glass and frame. Above the fireplace in the larger room is a card with gold and blue letters: "Feed My Lambs."

Without preliminary ceremony the guests take places at the tables which have already been set with thick china dishes and wooden handled steel cutlery. There are large bowls of cole slaw and pickles, and molasses in tin cans.

The faded blue curtains separating the kitchen from the larger room part, and Mehitable appears bearing a large platter of fried chitlins in each hand. She is followed by another Negro woman with pans of corn bread. A third carries cups of steaming coffee on a tin serving tray.

Immediately there is a cacophony of talk and laughter.

"Quit yer hollerin a minute," Mehitable shouts above the din, and when the noise subsides: "Jes help youselfs from the platters. And don't be 'fraid to eat. They's more where this come from."

"Won't take long to find how much is in the kitchen."

"Take some of them chitlins and leave some, and don't be all night."

Mehitable returns with another platter for the smaller room. Perspiration covers her coffee-colored face. Her heavy, shapeless body is encased in a grey gingham dress; her large spreading feet slide along within broken carpet slippers.

Onto each plate is taken a mound of the chitlins with helpings of the slaw and a mixture of pickled green tomatoes and cucumbers. The corn bread is broken open and eaten with molasses. Swigs of coffee follow mouthfuls of food.

Prodigious quantities of chitlins are consumed as Mehitable and her two helpers move between kitchen and the eating rooms. Several times Mehitable fries up more chitlins.

"Chitlins gettin low, Mehitable."

"More comin up, Zack."

Conversation flows without inhibition or restraint. Early efforts to shout across the room have been abandoned, and now only the strongest voiced are able to make themselves understood by their neighbor closest at hand.

For an hour the feasting continues, though a few have previously given up hope of eating any more. At last all have surrendered their plates except Moonstone Peeley, an enormous Negro with a bell-shaped head, spreading nostrils, and huge mouth.

"Put the chitlins to Moonstone."

"Don't weaken, Moonstone, else we know you gettin ol."

"Las time Moonstone done eat six plates smack clean. Betcha six bits he caint do it tonight."

"I calls you. Jasper, hold the money. Moon, I's bettin on you for six plates or better."

Moonstone has but little trouble in polishing off six big helpings, not only of chitlins, but of corn bread and all the trimmings.

As the bets are being paid, Aunt Orianna, an ancient neighborhood Negress, enters the cabin. She pauses on the threshold, and leaning on her persimmon-wood cane, sniffs the air. The brown skin of her wrinkled face is like old parchment. Beady dark eyes peer from sunken sockets. Grey wooly hair is covered with a man's hat, much the worse for wear. The old woman hobbles to the fireplace, where she sits on a low stool and takes a plate of chitlins brought to her by Doak.

Mehitable joins Aunt Orianna at the fire and settles near her on an overturned orange crate. "Back's down bad. I'll res me some while Doak and the others cleans up. Shuckin cawn and cotton-pickin parties all put together don equal chitlin doins," she says to her old friend. Mehitable's bulky figure is outlined in the glow from the fireplace. Her black hair is longer than that of most Negroes. She works out the kinks with possum oil.

Aunt Orianna nods assent. The two survey the gay scene before them. Aunt Orianna sucks her toothless gums over her chitlins and corn bread. Shadows flicker across their black, shining faces.

The guests wander restlessly between tables and fireplace, waiting for the banjo boys to finish their supper and tune up for the strut.

Presently the two women on the hearth are joined by Clossie Jones. She is the color of old brass, with thin lips, and resplendent in purple silk and white canvas shoes.

Settling herself by the fire, she addresses her hostess: "Mehitable, I wants to know how does you get these chitlins flavored so tasty? Howcome they's the beatingest chitlins I ever eat?"

"No flavor to it, 'cept natcheral flavor," Mehitable replies. "It's jes in the fixin. You got to get yore chitlins clean and sweet." Going to the fireplace, she throws on more pine knots from the boxful beside the hearth. "Them chitlins been done fussed with right smart. After the hawgs is kilt and scraped and the chitlins took out, I squeezes them chitlins clean as I can with my hands. Then I washes them through two waters. Then I cuts them open lengthwise and washes them two more times, then I scrapes 'em good and plenty with a dull knife. After that I washes them in two more waters and they is ready for the saltwater soakin. After soakin them two days they is boiled three hours 'fore I sets to fryin."

"Does you fry 'em in deep fat, Mehitable?" asks Clossie, much interested.

"After they soaks in the salt water I rinses 'em good ag'in, and cuts 'em in fo-inch lengths, and rolls 'em in meal, and I fries 'em in medium fat. Hawg lard's the bestest."

"And make sure to cook 'em crisp and brown," puts in Jordan Perdew, the undertaker from town, a bald little man with a nervous twitch to his upper lip. He stands staring into the fire.

"That's where you wrong, Jordan." Moonstone Peeley now joins the group. "You misses the good flavor by fryin you chitlins too brown. Jes so's they's cooked through makes the choicest chitlin eatin they is. I knows, because I's a real chitlin eater."

"Quit you fussin," Mehitable admonishes. "Some likes 'em brown, some likes 'em medium, and some likes 'em jes warmed through. Now the deacon there is the onliest one I knows what pours vinegar on his chitlins. Seem to me sour would spoil the taste."

Deacon Basswood, who is the shade of ginger cake, shakes his head. "I's perticular 'bout my chitlins."

Moonstone glances in the direction of Doak. "I knows of some folks what would eat 'em any way a'tall, jes like they come from the hawg, even."

This brings a round of uproarious laughter that drowns out Doak's reply.

Aunt Orianna has remained silent during this argument, scratching the wart on her ear meditatively. Now the old woman takes a dip of snuff, and peeping over the brass-rimmed glasses set aslant her flat nose, she speaks in a thin treble voice: "When I come in the do, I didn't smell no collards cookin, nor turnips neither. 'Course," she glances at Mehitable politely, then grins at the empty plate on her knee, "Mehitable's chitlins is purest and best of any in this whole Cape Fear country. They is most tasty as possum gravy."

Truletta Spoon, belle of chitlin struts for the past two seasons back, sits beside Aunt Orianna. Truletta is wearing a bright yellow cotton dress, which goes well with her russet skin. A wide red belt encircles her slim waist. Red slippers are dyed with "sto-bought" colors.

"My Granny say chitlin dinner sets better iffen a mess of collards and green vinegar pepper goes long with. I likes mine seasoned with red pepper. I have eat sweet taters and biscuit served at strut suppers, but my fambly likes to refresh our hawg meat with corn pone."

"Does you cut yo chitlins afore they is cooked, Auntie?" Mehitable asks respectfully, "or does you cook 'em afore you cuts 'em?"

"I cooks 'em whole, honey, and cuts 'em after. After we takes the intrils from the hawg, I rids* 'em and empties the waste in a big ol hole dug in my yawd. I gits back to where there is water aplenty, and I fills them chitlins full, and rinses 'em up and down, up and down." Aunt Orianna motions with her skinny arms, and makes a sucking noise with her lips to imitate the water washing through.

"My Granny soaks 'em in clean cold water without salt not less than four to six hour, then she soak 'em in salt water from twelve to fourteen hour. My Granny turn her chitlins on a switch.†"

Truletta shuffles her feet self-consciously. "I knows hawgs is moon-killed."

"Everybody know that, honey. Hawg meat aint fitten to eat if it aint killed either three days afore or after moon turns. Grease will all fry out iffen you kills a hawg on too ol a moon. Same's a body must mind not to pity no hawg at butcherin, lessen it die hard."

The women remove the table cloths and the men pitch in, moving chairs back against the walls and taking down the tables, which are carried outside the cabin. While the house is cleared for the dancing, jugs of cider are brought out and guests are served from tin cups.

The banjo boys are tuning up, taking much time in the process, while the guests fret for the fun to begin.

After a few preliminary flourishes the musicians swing into the rapid tempo of "Left Footed Shoo Round." The strut is on.

Hands clap softly, and bodies sway back and forth with the music. Men move toward the women, inviting partners. The leader, standing by the banjo boys, calls out in a sing-song tenor:

> *"Ketch you partner by the arm,*
> *Swing her round, 'twont do no harm."*

Into the center of the floor jumps Carter Dunlap, a town Negro who never misses a strut. Dunlap is dressed in a tightly fitting suit of black and

---

*Rids: Cleans.

†On a switch: Negro method of turning chitterlings inside out.

grey checks, padded substantially at the shoulders. His light tan shoes are well polished. Shirt and tie are checked, but of lighter tones than the suit.

With a glass of cider in each hand, and a third balanced on the top of his head, Carter begins shifting his feet on the floor. At first the tan shoes move but slightly. Then, as the banjoists swing into "Guinea Walk" Carter moves with more energy. He slides one foot forward and draws up with the other. Round he spins, faster and faster, now squatting, now leaping toward the rafters. Sometimes the glass on his head teeters precariously, but he finishes up without spilling a drop, a feat that draws a round of noisy applause.

Moonstone Peeley gives a demonstration of "cutting the buck," then turning, he takes Truletta Spoon in his arms and swings her dizzily in the middle of the room. Couples vie with each other in cutting didos. Some of the men lift their partners off their feet and whirl them rapidly around.

On goes the dance, the banjos strumming faster and faster. The hearth fires blaze brightly, and soon the dancers are perspiring freely. Men take off their coats and throw them over chairs. Sweat flows from cheek and jowl; shirts become wet through. The women mop their faces with damp handkerchiefs. The floor boards creak, the lanterns bob up and down. More tunes and more dances until past midnight, when the strut breaks up.

Mehitable and Doak stand at the door, bidding their guests good-night.

"She glad everthing went off good and social and no trouble."

"No use fightin like they done over to Uless Sherman's. Reckon Uless ever goin to get outten the jailhouse?"

"Caint rightly say. 'Tween chitlins, strut, and chin music,* I's ready to go to roost."

"Was sure a tasty feast, sister. Must have took a lot of cawn to fatten yall's pig-tail."

"Glad it set well. See you at meetin."

The slim crescent moon rides high behind the slender trunks of spindly pines. Bare gourd-vines on the cabin porch are dimly etched in the pale light. Across the river a hound bays. Mehitable and Doak turn to enter the cabin.

"Les let the dishes res till mornin come," sighs Mehitable.

---

*Chin music: Talking.

Menu for Chitterling Strut

(A North Carolina Negro Celebration)

25¢

Chitterlings—Cold boiled with vinegar and red pepper sauce.
Hot boiled with barbecue dressing.
Fried crisp and brown.
Cold slaw.
Cucumber pickle, sweet or sour.
Hot corn pone and butter.
Sweet potato custard.
Hard cider.

15¢

Chitterlings—Served any way.
Pickle.
Corn pone.
Cider.

These struts are held in the homes of the Negro for the purpose of making money to be used for anything from paying church to buying a winter coat. The meal is served on a long table reaching across the room. Wash tubs of cider sit on each end of the table where it is served with tin dippers. The pickle, slaw and potato custards are placed at intervals along the white cloth, but the chitterlings and corn pone are served hot from the kitchen.

The Negroes begin to gather by sundown. The host walks around barking:

> "Good fried hot chitlins crisp and brown,
> Ripe hard cider to wash dem down,
> Cold slaw, cold pickle, sweet tater pie,
> And hot corn pone to slap your eye."

By nine o'clock the feed is over and the shoo round strut begins. The table is pushed aside. The banjo pickers take their places back under the stair steps out of the way. With the first clear notes a high brown leaps to the center of the floor and cuts the buck. Couples form, then comes the steady shuffle of feet and the strut is on.

SHARECROPPER EATING NEAR CLARKSDALE, MISSISSIPPI.
(PHOTOGRAPH BY DOROTHEA LANGE)

Mississippi Chitlins

It has been said that hog meat, in one form or another, is the Mississippian's staple diet. And considering how we eat it fresh in winter, cured in spring, and salted in summer, and how we use the belly fat with vegetables the year round, we have to admit that pork is certainly our dish. It is all good eating, from the hog jowls to the squeal, but come a cold January day and hog-killing time, what we hanker after is the chitlins.

We favor the small intestines for our chitlin feast but the small ones come in right handy for casing the sausage meat, so the large intestines will do. It takes a keen knife to split the intestines from end to end, then they must be scraped and washed until they are good and white. They have to soak overnight in salted water but since we, ourselves, are too tired from hog sticking to do the dish justice, we can wait.

By sun-up Ma has drained the chitlins and put them to boil in fresh salted water. She does this outdoors since boiling chitlins have a right high stench and she won't have them smelling up her kitchen. After they boil tender, Ma takes them out and cuts them into pieces two or three inches long. She says you can meal them or flour them according to your fancy, but she always meals hers and fries them crisp in deep fat. Those that like 'em extra hot put red pepper and sage in the boiling water, and everybody sees that there's plenty of catsup and salt and pepper on the table.

There is a state organization which calls itself the Mississippi Chitlin Association. Mr. Dan B. Taylor is president and Mr. Pat V. James, of Hot Coffee, is secretary. Mr. Si Corley, State Commissioner of Agriculture and an enthusiastic member, says that the sole object of the meeting is chitlin eating and that the members waste no time getting down to the business at hand.

Kentucky Oysters

This was an interview by the Kentucky Writers' Project with G. R. Mayfield and his wife, whose name was not given. They had worked as cooks in a number of prominent Louisville restaurants for forty years, and at the time they were interviewed for America Eats *they were retired. Notice the delicacy with which the cut of meat in question is never identified by name.*

Negroes of Kentucky look forward to the fall of the year for their annual treat, "Kentucky Oysters." Every fall, just after the first frost, comes "hog killin'," a time when hogs on the farm are slaughtered for winter use. "Kentucky Oysters" are the porcine equivalent of lamb fries. Placed in cans for commercial use, this part of the hog is in season according to the same tradition as the salt water bivalve from which it gets its name. It is in season during all the calendar months with an "R" in the spelling.

G. R. Mayfield, long famous in Louisville as head cook at the old Willard Hotel (22 years), the Louisville Old Inn (4 years), Fontaine Ferry Park (5 years), and for the past decade, until his recent retirement, at the Municipal Airport at Bowman Field, where he prepared the meals for the airline passengers to be picked up here, has prepared hundreds of Kentucky oysters for both the Negro and white trade.

He said recently: "Yes, manys a time I've cooked 'em. There's two ways of cooking 'em. Some folks jist like 'em boiled in two waters, pouring the first water when they are about cooked and then using a second water to make 'em tender. Others like 'em parboiled, then wrapped in a batter of raw eggs with plenty bread crumbs and fried in deep fat. Course if you can get it, rich bacon grease is the best. Either way you cook 'em they is served with cabbage slaw and corndodgers or corn bread."

Another delicacy high in the esteem of Negroes in Kentucky is roast possum, which grows scarcer every year. According to Mr. Mayfield, the preparation of this dish is simple. The possum is roasted as a young pig is roasted, garnished with sweet potatoes. If dressing is desired it is prepared and cooked separately. But as Mr. Mayfield explained, the only trouble with this dish is "You'all got to cotch your pussum first."

Louisiana "Tête de Veau"

H. MICHINARD

H. Michinard wrote a great deal about New Orleans, includ-
ing reminiscences of Creole life in New Orleans, and worked
under Lyle Saxon for the Louisiana Writers' Project on "Negro
Narratives" and many other FWP projects.

I remember when a child, my grandfather was reputed as having the best table in town and of being a "fin gourmet." He prided himself of buying all the choicest things on the market; he believed also in variety, so there was always something new on the menu. One of the many things he was fond of, also my uncles (six of them), was a "Tête de Veau" (calf's head) a la _____.

We children refused flatly to partake of that dish, and I invariably made a grimace when grandfather began carving the ears and digging out the eyes, which it appears were the choicest morsels. There was a fight over who would have one of the eyes.

The children had great fun after there was only a carcass left to pull out one by one the remaining teeth, some of them having been lost during the process of boiling.

There is a saying that, "C'est la sauce qui fait le poisson," well to me it was the French dressing that gave rest to the calf's head.

Kentucky Wilted Lettuce

Throughout Kentucky, and particularly in the mountainous area, wilted lettuce is certain to appear on the table of most every household that has a garden. Fresh leaf lettuce is washed, cut crosswise in one-half inch strips and placed in the bowl from which it is to be served. Fresh green onions are cut over the top with sufficient salt and pepper. Hot bacon grease, containing small crisp pieces of bacon, is poured over the lettuce. After it has produced its wilting effect vinegar, diluted with water to the desired strength, is added.

Although this mode of preparing leaf lettuce salad may have been brought from Virginia, it nevertheless is a dish introduced into America by German cooks.

North Carolina Oyster Roasts

In the whiskey Greek section near Wilmington in Eastern North Carolina, what is known as oyster roasts are located in the countryside. These are built similar to road houses except that only oysters and their trimmings are served. The oysters are roasted outdoors on tiers of an iron frame, underneath which is built the wood fire. The oysters are then dished up, taken into the house, placed in a trench-like trough built of plank on either side of the table, with enough space left at the edge of the table for plates. The guests shuck the oysters as they eat them, seated around the table, and toss the shells to the center between the two trenches where they fall out of sight to the ground underneath. The trimmings are: slaw, vinegar, salt, pepper, catsup, lemons, horse-radish.

Eufaula, Alabama, Oyster Roast

GERTHA COURIC

Early in the FWP, Gertha Couric distinguished herself as a WPA folklorist working on ex-slave narratives and other oral histories, interviewing people in and around Eufaula, Alabama.

When oyster trucks from the coast begin penetrating Alabama's interior, the residents of Eufaula start plans for one of their favorite winter festivities, the oyster roast. Large or small groups may assemble to take part. Or the roast may be the principal food at a family dinner. Custom, however, dictates the choice of accompanying viands.

Roast oysters are highly appetizing if properly prepared. First, the oysters are placed in a hot oven, where they are allowed to remain until they pop open. Then, a sauce made of melted butter, lemon juice, Worcestershire sauce, salt and pepper is poured over the whole.

The oysters are eaten from the shell, piping hot, and baked Irish potatoes, Cheese Creole, pickle, hot biscuit and coffee are included in the meal.

The recipe for Cheese Creole follows:

Chop onions, green pepper and celery fine. Add a can of tomatoes, butter, cayenne pepper and salt. Then add grated cheese. When the cheese is melted, add milk and eggs beaten lightly. Cook, stirring, until smooth. Serve on toast, topped with crisp bacon.

Georgia Oyster Roast

LOUISE JONES DUBOSE

Louise Jones DuBose, born in 1901, was the director of the South Carolina Writers' Project, an assistant professor at the University of South Carolina, associate editor of South Carolina *magazine, the director of the University of South Carolina Press, and poet and author of several books, including a Who's Who of South Carolina.*

The oyster roast has been a favorite way of serving oysters since the Indians lived in Georgia. Evidence of this fact lies in the many pieces of broken grill and banks of oyster shells that are found all along the shores and that apparently have been there for many years.

There are many ways of preparing oysters—on the half shell, in a chowder, stewed, and fried. But because of the informality of the occasion, the ease of preparation and the appetizing results there is still no more popular way of cooking the oyster and of entertaining large groups of people than the oyster roast. These al fresco affairs are held during the "R" months when the oysters are plump, plentiful and delicious.

Last year a visitor from a Midwestern state, while in Savannah for a few weeks, was asked if he had ever been to an oyster roast. He replied that he had not but would like very much to go, since he had never heard of one. He wanted to know what they were like and how an oyster was to be roasted.

Next day his host set about making plans with a group of friends for one of these delightful gatherings. The following Wednesday was decided on for the day. Since one of the men owned a place on Wilmington Island, he invited the crowd to have the outing there.

Wednesday dawned clear and cold, an ideal December day for the roast. There was much excitement as the men in overcoats and mufflers started out at ten o'clock. They wanted to be at the island early, so the visitor could watch every step in the preparation of the oysters.

Early that morning, Uncle Ed, an old Negro servant, and his son, Mose, armed with oyster tongs, had gone out on the river in a bateau to get the oysters. This is usually done at low tide when the choice oysters may be seen more easily.

Another son, Silas, had stayed behind to look after preparations for the cooking. Long pieces of sheet metal were stretched on bricks or logs a few feet from the ground, wood was gathered for the fires, and long tables placed about the grounds.

While the men were busy with the oysters, Aunt Jane and fifteen-year-old Sarah had prepared a savory sauce to dip them in as they were eaten. This sauce was made of about one pound of butter, melted, four quarts of tomato catsup, a small bottle of Worcestershire sauce, one cup of lemon juice, some good dashes of Tabasco, and salt and pepper. Bowls of the steaming hot sauce, crackers, pickles of all kinds and plain catsup were placed at intervals on the tables.

When the guests arrived, the visitor was full of wonder, as he thought an oven was necessary to roast anything. He walked over to Uncle Ed and inquired, "Where are the oysters cooked?"

"We just pours 'em out on dat hot tin, kivers 'em up wid wet crocus sacks so as to steam, an in 'bout fifteen minutes you see 'em pop open. Dey's just right den, an you got to eat 'em right now. Dey ain't no good cold."

After a few minutes he saw Aunt Jane and Sarah bent over a big iron pot from which a savory steam was rising. Strolling over, he asked,

"What have you in the big pot, Aunt Jane?"

"Mister, dat sumpn' you aint never had befo' an I knows it. Dat gonna be shrimp pilau."

"How do you make it?"

"Well, I aint got it done yit, but it comin'. I tell you fur as I bin' an you can stay here an watch de res' fur yo'sef.

"I cut me up 'bout one pound of good bacon in little pieces on fry dat down to git all de fat. Den I put me in six big onions, four bell peppers, and a little stalk of celery—all done chopped up fine.

"W'en dat git kinda' brown lak, I dumps in six big cans of tomatoes all mashed up—Dat all in de pot now and it gonna stew down 'bout ten minutes."

Over on a table nearby were a bag of rice and some raw shrimps which had been picked.

"Is that the way the shrimp look when they are caught, Aunt Jane?"

"No, suh. W'en dey come out de river dey in a shell wid heads, feets, and beards. I pull de head off, and squeeze de body through the shell, cose I washes off de sand and grit too."

"Do you put in the rice and shrimp at the same time?"

"No, de rice come next, I washes it and washes it fo I puts it in. I gonna use twelve cups of rice, an when dis all cook 'bout fifteen minutes—I just kinda folds in my ten pounds of shrimps, make de fire low as I kin and let 'er cook 'bout one hour. After everything in de pot, I sprinkle in slow 'bout a big han' full o' salt, and some pepper—Fo it git good done ef dat aint 'nough, I adds some more. You doan never stir pilau while it cookin'. You must raise 'em up and down wid a long kitchen fork."

Sarah asked her mother if they were going to have "hoe cake."

"Chile, you know I's gonna have hoe cake. I wouldn't give dese w'ite folks no seafood widout a hoe cake."

Turning to the man who was watching and listening she said, "Have you ever et a hoe cake?"

"No," he said dubiously.

"Well I done mix up some corn meal dis mornin' and set it aside. I mix as much meal as I want wid bilin' hot water just so I can pat it out. I adds my salt and leave it set a w'ile. Jest fo it time to eat, I puts it on the greased griddle in cakes 'bout half an inch thick and browns both sides. We always has hoe cake wid our seafood and vegetable dinners down here whar we lives."

The man asked her how in the world it had ever come to be called hoe cake, so she told him, "Well a long time ago befo' dere was any stoves folks used to bake it on the iron end of a hoe set up before de fire. Dat why it called hoe cake—I didn't live then but my mammy tole me 'bout it."

By this time everyone was hungry and the steaming hot oysters were taken up in shovels and poured on the tables ready to be eaten. All had gathered around, each one armed with an oyster knife to open the oysters—and with a fork to take them out. Sometimes when the oysters are hard to pry open with the knife, the shell has to be chipped away. To do this, the handle of the knife or a piece of shell is used. Aunt Jane brought out the pilau and hoe cake in paper plates and cups of steaming hot coffee were plentiful.

The visitor soon found himself lifting the piping hot oysters out of their shells with as much ease as if he had had a lifetime of practice. The plump morsel, dipped in the spicy sauce and swallowed in one juicy mouthful, was a treat, he agreed, for the most jaded appetite. To his astonishment he put away several dozen oysters without even realizing it.

Late in the afternoon when they were ready to return to town, it was agreed that nothing could surpass an oyster roast for good things to eat and genuine fun. Aunt Jane was so elated when complimented on everything she had cooked that she tried to tell the visitor of all the good Southern dishes she could prepare.

"Nex time you come I gonna make you some crab stew and some oyster chowder like only me knows how to make. I also gonna make you some rice spider bread. I makes dis out of flour, rice an' eggs, an' cooks it in a spider."

"What in the world do you mean, Aunt Jane, by cooking it in a spider?"

She laughed and said, "I knowed dat would git you. A spider is a old time skillet but it got straight sides and stan' on three legs. Dat why it called a spider. De hot ashes could be raked under it so de bread git hot through."

As the party drove off up the road, all the Negroes stood waving good-bye with one hand while in the other they clutched the pieces of money which the men had given them.

Columbia, S.C.

October 9, 1941

South Carolina Pee Dee Fish Stew

LOUISE JONES DUBOSE

Receipts for fish stew are as numerous as the club houses on the Little and Big Pee Dee rivers and all their tributaries combined. In any receipt that might be given there is something found to bring out violent objection, which might develop into a physical dispute. On one thing everyone has agreed and that is, that a person must have fish before he has a fish stew, though somebody said the Pee Dee fish stew is so hot that, if you have no fish, you might use pine bark and nobody could tell the difference. Certain fish stews are sometimes called pine bark stews but the origin of the name is lost in folklore.

A Pee Dee fish supper has a very particular place in South Carolina gustatory annals. A guest invited to a fish stew will find three huge iron pots over bright coal beds of hard wood embers. One pot will be full of black coffee, another of rice cooked dry so that each grain can stand separate, the third pot will contain the fish stew. Only an hour or two previous the supper was begun. The rice takes much longer to cook than the stew, so it was well on its way before the latter was started. The rice was dumped into its big iron pot, covered about one and one-half inches in cold salted water, and allowed to steam until it became dry over the slowly burning fire.

Cooking a fish stew requires art that is to be learned only by experience. "Taste as you go" is the watch word, and before it is all done it must be hot enough so you can "hiccough and cry at the same time." Assuming that the blue or channel catfish have been caught and dressed, you will take about one pound of fat-back or salt pork to three pounds of fish, render the fat-back, or fry the grease out, and remove the meat. Into the boiling grease pour chopped up onions, about one and one-half large Spanish onions to each pound of fish. After the onions are brown, stuff each fish with them, put the fish into the large iron pot, fill in spaces between fish with additional onions and if any grease remains pour this over them with the bits of pork, then barely cover with water. This mixture should cook about ten minutes until the fish begins to come to pieces. Then with salt, tomato catsup, Worcestershire sauce, and Tabasco or red pepper begin to season to suit your taste and in order to preserve your reputation as an artist with fish stew. Proportions of these last condiments are individual matters and you must always remember the secret of success is to "taste as you go."

Sometimes there might be cornbread, though if the gathering approaches the hundreds in attendance there will be lightbread from a bakery. Corndodgers on the Pee Dee become redhorse bread in some other sections. To make the latter, small pieces of raw onions are cut into thin cornbread batter, with flour added by some cooks, and dropped a spoonful at a time in boiling fat. The results are small, brown, crisp corncakes. For the less enthusiastic guests, the cornbread is cooked without onions. Sometimes pickles are served but the old timer looks askance at such additions. The flavor of the fish stew is good enough for him.

President Taft in 1909 was guest of honor at a Pee Dee fish stew in Florence, South Carolina, and he pronounced it good.

Fish Fry on the
Levee, Mississippi

There are marble palaces up above, they say, for the good Negro who dies, but in Mississippi such birthrights could be bought at a premium with a good fish fry and nothing sought in exchange. There is always a cook working for one of the contractors on the levee whose ability to cook catfish compensates for whatever other shortcomings she may have.

If she is justly famous up and down the river for her fish fries she can supplement her cook-wages by pitching frequent Saturday night fish suppers, as they are elegantly termed along the levee. Connection with an outside bootlegger makes the venture even more profitable and if she can get in on the all-night dice game she does right well.

Fish fry night always follows pay day in the levee contractor's camp and has to be on a Saturday night if the outside Negroes are allowed to attend. The feast is staged purely and solely for profit, the cook having purchased some riverman's catfish with money furnished by the commissary and charged against her wages.

She will charge ten cents per plate for catfish and "hush puppies" and sell them as fast as she can get them off the griddle of her backyard fire. Cheap whiskey, locally known as "stoop-down," brings about twenty-five cents for a short half-pint; "two-block" wine is a little cheaper but just as potent since you can't drink it and walk more than two blocks.

The contractor views the proceedings with one eye closed and the other slightly drooped. There is always an overseer within pistol-hearing distance and if the sound of a blast is heard, all "warm-barrel" guns found on the person of the Negro participants are thrown into the Mississippi River.

The cook places her confidence in a big iron skillet and plenty of hot grease. Before hitting the skillet each slice of fish is properly salted, peppered, and mealed, constituting all of the precooking preliminaries after the delicacy has been scaled and cleaned.

"Hush puppies," a sort of highly seasoned hoecake with the added flavor of minced onions and green pepper, are fried in the same skillet with the fish. A catfish fryer worth her salt will never serve "wasp-nest," the local name for store-bought lightbread.

Singing has no part in the levee Negro's festivities, his famed river chants being too closely tied up with his daily labor. At the moment, his mind is centered on eating, drinking, and gambling and, although the fish fry will last all night, he has a lot of it to do before Monday morning.

Mississippi Mullet Salad

M ullet, not usually prized as food, is commonly eaten by Negroes. In the Coast region, however, many white people eat it and have come to call it Biloxi Bacon. Besides the most common way of preparing mullet—frying—the fish is often made into a salad. The mullet should be cleaned at once after catching, preferably while alive. Scale them, remove entrails, and scrape around the backbone. Drop fish into boiling water to which a sliced lemon, salt, bay leaf, thyme, and cayenne pepper have already been added. When fish is tender, cool, remove skin, and pick the meat from the bones. Chill this meat in icebox and serve on lettuce leaf with mayonnaise or oil and vinegar dressing.

The Baked Fish of Alabama's Coast

FRANÇOIS LEDGERE DIARD

François Ledgere Diard researched local history in his native Mobile, Alabama, for the FWP.

When Bienville had finished with his fish supper, he leaned back in his chair and exclaimed, "This would be a fitting meal for my emperor. Please, who originated this recipe?"

Madame Langlois, his cousin and housekeeper, smiled at his pleasure. She said, "I prepared the fish according to instructions given me by the Indians."

On Alabama's gulf shore today, years after Bienville's time, the fish is still the favorite of those who like something new in the cooking of fish. It is prepared in many homes, but the Mobile fishermen, cooking their catch out of doors, are principally responsible for its present fame.

The fishermen usually put out their hooks near a clay bank, because clay is important to the cooking. After the clay is left to burn until there is a heaping bed of red coals. Then the fish are cleaned, split down the sides, and covered with melted butter. Salt, thyme, garlic, sweet bay leaves, parsley, and sometimes red pepper are then stuffed inside the fish, and it is sewed together with thread.

The next step is to sprinkle the fish liberally with corn meal, and this is followed by wrapping the catch in heavy brown paper. This is the time for the clay to be applied, and it is placed over the brown paper to the thickness of an inch or more. The whole is then covered by the red coals, and when the clay dries and begins to crack, the fish is ready to serve steaming hot with coffee and potatoes.

According to descendants of Madame Langlois, the Indians used bark instead of brown paper, but the Frenchwoman found that the paper gave the fish a better appearance after it was baked, and also served as a shield against dust, grit, and ashes.

Conch Eats Conch and Grunts, Florida

STETSON KENNEDY

The conch, which in Florida is always pronounced konk, *is a Caribbean staple that became popular in Florida with the immigration of Caribbean people. In the Caribbean it is sometimes considered an aphrodisiac and is associated with prostitution. The shells are used as grave markers, which is why Bahamians consider them bad luck to have in the home. By making a hole in the tip, the shell can be played like a bugle, and such horns were used to signal slave uprisings, which is why today in Haiti they are still a symbol of freedom and defiance.*

The meat is tough and can be rubbery if not beaten until the fibers break down.

While Bahamians, Haitians, and other conch-eating people are still coming to Florida in large numbers, today conch is not the exotic food of immigrants that it was at the time of America Eats *but more of a universal Florida food. The quantities taken are far greater than Kennedy described in* America Eats. *But they are severely overfished and far too often taken before maturity. The mature conch shell has a wide lip that extends and spreads out far beyond the rosy opening. Left in nature, if they accidentally lose this lip they can grow another. Such mature shells, which are at least four years old, are rarely seen anymore, which may explain the decline in shells as the popular tourism item Kennedy described.*

Stetson Kennedy was born in Jacksonville, Florida, in 1916. Even before the WPA, as a teenager working at his father's furniture store, he interviewed elderly Floridians to collect their folklore. By the age of twenty-one he was a supervisor of folklore and oral history, promoted over the head of the more experienced writer and folklorist Zora Neale Hurston, with whom he worked. His first book, published in 1942, while the FWP was dying, was Palmetto County, *about which Woody Guthrie said, "Gives me a better trip and taste and look and feel for Florida than I got in the forty-seven states I've actually been in body and tramped in foot."*

After World War II Kennedy began writing about and exposing southern racism in such books as Southern Exposure *in 1946 and* I Rode with the Klan *in 1954. As a member of the NAACP, he ran for a Florida seat in the U.S. Senate as the "independent color-blind" candidate. In 1950 his book* The Jim Crow Guide *was published in France by Jean-Paul Sartre after he failed to find a U.S. publisher for it. In 1995* After Appomattox: How the South Won the War *was published.*

Kennedy still lives in Florida, where he was interviewed for this book.

W hen "Conch eats conch" nothing like cannibalism occurs, because the Conchs are a group of Anglo-Saxon people of Bahamian descent now living on the Florida Keys, who have come to be so-called because of their fondness for eating the conch shellfish. Some 5,000 Conchs live in Key West, Riviera, and along the Florida Keys, most of them eking a living from the sea by following their traditional occupations of fishing, sponging, and turtling. It is not surprising, therefore, that they are partial to seafoods.

On days "when the wind is walking right" Key waters are "as crystal as gin"—to use expressions of the Cockney-speaking Conchs. On such days conchs can be sighted at great depths on the ocean floor. Spongers, peering through glass-bottomed buckets, are able to bring up conchs with their sponge hooks from depths as great as 60 feet. But most Conchs are excellent swimmers, and capture many conchs by diving for them.

Some Conch fishermen and spongers are fond of eating the conch raw, as soon as it is caught. With a chisel or screw-driver, they pierce the shell near the spiral tip, and by inserting a knife blade they sever the muscle that binds the flesh to the shell. Grasping the protruding "heel" of the conch, they then draw out the mass of flesh.

Strips of the best parts are pared off, and dipped over the side of the boat to season them with the salty sea-water. Then the strips, perhaps still squirming a bit, are chewed and eaten with great gusto. It is popularly believed that raw conch is an aphrodisiac.

Conch meat is also eaten raw as a salad, with a dressing of lime juice, olive oil, vinegar, salt, and pepper. Similarly seasoned, it is made into sandwiches. It is also prepared as steaks, but the most popular conch dish is chowder made with tomatoes, onions, garlic, salt, and hot pepper. Conch in all these forms is served in most Key restaurants, and is popular with both natives and tourists, even more so than another Key delicacy, the "turtleburger," made from ground green turtle meat.

Countless souvenir shops along U.S. 1 maintain heaps of conch shells which they sell for 5¢ each, or give free to their best customers. Other shops make the shells into attractive lamps and similar curios. This market for conch shells so depleted the supply of conchs that the Florida Department of Conservation was forced to restrict the business. Strange to say, the Conchs who supplied the demand for conch shells believe that they bring bad luck, and will not allow them to remain in their houses.

"Besides conchs, grits and grunts is our favorite eats," the Conchs say. "We can't afford much else, but even if we could, I guess they would still be our favorites." The grunt's popularity is by no means confined to the Conchs—it is one of Florida's most important food fishes. In Key West, waterfront fish markets keep their grunts and other fishes alive in pens along the docks. Customers peer into the water, point out their preferences, and the fish are scooped up with a dip-net and sold either dressed or alive.

In former days, when ships piled up on the dangerous and then uncharted Florida Straits, the Conchs plied the lucrative trade of salvaging; and when a ship ran ashore the message was carried from one Key settlement to another by means of plaintive blasts blown on conch shell bugles. One wrecker became so prosperous that he took his wife to New York City and established residence at the old Waldorf-Astoria. His wife soon tired of the hotel's rich French cuisine, and announced indignantly that if he did not wire Key West immediately for "a sack of grits and barrel of grunts" she was going to return to the Keys "where she could get some decent eatin." The grits and grunts were sent for, and, in keeping with the tradition of American hotels to cater to the whims of their guests, were cheerfully prepared and served by the Waldorf-Astoria.

The grunt, it should be explained, is a small bottom-feeding fish (*Haemulon plumieri*), which derives its local name from its habit of emitting several loud grunts upon being pulled from the water. In other parts of Florida, this fish is known as a "croaker." Because of their small size, usually from 5 to 12 inches, a considerable number of grunts are required to feed a hungry Conch family. Fortunately the grunts are numerous, and are quickly and easily caught on small hand-lines.

In preparing grunts for the frying pan the Conchs scale and clean them but leave the heads on. They are then dipped in meal, and fried in deep fat until they are a crisp, golden brown. Heaping portions of grits (finely ground hominy) are placed in plates or soup bowls, and the grunts are stacked high on a platter in the center of the table. The grunts are seasoned with "sour," a bottle of juice from the small, fragrant Key limes, and the grits may or may not be eaten with butter, depending upon the family's income. The grits are eaten with a fork or large spoon, while the grunts are eaten entirely by hand.

The Conch develops his skill at eating grunts at an early age, as his speed determines the number of grunts he gets from the platter. For this reason, speed, rather than ceremony, keynotes the meal. Competition is keen, and the piles of bones mount very rapidly.

The Conch's knowledge of the grunt's anatomy is truly amazing. First the head is snapped off, and by dexterous plucking with the thumb nails the cerebral cavity is laid bare and the brains are sucked out. Before being discarded the head comes in for a nibbling, which removes the fleshy strips and tasty crust. The body of the grunt is then manually dissected. The backbone and dorsal fin-bones are removed, leaving two slabs of virtually boneless flesh and the crispy tail and fins, all of which is consumed. The number of grunts that can be eaten at a single sitting by a single Conch is almost incredible—a conservative estimate would exceed 30. The bones are picked so clean that Conch cats are notoriously undernourished.

Josephine's Mississippi Crabs

Josephine—ebony, middle-aged, a comfortably plump matron from "Quarters," serves as cook, maid, and mentor in the Benoit household. Sure, she could tell us how to fry hardshell crabs in the shell, a manner of preparing them unknown to inland Mississippians.

"First, you kill your crabs in boiling water—sounds sinful, don't it, but it's the best way. This sets the meat firm. Break off the claws an' legs; the dark meat's inside them. Break the body apart; save and clean the bottom part that's got the white meat in; roll in meal and fry in deep fat."

When served, the large claws may be laid by the plates in lieu of forks as useful and ornamental utensils for picking meat from shells. Hard-shelled crabs are more often left in the boiling water till done (about 30 minutes), then eaten, or meat is separated from shells to serve in crab gumbo, cocktail, stuffed crab, or other combinations.

Maryland Crabs

C rab has always been one of the favorites of Maryland sea food delicacies. The *soft shell* crab being considered the superlative in good eating. The only specie that is caught for commercial use is the *blue crab* and during the season which extends from May until November they assume an important place on the *menu* in Maryland.

The crab in various stages of its life sheds its shell. At which time it is called a "peeler." It next becomes a "soft shell" as the new shell stiffens, and finally a "hard shell."

Soft crabs are taken by three forms of apparatus: scrapes, scoop nets and small seines. A few are taken incidentally on trot lines together with hard crabs.

Crabs are sold by the fishermen principally in the "peeler" condition. Most of the hard crabs are obtained with trot lines.

There are many ways in which to prepare crabs and each has their adherents. Among the famous recipes are:

Crab Soup: Boil six crabs, break the shells of three and pick the others. Fry the three broken ones with two slices bacon, chop a small onion up fine and when the crabs and bacon are half fried, add the onion. All must be fried partly brown. Add half a pint of water and let stew slowly for half an hour. Add half a gallon of water and let boil down to three pints. After putting in water peel and cut a quart of tomatoes up fine and add. Add a large tablespoonful of butter wrapped in one of flour and a bunch of parsley cut.

Crab Imperial—1 pound "Flake" or "Lump" crabmeat, 1 cup cream, 1 cup finely chopped red or green pepper, preferably both, for color, 1 cup bread crumbs, 1 tablespoon Worcestershire sauce, ½ teaspoon dry mustard, 1 teaspoon vinegar, salt and red pepper, 1 tablespoon butter. Melt butter, add cream, salt, pepper, mustard, Worcestershire and vinegar. When thoroughly mixed and heated, add red and green peppers, bread crumbs; mix well, take from fire, and mix-in, very gently, the crabmeat. Stuff shells, mounding highly; and remembering not to break the *lumps* of crabmeat. Sprinkle lightly with bread crumbs, and run in hot oven to bake to a nice brown.

Florida Shrimp Pilau Supper (St. Augustine)

ROSE SHEPHERD

Though Rose Shepherd claims here that the origin of pilau is Minorcan, this does not seem likely. Variations on the dish are found throughout the Caribbean, from Trinidad, where it is a national dish, to Florida. The word comes from pilaf, *which comes from the medieval Farsi word* pulaw, *from which come the Turkish* pilav *and Central Asian* plov. *In Trinidad and other Caribbean places with large Indian populations the dish is recognized to be of Indian origin, though in India it is recognized as Muslim and originally from the Middle East.*

St. Augustine being the seat of the Florida shrimp industry, there is always a plentiful supply of the tasty crustaceans available at a very nominal price. Shrimp pilau, or "perlow," as it is more commonly referred to, is a favorite dish, particularly, for congregation suppers prepared for the churches.

A recipe handed down from the early Minorcan settlers is the one most ordinarily used. The proportions are:

2 pounds headed shrimp
⅓ pound salt pork
2 cups best rice
1 small can of tomatoes
4 medium sized onions
1 small green pepper, or red sweet pepper
1 small datil pepper (very hot)

In preparing the shrimp, the sand vein is first removed, and the shrimp thoroughly washed in cold water, and cut in two—medium size gives the best flavor. The salt pork is cut in small dice and fried, the can of tomatoes and peppers cut fine are added. Simmer until light brown. Raw shrimp are added and cooked for a few minutes, then water enough added to make three and one-half cups. Put all together in a heavy pot, and when the contents boil, add rice. Cook slowly until finished. Thyme and other spices may be added. The rice grains should be separate. Salt to taste and serve.

The committee gathers in the church kitchen early in the day the supper is to be served. The purchasing committee has ordered for a contemplated 100 persons a pound of shrimp each, or 100 pounds. It is known in advance how many may be expected, as tickets have been sold, usually at 35 cents each, so the committee may know from the sale of tickets just how many will be present. Other contents of pilau are ordered accordingly. Also French bread, two or three pounds of coffee, pickles, salad, five 1-gallon cans of beans for baking, and tarts or lemon pie for dessert.

When the pilau is ready, the supper is served at 6 p.m. or 6:30 p.m. Since it is a religious affair, the minister of the church and his family, with the elders or trustees, have the seats of honor.

The dinner is preceded by an invocation, and during the serving an improvised choir renders hymns and other sacred music, the diners joining often in the singing.

Such dinners often precede an important business meeting, or plans for a revival, and at the conclusion everybody adjourns to the church proper, where the matter in hand is discussed, or plans formulated for whatever action is contemplated. These are considered opportune occasions for getting the congregation together under very happy circumstances, especially the men of the congregation. The money derived from the sale of tickets, after deducting the necessary expenses, is turned into the coffers of the church.

South Carolina Chicken Bog

LOUISE JONES DUBOSE

Chicken Bog might be called the masculine version of chicken pilau in South Carolina. It is one of the principal dishes for out-door gatherings in and around Darlington. Each cook has his own particular way of preparing the "bog," which belies its name in being almost crumbly. The main ingredients are chicken and rice. Some like young chickens, some like more flavorsome old ones. They all agree that the chickens must be cut in pieces and boiled, seasoned with salt and pepper. When the meat is cooked so that it slips off the bone it is removed from the pot and thoroughly washed rice put in the stock.

Just at this point there are also divergences of opinion. One person adds butter and another insists on fat that has been fried out of salt pork. When the latter is preferred, the grease and bits of browned meat are added when the rice has begun to cook. Then the chicken is put back in the pot and the whole seasoned with salt and black pepper, a good deal of pepper. It must cook slowly until the liquid is absorbed by the rice that afterward steams dry.

A huge iron pot is called for when a big crowd attends the event. But, with small proportions, anyone who knows how to cook rice can make a chicken bog.

Virginia Chicken

JOHN W. THOMAS

There are many kinds of delicious food all over Virginia; but there is no food more valuable than the chicken; especially in Northern Neck, Virginia. In this section one can find all kinds of good things to eat; crisp fried oysters, soft shell crabs, fish pudding, corn on the cob and all kinds of foliage food. But there is none which takes the place of the chicken on the family menu. There is an annual revival meeting at every church in the state and in the rural districts; chicken assumes its proper place at these services. Here the sisters bring large baskets of food to church with chicken as the main course; chicken baked, fried, stewed, stuffed, and broiled. The very nature of the services demands chicken. After a half day of hilarious worship the services suddenly come to a halt. The chicken fat preacher will say: "Brothers and sisters we all done had a great time in Zion dis mornin'; now we come to another important part of de services, a greater time-amen! I see de sisters got a heap lot of baskets out on de hard, I jest knows 'tis chicken in dem-amen! We all goin' out and eat-amen! After we done ate we will be in some shape to receive de holy ghost-amen! and specially if 'tis chicken we done et."

Soon the little church is empty and hundreds of people are standing around a long row of tables, made of old boards covered with snow-white sheets. In the center there is a large platter of chicken, sometimes a small wash tub full of chicken. The person will ring his hands with a half hungry and holy-ghost look in his eyes and say: "Let us ask de blessin'. 'Lord, we knows 'tis a sin to kill; but we kilt dese chickens for a purpose. Therefore we thank you for dis food, Lawd, 'cause dose chickens gave their lives that we might have meat, as you gave your life dat we might have salvation, we thank you Lawd-amen.'"

Then everybody reaches for the chicken. A dozen of the sisters at one time help the preacher's plate with a chicken leg. Sister Mary, the head Deacon's wife, is begging the pastor to have some of her chicken that was especially fried for him.

Everybody is eating and happy when suddenly some sinner boy who has enough embarrasses everybody by yelling, "Chicken ain't nothing but a bird." There are Christians standing at the table, sitting on the grass in automobiles; but all have chicken. There are certain unwelcome worshippers; flies, ants, dogs, cats, and even church mice attracted from miles around by the aroma of chicken. Legend says that the chicken is a holy bird, a gospel fowl. Country folk use the roosters instead of an alarm clock. If a rooster crows on the fence, it will clear and the rain is over; if he is on the ground there is sure to be a heavy rain; and if a rooster crows under a window, someone in the family is sure to die. These chicken worshippers say that in the spring time if a rooster sees a preacher coming he will warn all the chickens to hide and will declare war on the parson. I conclude that chicken is an indispensable food in Virginia. Not for all the crisp fried chicken, it might even be baked and some cavalier might broil this holy bird, but not me, no, sir, as a preacher, I would not think of approaching the chicken house after dark—unarmed.

Note: This contribution is from a Negro man who is a Baptist preacher.

The Use and Manufacture of Filé in Mississippi

JACK BATHIA, D'IBERVILLE, MISSISSIPPI

Almost the only use of filé is to thicken, color, and faintly flavor gumbo. A level teaspoonful of filé is enough for a large pot of gumbo; too much makes it ropey.

Actually, filé is made of sassafras leaves and nothing more, although some people add bay leaves to it. Most cooks prefer to add their bay and other herbs and spices separately so that they know exactly what is going into the soup. In June or July the leaves are pulled from sassafras saplings and hung up in the shade, usually inside the house, to dry. Sun drying or even heating destroys the oils essential to good filé. The plants that are too young, those that look almost like weeds are not stripped for making filé. Some people pull each leaf separately and string them on thread which is hung up; others break off small twigs with many leaves on them and hang the whole twig, pulling the leaves off when they are dry.

Drying usually takes about two or three weeks, after which the leaves are placed for a few hours in the sun just to make them crisp. When crisp, the leaves are crushed between the hands and dropped into the bowl of an upright log, about three feet high. This bowl has been cut out in one end of the log to form a cup about eight inches deep, and then burned inside to smooth the sides. The broken leaves are pounded in this bowl with a long club until they are very nearly pulverized. Afterward, the stems and tough fibers are picked out, and the remainder sifted through a fine-meshed tea strainer. The rough powder is then bottled in clean half-pint whiskey bottles, with no labels, and sold at prices varying from 15¢ in ordinary years to 25¢ at the present time.

The manufacture of filé involves much labor of cleaning clothes and hands afterward. The powder forms a gummy substance like cornstarch when wet and it is almost impossible to wash out of clothes. To clean the hands that are covered with filé powder requires about six or seven separate washings.

Grandma Smith's Mississippi Hoecake

Marjorie Kinnan Rawlings, in her book Cross Creek—*which, published in 1942, would have been a contemporary of Amer-ica Eats—attempted to rate the various forms of cornbread and concluded that hoecake was the lowest form. It derives its name from having been cooked on a shovel or hoe held over a fire. It was the bread of slaves and the bread of Civil War soldiers.*

On the other hand, she could not rate hush puppies. She wrote: "I do not know where, among the cornbreads, to place hush-puppies. There are elevated Floridians who turn up their noses at hush-puppies, but any huntsman would not exchange a plate of them for crêpe suzettes. They are made and served only in camp, or when one is frying fresh-caught fish informally at home, with the returned fishermen clustered comfortably in the kitchen while the cook works."

Today hush puppies are commonplace in Florida and much of the South, whereas hoecakes are increasingly rare.

Grandma Smith, sprightly, deeply wrinkled and bronzed by out-door life, and with a bit of Choctaw ancestry, gives this recipe for hoecake:

"Take you about a quart of meal; a teaspoon salt (it mightn't be salt enough for you an' again it might); make it up (not too soft) with water (some folks use hot water to make it stick together but I don't have no such trouble iffen I bake it good an' brown—an' to my mind hot water gives it a gummy taste); put in hot pot or pan that's well greased (Indians used to use hot stones); put it down with your spoon flat; let it lie over that fire till you know there is a good crust on the under side; turn it over an' brown the other side; then eat."

Grandma Smith

Route 1

Gulfport, Miss.

Florida Hush Puppies

Wampus or hush puppies: corn meal scalded in milk, mixed with egg, baking powder, and onion, and cooked in the grease of frying fish. In early Florida days when fish were fried in large pans out of doors, the savory odor caused the family's pack of hounds to whine and yelp with hunger. As a means of quieting the dogs, the cook would hastily scald corn meal, pat it into cakes without salt or shortening, and cook it in the grease of frying fish. When done, it was thrown to the dogs, after which silence prevailed, hence the name, hush puppies.

Kentucky Spoon Bread

This type of cornbread has long been popular in Kentucky. The appeal of its taste is accentuated by its rich brown crust. Its consistency requires that it be eaten with a spoon, hence its name.

Three tablespoons butter, three eggs, one pint sweet milk, three-fourths cup corn meal and one teaspoon salt.

Heat milk, gradually add meal and cook slowly until thick and smooth. Remove from fire, add butter and salt and let cool while beating egg whites. Beat egg yolks and add to corn meal mixture, then fold in beaten whites and bake about 35 minutes in slow oven.

Recipe by—Mrs. S. B. Fowler, Glasgow, Ky.

Mississippi Molasses Pie

3 whole eggs
3 tablespoons light cream
3 tablespoons melted butter
1 cup molasses
1 cup sugar
1 tablespoon meal (corn)
1 teaspoon vanilla

Beat eggs enough to mix well (be sure not to fluff, just well-mixed, and put white and yellow together), add sugar, molasses, butter, cream, vanilla and corn meal last. Mix all well. Bake in uncooked pie shell, in moderate oven until knife stuck into it does not stick.

Mrs. J. B. Black
Colonial Tea Room
Jackson, Mississippi

Divinity Chocolates of Kentucky

Before the World War Miss Mayme Holladay, of Paris, Ky., produced a wide variety of candies. No candies were carried in stock but any order received, from her widely scattered patronage, was filled out of stock especially prepared for that particular customer. Divinity chocolates, her most popular confection, were made as follows:

3 pounds of granulated sugar, 1⅓ pounds of corn syrup, 1 cupful of water, 5 egg whites, 1 tablespoonful of vanilla, ½ pound of pecan meats, about 3 pounds of unsweetened coating chocolate. Cook the sugar, syrup and water to the stiff-ball stage—244 F. Beat the egg whites to a stiff, dry froth and add half of the hot mixture to them, beating constantly; then pour into the other half of the syrup and beat some more. When cool add the vanilla and broken nut meats, and place in an air tight can or crock to mellow over-night. Then prepare for dipping in coating chocolate by making into shapes, and let stand another night in a cool place to become dry on the outside. It is also important to keep the temperature of the chocolate about 80 F., slightly cooler than the hands.

Alabama Cane Grindings
and Candy Pullings

GERTHA COURIC

November is a cane-grinding season in Barbour County, Ala., with mills running from early until late. The best place to get "all stuck up" is at an old-fashioned cane grinding and candy pulling. Everyone goes dressed for the occasion, in clothing that will stand a tubbing or may be discarded. Standing around the smoking and steaming fumes, one is covered with both the smoke and sweet vapor of cooking juice.

To drink the juice as it comes from the mill is a pleasant pastime. Then to cook candy and have an old-fashioned "candy pull" with all doing their best to get it off their hands, is an amusing sight.

An old Negro mammy usually stirs the boiling syrup candy. In another pot is peanut candy. The peanuts are put into the boiling syrup, and when cooked it is poured into tin plates to cool. Into another pot of boiling syrup, popcorn is dropped, and is then taken out quickly with long handled spoons, and put on large platters. When cool, it is rolled into balls.

Alabama Eggnog

JACK KYTLE

An Alabama eggnog is one that caresses the palate with velvety
gentleness, and then once it is within the stomach, suddenly
becomes the counterpart of a kicking mule. It is a fluffy, saffron-colored
beverage, delicate in fragrance, daintily blended, and pungently persua-
sive. It is as Uncle Nat says, "Lak a yaller gal wid a new dress—smooth
as cawnsilk, purty as de warbler's breas', but lightnin' on de rebound."

Uncle Nat should know, for he has been an eggnog specialist for more
than sixty years. He is one among scores of such specialists—stooped
and gray-bearded old Negroes, betraying a little weariness under the
weight of years, but very proud in a quiet dignity of their roles in keeping burning this light of tradition.

Somewhere in Alabama's past—probably during the glittery years
that immediately preceded the war between the states—the Christmas
eggnog custom became solidly established. It was not an innovation—
Christmas eggnog had been served for many years—but Alabamians
claimed then, and still do, that no eggnog parties approached their own
in lavishness and hospitality.

Beginning in the big-houses, in the majestic Greek Revival designed
mansions such as Gaineswood, Rosemont, and Thornhill, the custom
branched out to the cabins of the poorest farmers, and, where planters
were benevolent, to the slave quarters.

In these latter instances, the amount of whiskey was held to a mini-
mum, but on many plantations the Negroes were allowed sufficient
Christmas "nog" to bolster their spirits for "jig-tune" singing and buck
dancing to the rhythmic twanging of banjos.

However, it was in the big-houses that parties attained proportions approaching splendor. On Christmas Eve, great log fires were kindled in the marble-trimmed fireplaces of spacious living rooms; candles gleamed above shiny chandelier pendants, and red-berried holly hung in generous wreaths above all entrances. Hundreds of eggs were gathered, to be blended with choice, well-aged whiskies that the planters had ordered from distant distilleries.

It was the custom for guests—people from all the adjacent countryside—to begin "dropping in" around nine o'clock of Christmas Eve morning. They came dressed in all their finery; some came with extra clothing, for the parties continued unabated until nightfall of Christmas day. At the great double doors, they were greeted by their hosts, and then they were shown into the living rooms where huge crystal bowls, brimming with eggnog, were lined upon broad central tables.

This, then, was how the annual festive occasions came into being, during a period when Southern affluence reached its zenith. The affluence has waned; perhaps the parties are not so widespread as in the old days, but they may still be found at Christmas time in every section of the state. It is at this time that many persons, who never take alcohol at any other time of the year, see nothing wrong in drinking one or more richly stimulating eggnogs.

Prohibition, which is still enforced in several Alabama counties, never succeeded in halting the parties. The only difference was the substitution of "moonshine" corn for branded liquors. And the corn, when properly aged in a charred keg, proved very palatable. The Negroes sing about it:

> Bossman wants er keg o' cawn,
> Hi de do—hi de do;
> Been drinkin' grog since he wuz bawn—
> Hi de do—hi de do;
> Po-leece say, "Hit's ag'in de law!"
> Bossman say, "Gainst de law!—Ah, Pshaw,
> I's gont'er drink ef hit's aged er raw."—
> Hi de do—hi de do!

Several sections of Alabama are famed for the hospitable charm of their eggnog parties. The quietly dignified town of Eufaula is an example. There, the visitor will find warm generosity, gracious conversation, many new friends who will "drop in" for a few minutes of gossip, and the best eggnog and cake that skilled hands can create.

At Eufaula, also, will be found many of the "keepers of the spirits"— the aged Negroes who remain unequaled at their art of preparing nog. They know that they are good and they will tell a visitor with serious confidence, "Don'no whut de fo'ks hyar'll do when I's gone. Ain't nobody but me know how 'zactly to mix de nog wid de eggs."

Then, if asked, they will give the recipe:

Take a dozen eggs, and beat the yellows and whites separately, both very light. Put half the sugar in the whites, and half in the yellows. When the yellows and the sugar are beaten together very light, add the whiskey, two tablespoonfuls to an egg. Then fold in the beaten whites, and at last fold in one pint of whipped cream, adding more whiskey to taste. This proportion can be used to make any amount of eggnog.

They usually begin with 100 eggs and along with their product, they always serve fruit cake, Lane Cake, coconut cake, and salted nuts.

At such ante-bellum mansions as Roseland, Buena Vista, Elmoreland, Lockeland, Weelawnee, and Magnolia Vale, the parties have been an integral part of social life for more than 100 years. Surrounded by a background of Christmas greens, the great bowls are kept full, and foamy nog is served to every caller. The serving, as of old, takes place in the living rooms, where everyone with a speaking acquaintance is welcome.

Just as the town is widely known for its eggnog, the rural sections of Barbour County are famous for their syllabub. This is made with a syllabub churn. Cream is placed in the churn, and sugar and home-made wine are added. As fast as the syllabub is churned, it is taken out and put into tall glasses, and is served all day to neighbors and friends. All sorts of cakes, candies, and nuts are accompanying treats. One of the famous fruit cakes of that region is made this way:

One pound of butter; one pound of sugar; one pound of flour; twelve eggs; six tablespoonfuls of buttermilk; one teaspoon of soda; one cup of syrup; one pint of whiskey; one tablespoonful of cinnamon; one teaspoonful of allspice; one tablespoonful of nutmeg; one-half teaspoonful of cloves; four pounds of raisins; two pounds of currants; one pound of almonds; one pound of pecan meats; one pound of citron; one pound of crystallized cherries; and one pound of pineapple.

The fruit is prepared by cutting citron and pineapple in small pieces. Cherries must be whole. Wash and dry raisins and currants, several days before making cake so they will be thoroughly dry. Blanch and slice the almonds and prepare the raisins by pouring boiling water over them. Allow them to drain and afterward cut into small pieces. Clean the currants by placing and shaking flour over them and rubbing it carefully. Put them into a pan of clean water and rinse them until the water is clear. Dry in the steam of the oven.

Sift the flour, add soda, salt, spice, nuts and fruit, and stir well in order to distribute the flour. Add sugar gradually, constantly beating. Beat the eggs and add a little at a time to the butter and sugar. If this mixture curdles, add a little flour. Add syrup, flour, salt, soda and slices of fruit, beating thoroughly. Last of all, stir in the whiskey. Line the cake pan with three layers of brown paper, greased with fat. Do not use butter. Bake four hours. While warm, pour more whiskey over the top and cover with a cloth.

However, few of the old Negroes know the secret of making fruit cake, and they scorn the prospect of being enlightened. They protest vehemently that whiskey should never be mixed with cake.

"De women folks is 'sponsible," they say. "De manfolks, dey lak de nog strong, wid nothin' to weaken it down. But de mistuses, dey watch de men close, an' 'bout de time everybody gits to fightin' de Yanks, de mistuses call out, 'Pass de cake aroun'—dey's moufs hyar need stuffin' up."

Kentucky Eggnog

Before prohibition on every Kentucky bar there was a giant punch-bowl full of eggnog from a week or so before Christmas until well after the New Year. In the home it made its appearance on Christmas morning and there was always an ample supply, even for the darkies— the slaves and in later years the tenants. The usual ingredients were:

12 eggs
12 tablespoonfuls best whiskey
12 tablespoonfuls of sugar
12 tablespoonfuls Jamaica rum

Beat the yolks and sugar together until very light; then add the liquor slowly, next the whites, beaten to a stiff froth, and then one pint and a half of cream, whipped.

Old Fashioned Cocktail

Originated by "Martin" (full name, Martin Cuneo), a bartender for the Pendennis Club of Louisville, Kentucky, about 35 years ago. The old fashioned cocktail is really a development from what was known as an old fashioned toddy. Certain patrons of the club, those gentlemen who knew exactly what they wanted in a drink, began to ask from time to time for certain additions to their toddy, such as a slice of orange, a cherry, etc. Ultimately, the bartender, upon receiving an order for a toddy for Colonel Whosis, would know that the Colonel expected the drink to be fashioned in a certain manner. Finally, in order to eliminate confusion in filling orders, the old fashioned cocktail was evolved to differ from the toddy. The following recipe, furnished by Martin, the bartender, now retired, is the original (as far as Kentucky is concerned) old fashioned cocktail.

½ lump sugar, dissolved
1 dash Angostura Bitters
1 or 2 lumps ice; stir well to chill

Add

1 jigger (1½ oz.) Kentucky Bourbon Whiskey (this should
   be well aged in wood)

Add

½ slice of orange
1 cherry with stem

Stir well; serve with a glass of pure spring water on the side.

A stick of pineapple may be added if desired, but the original recipe did not include any pineapple. If pineapple is used, it should be fresh so as to prevent any addition of sugar which would be included in the prepared fruit.

Mississippi Pear Wine

CLARENCE KERNS

Clarence Kerns was a Mississippi writer who coauthored with Jean Walsh a history of steamboats on the Mississippi.

Though probably not legal under Mississippi's rigid prohibition laws, pear wine is a common home-made beverage of real merit. Sand or "pineapple" pears are a superior fruit for cooking, especially preserving like quinces, but are so plentiful that they frequently rot on the ground, are fed to stock, or sold for as low as ten cents per bushel. Consequently the home-owner usually figures the cost of his champagne-like beverage at only 12 to 15 cents per gallon, the price of the sugar needed for it.

Juice may be obtained by grinding and pressing the raw fruit. The commoner and better way is to dice fruit, including some of the peel, and stew slowly in limited water till tender; squeeze out juice through bags; strain carefully; add 2½ to 3 pounds sugar per gallon; put into narrow-mouth containers of glass, stone, or wood; leave open for several days till fermentation is well started; cork (leaving a vent for gasses—preferably rubber tube with end immersed in water); store in cool, dark place; cork tightly when vinous fermentation (bubbling) ceases (2 to 3 weeks). Improves with further ageing.

Good ripe fruit, cleanliness, freedom from dregs or floating particles, proper moderate temperature, and exclusion of air, so that alcohol does not escape or acetic (vinegar) fermentation set in, are important factors toward best results. It is often advisable to drain from dregs and re-bottle for ageing.

The Mint Julep Controversy

K entucky Colonels eat as well as drink, but the annual Colonels'
Dinner, during Derby Week in Louisville, is built around the
mint julep, and Colonels have been known, at the conclusion of the banquet, to have remarked, "That's the finest meal I ever drunk." The Colonels, from every state in the Union, Canada, and Hawaii, discuss two
subjects—horses and the correct way to make a Kentucky Mint Julep—
the three or eight correct ways.

Historically, the mint julep was probably born in Virginia, but Ken-
tuckians will stoutly insist it is a product of their state. There are,
broadly speaking, two schools of thought regarding their preparation—
the don't-crush school and the do-crush school. The don't-crushers aus-
terely contend that an abundance of mint sprigs in the top of the glass,
to give the partaker a fragrant aroma of mint as he sips the drink, is
sufficient. The do-crushers insist that the mint should be bruised and
crushed so that its flavor is incorporated in the drink itself. But here

there are numerous differences as well.
Irvin S. Cobb would crush his mint leaves
around the interior of the glass with a spoon.
The Sealback Hotel of Louisville practice is
to bruise the mint on top of the crushed ice
in the glass, then pour in the whiskey. The
Louisville Pendennis Club would have the
mint leaves crushed thoroughly in the bottom of the glass with sugar and a little
water, to create a mint-flavored syrup,
before the ice and whiskey are put in.

Arkansas planters were fond of cherry

bounce. The manufacture of this is supposed to have come about when Negro houseboys would gather up partly used bottles of whiskey belonging to their masters—after their masters were past noticing the bottles—and fill them with freshly picked cherries, and let the mixture steep until Christmas.

"Original Kentucky" Mint Julep
(Recipe Furnished by Frankfort Distilleries)

Put 12 sprigs fresh mint in bowl, covered with powdered sugar and just enough water to dissolve the sugar, and crush with wooden pestle. Place half the crushed mint and liquid in the bottom of a crackled glass tumbler, or in a sterling silver or pewter tankard. Fill glass half full of finely crushed ice. Add rest of crushed mint and fill remainder of glass with crushed ice. Pour in (trade name omitted) whiskey until glass is brimming. Place in ice-box for at least an hour (preferably two or three hours—if you can wait that long). Decorate with sprigs of mint covered with powdered sugar when ready to serve.

"Original Kentucky" Mint Julep

(As Given by John Coyne, Bartender at Drake Hotel, Lexington)

Take ten-ounce container, two teaspoons sugar, one ounce of water, glass full of chipped ice. Pour in four ounces of bourbon whiskey. Stir thoroughly. Decorate with plenty of mint (no fruit). Serve with or without straws.

Mississippi Mint Juleps

The epicureans of other cities seem 'to keep their eyes skinned' in regard to the style with which we do up small matters in Natchez. One of the last numbers of the *Philadelphia North American* has the following:

"'*Refinement*—In Natchez they ornament the glasses containing mint juleps with moss roses.'

"This was a fact at the time we made the record; but, now at the present writing, we have newer and more exquisite delicacies. That same 'moss rose' house, 'the Shakespeare,' now puts strawberries in their milk toddies.

"Mr. Alexander, at the Steam-Boat Hotel, puts strawberries in his mint juleps, and it affords one of the strongest arguments in favor of temperance to see with what avidity the drinkers will dig among the lumps of ice for the strawberries, after the julep has evaporated."

Mississippi Free Trader and Natchez Gazette, Natchez, Miss., April 16, 1840, p. 3.

THE
MIDDLE WEST EATS

ILLINOIS—*responsible for the region*

OHIO

INDIANA

MICHIGAN

MINNESOTA

WISCONSIN

IOWA

NEBRASKA

KANSAS

MISSOURI

SOUTH DAKOTA

NORTH DAKOTA

The Middle West

The Midwest is often thought of as the part of the country that isn't a part of anywhere else. But midwesterners do have a sense of themselves and their own regional identity. And though today the cuisine has been ravaged by fast food, it was a region with a very strong sense of its own food. It was a simple food, based on local products and local traditions, often connected with a specific town. Sometimes it was connected with a certain immigrant group, such as Scandinavian lutefisk. But that was unusual. It was the kind of food best found in people's homes and not restaurants. Today it is not easy to find local specialties in the Midwest, but it is surprising how strong that sense of regional cuisine was in 1940.

There are many noticeable gaps in the manuscripts left behind by the midwestern part of the project. Not only are certain states, such as Missouri, not represented, but there is nothing on Chicago, not even from Nelson Algren's original ninety-eight-page manuscript. Had the FWP stayed together and the book been completed, such omissions doubtless would have been corrected.

But despite these deficiencies, the midwestern section seems to hold its own with as interesting and varied a cuisine as other regions, something that seems unimaginable today.

Of course, the Midwest is that part of the country that people long to leave, and midwesterners have a self-mocking charm to their humor. No other region would have produced a piece like "Nebraskans Eat the Weiners."

Nebraskans Eat the Weiners

HANS CHRISTENSEN

Nebraskans eat the weiners,
And are they considered swell?
They are eaten by the millions,
That is one way you can tell.
Some fry them in a skillet,
Others boil them deep in kraut,
But the man who knows his weiners,
And what it's all about,
Is the one who builds a fire,
In the forest or a park,
Then watch them sizzle to a brown,
As the dusk turns into dark,
And as the center of attraction,
Here are solid facts we own.
For a tasty outdoor morsel
The weiner's in a class alone.
This is true in town or city,
That when folks go out to play,
Ol' Mr. Weiner goes along,
And is the hero of the day.
Then while he's turning juicy
Folks sing songs of long ago.
Like Auld Lang Syne and Annie Laurie
Moonlight Bay and Old Black Joe.
We believe that if Napoleon
In retreating from the cold
Could have had Nebraska hot dogs
He would have made it to the fold.

Urban Kansas Eats and Drinks

W hile most Kansans are good trenchermen, few could be regarded as gourmets. The average male Kansan likes to look upon food in quantity, and is not one to bother about the intricacies of the culinary art, although he insists upon good cooking. Heavier foods appeal to him more than the vitamin-laden, but often scantily-portioned dishes prepared by the daughter who has returned from the state college with a degree in "Home Ec."

A lover of beefsteak is Mr. Average Kansan, with potatoes and gravy, coffee, and pastries for dessert. The urban dweller eats his heaviest meal in the evening and it is known as dinner. Lunch, in the larger cities, is eaten at a downtown restaurant. Breakfast is a hurried affair, usually consisting of toast, cereal and coffee. The evening meal is the most leisurely and its menu often displays a certain degree of culinary sophistication, especially when there are guests to be impressed.

The usual dinner consists of a meat (usually beef), potatoes baked, mashed or fried; a salad, a side dish of vegetables (fresh in season, otherwise canned), coffee and dessert. The average Kansas housewife seldom serves a soup or an appetizer except for a company dinner, then there is apt to be a fruit or tomato juice cocktail to start the meal. Chicken is considered a treat, and is consumed at Sunday dinners. Turkey is the traditional Thanksgiving fowl and most families prefer it at Christmas, although roast goose has many devotees.

To the Kansan, rural or urban, fried chicken is always associated with the 4th of July as is turkey with Thanksgiving. There is a good reason for this. Spring friers are ready for the pan at this time of the year. Corn on the cob goes well with fried chicken. Corn in the home fields is rarely ready for consumption so early in the season, but the groceryman has it and it's cheap, so a platter of steaming golden ears inevitably adorns the table when the family sits down for the 4th of July dinner. Probably no dish is so widely acclaimed in Kansas as corn on the cob. Sometimes they are called roasting ears, for in the early days they were actually roasted in an oven or in a bed of coals. Now they are boiled until tender, piled high on a platter or in a vegetable dish, and eaten with the fingers. Butter is spread profusely on the ear, and it is salted and peppered to taste. Sliced tomatoes, green beans and green onions are on the table. Iced tea is the accepted beverage, and it is consumed in large quantities.

The holiday picnic in the summer season, usually 4th of July or Labor Day, is often laid in one of the city parks where there are facilities for that purpose. Outdoor eating is more fun, however, in the early spring or in the fall, when hot food may be prepared over a picnic stove or an open fire. The cool, frosty evenings are best for the steak roast or the weinie roast.

The city dweller welcomes this opportunity to get out of doors, work up an appetite and gorge himself with good, red meat. The method of preparing beefsteak has been undergoing a minor revolution in recent years. Many households are using the grill instead of the skillet and sirloin is fast replacing round steak on the family menu. The steak roast is a traditional social function. In the early days the steak was roasted by holding it over the fire on the end of a pointed stick. More recently it was pan fried. Now it is broiled on a grill over a bed of glowing coals, basted with barbecue sauce and eaten between a sliced bun with fried potatoes and a salad. Most popular of the salads for an outdoor feast of this kind is made with tomatoes, head lettuce, onions, sometimes a bit of garlic. These ingredients are chopped up in a bowl and served on the plate with French dressing.

In every crowd there is one expert, who builds the fire, prepares the meat, lays the grill over the coals when the blaze has burned down to a tiny flicker, then places the steaks on the grill and tends them with a long handled fork as they sizzle. Loin steak, cut from one-half to three-fourths of an inch thick is used. Hungry guests often eat a half pound at a sitting. Usually tending the steaks is a man's job. The women prepare the salad, fry the potatoes and make the coffee.

The potatoes are first boiled at home and brought out to the picnic spot in a kettle. Then they are sliced and placed in a skillet with a large dab of grease. If there is room on the grill the skillet occupies a corner and the "spuds" are allowed to fry slowly. Coffee, sometimes prepared at home and brought out in a thermos jug, is better if boiled and served fresh. In that event it is made in the old fashioned way, that is, boiled in an open kettle, the grounds in a muslin sack.

Kansas is a prohibition state where the sale of 5.2 beer is legal; beverages of higher alcoholic content are banned. If there are drinks at the steak roast they are usually poured from a bottle. The men often take their whiskey straight or with plain water, women prefer it with soda and lemon. Few of the sophisticated drinks are served, although a hostess in one of the larger cities used to mix a thermos jug full of martinis for these outdoor celebrations.

Kansans are becoming increasingly addicted to the "Cup that cheers but does not inebriate." Most office workers go out for coffee at least twice during the day, executives frequently adjourn to the corner coffee shop for a conference over a steaming cup. Mid-morning coffee is popular even in the summer, but the afternoon recess is usually accompanied by iced tea or Coca-Cola. Few Kansans care for hot tea, but consume many glasses of the iced beverage, usually with lemon, with or without sugar. Mint leaves sometimes provide an added flavor. In comparatively recent years iced coffee has attained a degree of popularity as a hot weather beverage.

END OF THE PIE-EATING CONTEST. WINNER'S HAND IS RAISED. 4-H CLUB
FAIR, CIMARRON, KANSAS. (PHOTOGRAPH BY RUSSELL LEE)

Sioux and Chippewa Food

FRANCES DENSMORE

Frances Densmore was born on May 21, 1867, in Red Wing, Minnesota, where she also died ninety years later almost to the day, on June 5, 1957. In between she was one of the distinguished American women of her generation, translating a lifelong love of music into a celebrated career in anthropology.

She began with music, studying at Oberlin College's Conservatory of Music, after which she worked as a piano teacher in St. Paul. In 1889 she moved to Boston to study at Harvard under composers John Knowles Paine and Carl Baermann.

In 1893 she attended the Chicago World's Fair, where she saw the great Apache leader Geronimo, and she heard him humming a tune. That tune marked the beginning of a lifelong fascination with Indian music. In 1907 she published her first anthropological writing, an article in American Anthropologist *on a 1905 visit to a Chippewa village in Minnesota near the Canadian border. With grants from the Smithsonian, she began recording Indian music. The Smithsonian backed her work for many decades as she recorded on wax cylinders almost 2,500 songs of not only the Chippewa but the Sioux, Pawnee, Yuma, Yaqui, Cocopa, Northern Ute, and some twenty-three other tribes. She did this work at a time when most of the tribes still had rich cultures, but they were soon to fade. Her extensive collection of traditional Indian musical instruments is at the Smithsonian, which has also issued her recordings. The Smithsonian has published her numerous monographs on Indian music as well. Her two volumes on the*

Chippewa, published in 1910 and 1915, are considered some of her most important work.

This manuscript on Chippewa and Sioux food was written by Densmore for America Eats *and edited by the Minnesota Writers' Project.*

The principal food of the early Sioux was meat. In the winter they ate muskrats, badgers, otters and raccoons, in the spring they ate fish and the roots of certain wild plants, in the summer they had wild pigeons and cranes as well as fish and certain roots and in the autumn they killed wild ducks, geese and muskrats. These were animals that were plentiful at different seasons of the year. The buffalo was hunted twice a year, and the meat was eaten fresh or dried and prepared in various ways. The tongue of the buffalo was considered the nicest part. In the earliest times the Sioux boiled meat by digging a hole in the ground and lining it with a fresh hide. They put water in this, with the meat, and added stones that were heated in the fire. These heated the water, cooking the meat.

Buffalo meat was cut in strips and dried in the sun or over a fire. This was called "jerked meat" and used by many tribes living on the plains. But the favorite way of preparing buffalo meat was in the form of pemmican. For this, thin buffalo steaks were dried, then laid on a broad, flat stone and pounded with a smaller stone. In the old days, the Indians dug a hole like a large bowl in the ground and lined it with a piece of hide, fitting it neatly all around. Then they put in the dried meat and pounded it with a heavy stone. The pounded meat is like a powder with many shreds of threads or fiber in it. This was usually mixed with melted fat, but marrow made even nicer pemmican. Sometimes the Indian women pounded wild cherries, stones and all, and mixed them with the pemmican. The mixture was put in bags made of hide, and melted fat was poured on the top to seal it tightly. Buffalo hide was often used for these bags, with the hair on the outside. Pemmican was very nourishing and could be kept in the sealed bags for three or four years. The bags were of various sizes, those in common use weighing from 100 to 300 pounds.

The Sioux, like other tribes of Indians, had no salt until the traders came, and it took them a long time to learn to like it. Even in 1912 the older members of the tribe did not like the taste of salt.

Some of the Sioux who lived around the upper water of the Minnesota River had a small quantity of corn and beans, but their chief vegetable food was a root that was commonly called "Dakota turnip" or "tipsinna," although it has several other names. This root was dug in August and was about as large as a hen's egg. The Sioux ate it raw, or boiled it or roasted it in the ashes; they also dried it and stored it for winter. The dried root was mashed between stones until it was like flour; then mixed with water, this was made into little cakes and baked over the coals. It did not have much taste, yet it was not unpleasant to eat and was very nourishing. Two interesting travelers came to Minnesota in 1823 and mentioned this root in their description of their trip. These men were Major Stephen H. Long and Professor William H. Keating. Near Lake Traverse, they became acquainted with Chief Wanotan, who invited them to a feast. There were many large kettles and the food was emptied into "dozens of wooden dishes which were placed all around the lodge." The food "consisted of buffalo meat boiled with tepsin, also the same vegetable boiled without meat in buffalo grease, and finally the much-esteemed dog meat, all which were dressed without salt." The white men were polite and tasted of the dog meat. They did not enjoy eating it, but Keating wrote that it was very fat as well as "sweet and palatable" and quite dark in color. The Sioux considered it a great honor to a guest when they placed a dish of nicely cooked dog meat before him. The writer has seen this custom among both the Sioux and the Chippewa. A small dog, when cooked, looks somewhat like a platter of large chicken.

When the Sioux lived in northern Minnesota, they ate the wild rice that grows in the shallow lakes. This was a nourishing food and easy to gather.

After they learned to raise corn and beans, the work in the field was done by the women. They never planted corn until the wild strawberries were ripe. That was supposed to be exactly the right time to plant corn, and they soaked the seed corn until it sprouted before they put it in the ground. The women planted it quite deep, and when the little plants had two or three leaves the women loosened the earth around the roots with their fingers. When the plants were taller the women made the earth into a little hill around each plant, using hoes for the work. White people gave the Indians several sorts of seed corn, but they usually planted a small kind of corn that ripened quickly.

The women gathered the ripe ears of corn in their blankets and spread them on platforms or scaffolds. The women and children had to stand on the platforms to drive away the birds that came to get the corn. When the husks began to wither, they took off the outer husks and braided the rest in stiff braids as they had been taught to do by the white people. These were hung up so the corn would dry. Some of the corn was boiled, dried and put in bags that contained 1 or 2 bushels. A round hole was dug in the ground, and the bottom and sides were lined with dry grass. The bags of corn were put in the hole, which was filled with earth and firmly stamped down. Corn stored in this way is said to have kept dry and fresh from September until the next April. The hole containing the corn was covered in such a way that no one could see it, but the man who hid the corn could find it even though the ground was covered deep with snow.

The food of an Indian family depended on where the tribe lived. The Chippewa lived on the shores of Lake Superior and along the rivers, so their principal food was fish. They ate fresh fish in summer and dried or smoked fish in winter. They were satisfied in the old days if they had nothing but fish for a meal. The littlest babies were given fish soup, and the heads of fish were said to be very nice when boiled and seasoned with maple sugar.

The Chippewa had many ways of cooking fish, from the little sunfish to the large pickerel. Fresh fish were cleaned and put between the sections of a split stick that was placed in the ground, leaning over the fire. Sometimes the fish, without being cleaned, were stuck through with a sharp stick, head uppermost, and the stick slanted above the fire so that it could be turned and the fish cooked on all sides. Fish eggs were boiled or fried with the fish.

In the fall, the Chippewa strung the sunfish in bunches of 10 or 12

and froze them for winter use. When the snow was deep around the wig-
wam, they peeled the skin from these little fish and cooked them. Sometimes they strung small fish on strips of basswood bark and hung them
in the sun to dry, then packed them in layers, without salt.

The Chippewa had no special food for children, and little children
were given very strong tea and meat. It was thought that the meat would
make them strong.

Maple sugar was used to sweeten and season all food. Like the Sioux,
these Indians had no salt until it was brought by the white men, but
they learned to like it. In a treaty made with the Chippewa in 1847, the
government promised to give them five barrels of salt every year for five
years. This is known as the "Salt Treaty."

Ducks, wild pigeons and other birds came in the fall, and the Chippewa cooked them in various ways. Sometimes they cooked little birds
in hot ashes without removing the feathers, and sometimes they put a
sharp stick through the bird, after removing the feathers, and put the
stick upright in front of the fire. They also boiled birds with rice, potatoes and meat.

The deer was the principal game hunted by the Chippewa, though
they also killed mouse, bear, rabbits and other animals at various seasons. Beaver tails were considered a great luxury because they were so
fat. Fresh venison was sometimes boiled with wild rice and sometimes
cut in thin slices, roasted and then pounded on a flat stone. Then it was
stored in boxes, *ma-kuks*, and the covers sewed down with split spruce
root. If the deer was killed in the fall, they cut a portion of the meat in
strips, dried it over a fire and wrapped it in the hide. In the winter they
boiled this meat or prepared it in other ways. Sometimes they cut the
dried meat in pieces, spread it on birchbark and covered it with another
piece of the bark. A man then stamped heavily on the upper piece of bark
until the meat was crushed. Meat prepared this way was called by a
name meaning "foot-trodden meat."

If a deer was killed during the winter, they dried the meat enough
so that it would keep until spring. Then they put it in the sun to finish
drying.

After the Chippewa had driven the Sioux out of northern Minnesota, they had plenty of wild rice. Here, as in Wisconsin, were quantities of strawberries, blueberries, cranberries, wild plums and cherries, as well as other fruits. They had several recipes for cooking acorns and dug certain roots commonly called "Indian potatoes." In the spring they made maple sugar and syrup, and in early summer they planted corn, pumpkins and squash. We do not know how much gardening they learned from early white traders and settlers but they made gardens many years ago.

It is said that the Chippewa women were very good cooks and knew how to use all sorts of seasonings, though they had no pepper nor salt. They used wild ginger a great deal in seasoning meat and other food. They made tea out of wintergreen or raspberry leaves, or little twigs of spruce, and in summer they made a refreshing drink by putting a little maple sugar in a cup of cold water.

Before the traders brought steel knives, the Chippewa made knives of the ribs or other bones of animals. These were sharp enough to cut meat. They often used clam shells for spoons. Pointed sticks were used to take meat out of a kettle if it was too hot to take with the fingers. Cups and all sorts of dishes were made of birchbark, and it is said they could heat water in freshly cut birchbark. To do this they made a "kettle" of folded birchbark, fastened at the ends with strips of bark. The inside of the birchbark was on the outside of the "kettle." This was cool and moist. The Indian women put water in it and hung it over the fire, and the water heated before the bark was dry enough to take fire.

The old-time Chippewa ate only once a day, usually about the middle of the morning, but children could get food whenever they were hungry. If food was plentiful, the Indians ate as much as possible. A man might go to seven feasts in one day, and he was expected to eat everything that was put in his dish. If food was scarce, the people suffered terribly. They did not know how to store food when they had plenty in order that they might not starve when winter came and the hunting failed.

The first time a Chippewa woman saw a pie, she was very curious to know how it was made. She had bought flour at the trader's store and tried to make bread like that made by the white women, but there was blackberry sauce in the middle of what looked like a flat piece of bread.

How did it get there? These Indians make up a name for whatever is new to them and the word describes the object. So the Chippewa made up a name for blackberry pie and it is one of the longest words in the Chippewa language. It tells all about the pie except how to make it. This is the Chippewa word—*muckode-tututs-gominun* (blackberries), *bashko-minisigun* (sauce), *bukwezhigun* (bread). A Chippewa can say this whole word without stopping for breath.

A funny story is told about an old chief who went to Washington with others to sign a treaty. Usually the Indians who go to Washington enjoy eating many good things that they do not have at home. When they sit down to dinner they order more than they can eat. This chief, it is said, knew only one English word for food and did not like to show his ignorance. His word was "rosbif." So whenever he was asked what he would like to eat [he] said "rosbif." He ate roast beef day after day and watched the others eating also interesting new kinds of food. He was very tired of roast beef when he got home, but all the same [was proud] that he had been able to order his food in English.

Nebraska Buffalo Barbecue

The American bison first got its wrong name from a Spaniard, the explorer Hernando de Soto, who first saw one in 1544 and called it a buffalo. It is only very distantly related to buffalo. Its scientific name is Bison bison. *The estimated 60 million (some estimate as high as 100 million) of these more than two-ton animals that grazed in much of eastern and western North America before the nineteenth century was the largest land herd ever recorded on earth. There are descriptions of men standing on a ridge looking across the Great Plains and seeing nothing but the dark woolly backs of bison all the way to the horizon—millions of animals.*

The white man's interest in the bison was not gastronomic except for a certain gourmetlike preference for the tongues and the humps. While commercializing pelts, they had little interest in meat. Most bison that were shot by white men rotted on the plains where they fell. The U.S. Army wanted the bison exterminated to starve the Indians, who depended on these animals for food and clothing. In addition, the railroad wanted these 2,500-pound beasts out of their way and took easterners on trips in which they could shoot the animals from train windows as they chugged by. In fact, curiously, the extermination of the bison began in mid-nineteenth-century America at the same time that other Americans were starting to build up the great beef herds to feed the nation.

In 1886, with few bison left in North America, a herd of six hundred—decades earlier a few million had been called "a family"—found sanctuary in Yellowstone National Park. Eight years later all but twenty had been killed by poachers. At the time there were 1,094 American bison left in the United States, and by the beginning of the twentieth century, twenty-one bison in Yellowstone Park and a small herd by Lake Athabasca in Canada protected by North West Mounted Police were all that was left of the wild species.

In 1905 Theodore Roosevelt created a bison reservation near Wichita, Kansas, with a donation of twelve animals from the New York Zoological Society. Soon after another reserve was created in Montana. Most of the stock came from the 969 captive bison in zoo cages around the country. A bison can produce one calf a year for up to forty years, and by the time of America Eats *there were twelve thousand bison in the United States. The reserves did not have enough grazing land for more, and so each year bison were killed off to maintain the size of the herds, creating for the first time the novelty of bison meat.*

Buffalo steaks, buffalo burgers, and buffalo barbecues
became popular and have remained so since there are now
domestic herds to keep up with the demand. But even wild
buffalo meat does not taste very gamy.

A half-century and more after the last straggling remnants of free ranging buffalo herds were slaughtered in Western Nebraska, buffalo meat is reappearing on Nebraska menus.

A traveler will seldom find it on a restaurant bill-of-fare but he may read an invitation in the newspaper to come and get a free helping of barbecued buffalo at some community celebration.

Return of this meat—once a mainstay in the diet of pioneer plainsmen and farmers—is due to conservation of the animals by federal and state governments. Herds of buffalo in some cases are increasing in numbers beyond the pasture capacity of the game refuges and the surplus animals are butchered and sold. Applications for the meat are received by the U.S. Department of the Interior and the Nebraska State Game, Forestation and Parks Commission.

"Barbecued buffalo" announced in connection with community celebrations is a powerful advertising drawing card, as indicated by the attached accounts of such affairs.

Mr. S. R. Danekas, who lives at Thedford, Neb., Thomas County, in the heart of Nebraska sandhills cattle country, has considerable reputation as a master of ceremonies at barbecues. Invited by letter to describe his system, he responded as follows:

"The first step is to select the meat animal. Naturally the better the grade of meat used the better the finished product. In the particular barbecue on which you asked information we happened to use two buffalo.

"After the carcass has been thoroughly chilled and cured, preferably six days or a week, in a meat cooler, the bones are removed and the meat rolled into uniform pieces 6 to 8 inches in diameter, no piece to exceed 26 pounds in weight.

"Then for seasoning, I like to use just plain salt and pepper rubbed into the meat, the amount used depending upon the age of the meat animal and degree of seasoning desired.

"The meat is then wrapped, each meat roll individually in clean muslin or cheese cloth, then wrapped in clean burlap. These bundles are then ready and must be kept cool until it is time to be put in the pit.

"A well-drained location should be selected for the pit. A pit 4 ft. deep and 3½ to 4 ft. wide and 4 to 5 ft. in length should be allowed for each 200 pounds of boneless meat.

"The best fuel is hardwood worked up into uniform pieces. I list a few of them in order of their preference: hickory, oak, ash, hard maple, elm, willow and cottonwood. These are the common varieties used. Pine or fir or other resinous, pitchy, or turpentine trees cannot be used as they injure the flavor of the meat. The same is true of walnut and other woods which produce an offensive odor in burning. Even cedar, cypress and the like should be avoided if anything better is available.

"The fire should be started in the bottom of the pit 20 to 30 hours before serving time. Seven to 12 hours time is necessary to get a bed of live coals three feet deep, depending on the dryness of the wood, the draft to the pit, etc. Ten to 20 hours cooking time must be figured, depending on the age and quality of the meat and the liveness of the coals. Some woods give better coals than others.

"The next step is levelling off the bed of coals and removing all unburned pieces. Then one to two inches of coarse dry sand is spread evenly over the coals. The bundles of wrapped meat are then placed on top of the sand, allowing an inch or so between the bundles so that the heat can penetrate each chunk of meat uniformly. As quickly as possible the trench is covered with sheet iron or some durable material supported by iron rafters or pipes to hold up the 12 to 16 inches of dirt that is to be put on top of the chest iron to completely insulate the barbecuing process. The heat is thus retained and all meat juices are under seal in each package.

"The meat is left in the pit 10 to 20 hours, for the reasons mentioned.

"When a small portion of the pit is uncovered, with the aid of a pitchfork I hook a chunk of the wrapped meat and place it in a tub ready to unwind the burlap and muslin. Then place the savory smelling chunk of cooked meat on the slicing table.

"The meat is sliced cross-grained into slices to be put into buns or bread. From 350 to 400 servings can be expected for each 100 lbs. of boneless meat.

"I might add that this method of barbecuing eradicates waste and conserves the natural properties of the meat, while the main objection to the open fire method is that the meat burns to a crisp on the outside and the inside may remain raw."

Nebraska Pop Corn Days

M. C. NELSON

Nebraska has long been America's leading producer of popcorn, with Indiana as its only serious rival, although the Popcorn Institute is in Chicago and the Popcorn Museum in Marion, Ohio. Like most of the stories surrounding "the first Thanksgiving" in 1621 the legend of the Indian Quadequina bringing out popcorn to serve the Pilgrims seems dubious. But it probably was an Indian invention made from hard flint corn, which has a starch casing that expands with heat and explodes. Cortés and his men saw the Aztecs use it as ornament and Puritan governor John Winthrop of Massachusetts saw Indians making it. It was embraced by the early New England settlers, who, apparently more fastidious about questions of grammar than today's Americans, kept calling it "popped corn." It was always popular, both as a snack at public events and as ornaments at Christmas time.

But although popcorn was popular at the time of America Eats, *it was not nearly as popular as it is today. According to Betty Fussell, who wrote the 1992* The Story of Corn, *dur-*

ing World War II candy was shipped overseas to G.I.s, leaving the homefront to eat popcorn. Consumption rose dramatically and continued rising, and according to Fussell, today fifty-six popped quarts per capita are eaten every year in America.

Hollywood sometimes uses hundreds of bushels of corn flakes to create the illusion of a snow storm but there is no illusion when five or six hundred bushels of snow-white pop corn fluff out of the poppers and into the mouths of several thousand celebrants during Pop Corn Days in North Loup, Nebraska, every autumn.

This community on the North Loup River wants the world to know that Valley County in the north-east central part of the state specializes in this crop. Crop statistics reveal that it has harvested as high as 7,910 acres and 6,478,290 pounds of pop corn in one year (1926). Since there are about 56 pounds of shelled pop corn in one bushel, and a kernel increases about 18 times in size when popped, this bumper crop had a potential of some 2 million bushels of popped fluffiness.

This would make quite a "snow storm" even in Hollywood.

Three days late in September usually are reserved for the festival. The first day is "Entry Day" when exhibits of farm crops, cooking, canning, school work and fancy work are arranged. School is dismissed and crowds of people from neighboring communities go to North Loup to test the meaning of its invitation: "Free Pop Corn—Free Admission—Free Entertainment."

Entertainment includes the coronation of the Pop Corn Queen. A typical description of this ceremony is contained in the Sept. 24, 1937, issue of the *North Loup Loyalist* in part as follows:

"The procession started from the school house. Heralded by buglers with green capes over their uniforms, the Queen was announced. The buglers were answered by the roll of drums . . .

"The Queen was regal in her robes of lustrous gold satin, her long train of green velvet bound with gold was carried by her ladies in waiting, who were dressed in white with green streamers tied Grecian fashion . . .

"In the procession was the crown bearer, dressed in green and yellow, bearing the crown on a satin pillow. He was dressed in a green and yellow cutaway with white trousers. Two flower girls in white strewed pop corn in the path of the Queen."

This has been going on at North Loup since 1902. Free pop corn, all you can eat and free coffee is the big attraction each year. Going back through the newspaper files we find that in 1911 a total of 13,000 sacks of pop corn were given away. In 1912 the amount eaten was estimated at 306 bushels (of pop corn). In 1920, 1,800 pounds of shelled kernels were popped. Last year, 1940, the amount was 1,400 pounds. The population of North Loup in 1940 was 567.

Wisconsin Sour-Dough Pancakes

Sourdough has been around for thousands of years, and it is said—and might be true—that Christopher Columbus brought starter with him on one of his voyages. The characteristic sourness originally came from leaving wild yeast in a warm place so that it would ferment slowly over a few days. Starter then became flour and water that fermented over a few days with yeast that with luck was naturally present. Sometimes milk or mashed potatoes was included to stimulate fermentation. The idea was that it was a way of baking where yeast was not available and so it is a technique that was associated with pioneers and, later, gold prospectors. In modern times, with no lack of industrial yeast, those who want the sour taste simply add yeast to a fermenting batter. Then a portion of this is kept and added to more flour and water and the portion always saved for the next batch is the "starter," to which this piece from America Eats *refers.*

There are two kinds of lumber camp cooks, the Baking Powder Buns and the Sour-dough Stiffs. Sour-dough Sam belonged to the latter school. He made everything but coffee out of sour-dough. He had only one arm and one leg, the other members having been lost when his sour-dough barrel blew up."

So reads a passage in one of the Paul Bunyan stories. And, as in all tall tales, the hyperbole serves to emphasize a truth. The sour-dough pancake has always been a favorite food among Wisconsin lumberjacks, and few bull cooks worthy of the name fail to decorate their breakfast tables with huge platters stacked high with steaming, golden, sour-dough cakes. To the camp cook a continuous supply of sour-dough is an indispensable part of camp equipment, and he is never without his batch of "starter." The "starter" is a portion of dough reserved from previous mixtures and stored in the kind of barrel that proved disastrous to Sour-dough Sam. Zealously guarded, the "starter" can be kept for weeks in ordinary temperatures, lively though it gets.

The night before the pancakes are to be fried, the cook assembles his batter, using the "starter" as a leavening agent. Flour and water are added to the "starter," and the mixture is left near the stove to rise. By morning it is a light and frothy mass smelling pungently of fermentation. After reserving from the batch a "starter" for the next morning's pancakes, the cook adds salt, sugar, eggs, a little fat, and a pinch of soda. He pours large spoonfuls of the batter on a huge, fire-blackened griddle, abundantly greased with smoking pork rind and very hot. Then, after the griddlecake has fried a few moments, he flips it expertly. Soon the sour-dough pancake emerges to greet the morning appetite of the lumberjack.

In the old camps it was customary for the cook to install, near the door of the shanty, a crock containing sour-dough batter in various stages of fermentation. Into the crock went all left-over batter, and scraps of bread, doughnuts, cake, or pancakes, which quickly attained the semi-liquid consistency of the batter.

Nebraska Baked Beans

J. WILLIS KRATZER

Now, just what beats a big pan of steaming hot baked beans? Nothing, for there is nothing better. But they have to be baked right.

Why has Boston all the fame for baked beans? One need not go beyond that oven right over there to taste beans that make Boston take a poor second. Is that judgment too rash? No, for the taste of Boston beans never appealed to yours truly. I want them baked right.

It takes about four hours to slow cook beans right, and that before one thinks of baking them. Mind you, I said "slow cook." That roiling and boiling on a rip-snorting fire was never meant for the cooking of beans. Then take those beans and add minced onion, salt and pepper, mustard, vinegar, brown sugar and bacon. Then if you make about a half gallon of baked beans, pour in a full bottle of good tomato catsup; don't be stingy on that, either. Then bake in a slow oven, hot enough to cook but not to blister the beans, for from one to two hours as needed.

I'll dub these "Nebraska baked beans" and if the world will try them they will be down on Boston's forevermore.

Cooking for the Threshers
in Nebraska

ESTELLA TENBRINK

The huge threshing machine with its coat of bright red paint, chugging down the road behind the puffing steam engine, was a thrilling sight to one little girl on a Gage County, Nebraska, farm in the late '90s. With keen interest she watched it turn into her father's grain field. By this time the men of the neighborhood—brawny, sun-tanned fellows, clad in blue overalls and broad brimmed straw hats, their necks protected with red bandanna handkerchiefs—were arriving. Some came with hay racks and pitch forks; others with lumber wagons and shovels. Even the horses seemed to sense the excitement as they pricked up their ears and pulled at the reins. Eagerly the little girl listened for the blast of the shrill whistle, and the hum of machinery which announced that at last the long-anticipated day was here:

The threshing field was a scene of busy activity never to be forgotten. The cooperation of all was required to keep the work running smoothly. Some of the men with their long pitch forks piled high the yellow sheaves of grain on the tall hay racks. There was keen competition as the men raced to see who would be the first to feed his rack of sheaves into the machine which separated the grain from the straw. Other men hauled the oats or wheat to the granary and shoveled it into the bins. Usually a flock of hungry chickens, determined not to let a single grain that fell on the ground go to waste, had to be shooed away.

As the threshing continued, the pile of yellow straw rose higher and higher. To the little girl, who missed not a single detail of the scene, it was a mountain—her mountain, with its delightful bumps and hollows. It was a perfect place to climb during the sunny hours of day, but a place to be shunned at nightfall for that was where the bears and wolves slept. The little girl knew, for had she not seen their holes, deep and dark on the sides of the mountain?

But on this red-letter day the little girl could not spend all the time watching her straw mountain grow. She must help mother cook for the threshers. All the previous day she had been busy helping mother with the preparations. She felt happy anticipation, getting ready for the threshers—like dressing for a party. At last they were really coming!

How good the loaves of home-made bread smelled when mother took them from the oven. It was fun to dip a small white cloth into some butter and rub the brown crusts with it so that they would be soft and shiny. To see the big pile of loaves wrapped in a snowy cloth gave her a feeling of preparedness. It was fun to take the sugar cookies from the pans and pile them on plates to cool. And what little girl would not feel important when she was asked to beat the whites of eggs while mother cooked the syrup of sugar and water until it dripped in threads from the spoon? She felt quite grown-up as she slowly poured the syrup over the stiffly beaten egg whites while mother beat as hard as she could until the frosting was just right to spread on the spice cake. There were always two or three cakes. Sometimes there was a brownstone front, a reddish brown chocolate cake with a creamy brown sugar frosting. Sometimes there was a marble cake or a yellow sponge cake. The little girl liked to measure the sugar and flour, she liked to grease the cake pans; but best of all she liked to "lick" the frosting pan and the cake crock.

The day before the threshers came was a busy one. There was the house to sweep and sut and the kitchen floor to scrub until the bare boards shone. The cream was churned up and down with a dasher until the little balls of butter appeared. Then it was worked into round pats, decorated with the edge of the butter paddle, and put away in a cool cave. Potatoes were dug from the patch in the garden—enough to last until the threshers left. They usually stayed two days. A big bucket of beets was pulled from the patch in the garden, washed and boiled until tender. The little girl liked to slide off the skins after mother had poured some cold water on a pan full, she liked to slice the beets into the stone jar and watch mother pour on the hot vinegar to which had been added salt, pepper and a little sugar.

With eager anticipation the little girl looked forward to the trip in the spring wagon to the nearest town for a roast of beef. Mother always selected a nice big one. It was wrapped in brown paper and kept covered with a thick blanket all the way home and then it was hurried to the cave for there were no refrigerators on the farms in those days.

Mother had the pies in the oven very early in the morning on the day that the threshers came. There were always plenty of them—at least a half dozen. Mince, apple, peach, cherry, raisin, and custard were favorites. Sometimes cream fillings full of coconut or chocolate, or a lemon filling was poured into a crust which had been baked the day before. The little girl loved to see a row of delicious pies placed on a shelf to cool. The pies must be out of the oven early so as to make room for the roast for it took a long time to cook such a big roast tender. Mother said that it wasn't good if it cooked too fast. Odors that made the little girl's mouth water came from the oven every time it was opened.

To work alone with mother getting ready for the threshers made one feel important and necessary. But when the threshers came, it was nice to have two grown-up ladies dressed in crisp "calico" dresses and aprons in the kitchen helping mother. A little girl needed some time to watch the straw mountain grow, and then it was such fun to go with mother when she helped the neighbor in return, especially if there was a little girl one's own age to play with. It was so much nicer to have a little playmate along when one went to the garden for the vegetables. There were green beans, cucumbers, onions, cabbage, sweet potatoes and tomatoes and if it was not too late in the season, there was sweet corn. Mother always cooked every kind of vegetable that she had for the threshers. And they must be gathered on the morning that they were used so that they would be "nice and fresh," mother said. Two little girls enjoyed sitting under the shade of a tree while they snapped the beans. How delicious they were cooked slowly with a ham bone. They enjoyed peeling the cucumbers and slicing them very thin into some salty water to "draw out the green." Pepper, salt and vinegar was added and then they were ready for the table. There was always a big dish of stewed tomatoes well seasoned with butter, pepper and salt, as well as a dish of sliced fresh ones. Sometimes there was a big dish of sweet potatoes candied in brown sugar and butter and a dish of buttered beets. The dinner would not have been complete without a dish of cole slaw. And such slaw: The little girl chopped the crisp, white cabbage very fine on a wooden board with a slaw cutter. Mother added salt, pepper, sugar and vinegar until it tasted just right. Then she sent the little girl to the sour cream can in the cave. With a ladle she dipped the thick, sour cream from the can, a little at a time, and stirred it through the slaw with a spoon. "One had to be careful so as not to get too much cream," Mother said, and the little girl was anxious to have it perfect so the threshers would eat lots of it. Mother liked to have the men eat lots because then she knew that they liked her cooking.

By eleven-thirty all was hustle and bustle. Dishes of preserves, quivering jelly—several kinds of each, chopped pickles and beet pickles and the dish of cole slaw were all on the table, which had been stretched its full length and spread with a red and white plaid cloth. If only the flies didn't get in, thought the little girl: One didn't like to have to shoo them off the table with a branch from the maple tree. The roast was sliced and placed in the warming oven where it would stay hot. Time was moving fast. Soon the whistle would blow for dinner. The big kettle of potatoes was mashed, seasoned with salt, pepper and a piece of butter, then some rich, sweet cream added, and the whole beat until it was fluffy. The dripping from the roast was thickened and made into delicious brown gravy. The pies and cakes were cut. A big plate of home-made bread was on the table.

There was a blast from the whistle, the machine stopped; and the men, hungry and dirty, hurried to the house. There were always at least twenty of them—so many that some had to wait for the second table.

Mother and the neighbor ladies busied themselves "dishing-up" while the men "washed-up" in the tin basin which had been placed on the bench under the shade tree. They jostled one another and cracked jokes as they wiped on the roller towels provided for them.

Mother always sent the little girl to the cave for a pat of butter while the men were washing, for it would have been disgraceful to serve soft butter to the first table. One couldn't help it if the butter turned to oil in a little while. As the little girl, clad in a crisp, blue "calico" dress which mother had her put on after the table was set so that it would be spotless at dinner time, slipped quietly by the threshers on her way to the cave, she wondered why such big men wiped so much dirt off on mother's clean towels—like little boys. There was plenty of tar soap and a big tub of water had been warming in the sun all morning. Mother said that there "just wasn't any sense in it": It made the washing so hard.

How the hungry men "stored away the food": It was all on the table—meat, vegetables, pickles, preserves, gravy, cups of steaming hot coffee, pitchers of thick cream. Even the cakes and pies and cookies were on the table. It was so full that it fairly groaned under the weight. The little girl and her playmate were kept busy filling the bread plate and the water glasses. Mother said they mustn't forget—that it was their responsibility. The grown-up ladies kept all the other dishes filled and watched to see that everything was passed a sufficient number of times.

Dirty dishes were hurried from the table as soon as a place was vacant. They were washed and put back, ready for the next hungry man. The threshers laughed and joked and ate until they could eat no more. One by one they retired to a shade tree where they rested and told stories until the whistle blew. That was the signal for threshing to start again.

There was always plenty of food left for the cooks, even if it wasn't quite so hot as when it was served to the first table. The "little cooks" ate and ate until they could hold no more. It was the best dinner one could imagine: It was even better than a "company" dinner because there was lots more excitement. Mother always let the little girls play while the table was being cleared and the dishes washed. She said they had been such "good little helpers" all morning and they would be needed again when the hungry men came in for supper.

A big kettle of small potatoes in the jackets was boiled while the dishes were being washed. The women relaxed a little now that the rush was over and visited while they cleaned away the dinner. In the middle of the afternoon there was time for a short rest in the "sitting" room. Then

the table must be set again, the big slices of home-cured ham fried—
heaping platters of it. The potatoes which had been peeled and sliced
were browned in the fresh ham grease. A big pot of steaming coffee was
made, the left-overs from dinner were warmed, another dish of cole slaw
was made, and the table again groaned with food when the whistle blew
for supper. It never blew until after the sun went down unless the job
was finished early. Sometimes the big red machine threshed away until
it was dark. This was when they wanted to finish so that they could
pull to the next place that night. Then it was very late when the supper
dishes were washed by the dim light of a kerosene lamp. It was always
late when the dishes were washed, thought the little girl. And it wasn't
any fun then. The excitement was all over and she was so sleepy that
mother always sent her to bed.

The men with the machine stayed all night. Very early while it was
still dark, they were out at the machine "getting up steam." Mother was
up early too, because they had to have a *big* breakfast—hot biscuits,
fried potatoes, fried-down sausage and oatmeal served with plenty of
cream and sugar. Mother had another row of pies baked when the little
girl came down stairs, still a little sleepy but ready for another delightful
day. The dinner was much the same as the day before, except that there
were big platters of fried chicken instead of roast beef. It took a long time
to dress so many chickens. The little girl wondered why chickens had
so many pin feathers as she picked them out of the pieces that mother
dropped into the big crock of cold water. The neighbor ladies came again
and the little playmate. The threshers wiped some more dirt on fresh
towels and ate until they could eat no more just as they had done the day
before. The little girls again kept the water glasses and the bread plate
full and felt important and almost grown-up.

The straw mountain grew very high and very bumpy. The last sheaf
of grain was fed into the big machine. A shrill blast from the whistle
announced that the job was finished. As the little girl watched the big
red threshing machine chug down the road behind the little puffing
engine, she felt sorry for all the little girls who never had a chance to
help cook for the threshers.

The threshing scene in Nebraska has undergone many changes since

the '90s. There were no cars in those days. Social life centered in the
community and people made their own entertainment. Opportunities for
social contacts were not so frequent as today. Even though the threshing season was a period of long hours and strenuous work, it nevertheless had its social aspects. Men "swapped" stories as they paused for a
drink of water from the brown jug or waited their turns at the machine.
Women took advantage of the rare opportunity to get together and
exchange recipes and quilt patterns. They talked of the homely details
that made up their lives—the latest baby in the neighborhood, the new
rag carpet Grandma Stance was making, their shelves of canned fruit,
pickles, preserves and jelly, the number of chickens in their flocks. They
vied with each other to see who could get up the best dinner. The best
that the home afforded was none too good for the threshers.

Combines, which are used in many localities, have reduced the number of men in the threshing crews. Farm women are not so starved for
social contacts as they were in the '90s. They no longer exchange work at
threshing time as frequently as they did in the old days.

"Calories" were unheard of in the '90s. Everything that the farm
afforded was prepared in large quantities. Now many of the farm women
have become calorie conscious and they plan balanced meals. They
are not so dependent upon the home-prepared foods as they once were.
Bread may be delivered at the mail box in time for dinner. The cream
may be sold at the cream station and butter purchased from the grocer-
man. Canned vegetables are replacing the home-grown ones to a large
extent. Meals have become much simpler. Refreshing salads are replacing some of the heavier dishes. The trend is toward serving a single dessert instead of several kinds of cake and pie. Fruit salad, fresh fruit, or
ice cream are quite frequently served now.

An effort is being made to cut down on the work of cooking for the
threshers. Some women are beginning to serve cafeteria style and in a
few cases paper plates are being used.

Wisconsin and Minnesota Lutefisk

Lutefisk is a traditional winter food in Norway, Sweden, and the Swedish-speaking part of Finland. Both Swedes and Norwegians say that it was invented in their country, the claims usually accompanied by an apocryphal story about a mishap in a medieval kitchen. Eating dried codfish cured in lye is counterintuitive enough to assume it began as a mishap.

Lutefisk is made from the effect of alkali on the fish. In the Middle Ages this was accomplished with potash made from boiling wood. Beech was the wood of choice for lutefisk. Today's lye is a caustic soda.

Originally lutefisk was a dish for all the important religious holidays, such as Christmas, Good Friday, and Easter. In North America it became the dish for Christmas Eve. This was still popular at the time of America Eats. *But since then the tradition started to fade and there was a public relations campaign in the late twentieth century to revive the tradition, which was extremely successful. This may have been due to the implication that lutefisk, like most everything, is an aphrodisiac.*

Both the Wisconsin and Minnesota Writers' Projects contributed similar unsigned articles about Norwegians and Norwegian Americans having church-sponsored lutefisk suppers. The Minnesota one pointed out that such suppers were still common even in churches where the sermon was no longer preached in a Scandinavian language. The Minnesota story said that lutefisk provided "a sentimental link with the

*Scandinavian homeland," and also made the dubious claim
that the slimy gelatinous fish "could safely be counted on to
appeal to even the most finicky appetite." The Wisconsin report,
with more candor, asserted, "Nobody likes lutefisk at first."*

The Lutefisk Supper: Wisconsin

When the fall days become really crisp, people in all the Scandinavian-settled regions of Wisconsin begin to scan their local newspapers for announcements of *lutefisk* suppers. Such announcements are not hard to find, because almost every Norwegian church gives at least one such supper between October and the end of the year, and there are many Norwegian churches. From miles away, often as many as fifty, lovers of *lutefisk* drive to the church where the supper is to be given. And they are not all Scandinavians, by any means. So popular have *lutefisk* suppers become that in Dane County a group of Norwegians have humorously formed what they call a "Norwegian Lutefisk Protective Association" to guard the suppers from the invasion of non-Norwegian epicures. "Germans and Irish are again invading the sacred lutefisk domains," wrote one Norwegian-American editor in 1941, "and appropriating the usual disproportionate share of the traditional Christmas delicacy." But the ladies of the Norwegian churches are glad to have the strangers come, for the receipts from the suppers go to pay the church debts. It is not uncommon for as many as two thousand people to attend a single supper, and a crowd of five hundred has come to be considered almost trifling.

These church suppers, so eagerly awaited, so widely attended, are a comparatively recent innovation. But though the custom of the public *lutefisk* supper is only about fifteen years old, *lutefisk* itself has always been, and still is, a winter delicacy in the Scandinavian home. It is a "company" dish and a Christmas dish; in many a Norwegian home it takes the place of the Christmas turkey.

Its preparation is not complicated, but it takes many days—so many days that it must be confined to cold weather, when the fish will not spoil. The codfish arrives already dried. Formerly it was imported from

Norway, where it was sun-dried, but now it is gotten from Iceland, where it is electrically dried. The dry codfish is cooked in soft water for about a week (or for a longer period if the water is hard), and the water is changed each night and morning. Then the fish is removed and placed in a solution of lye and water (a gallon of soft water to two tablespoons full of lye), where it is cooked for another week. It is then removed from the lye solution, washed, and soaked in clean water for two days and nights. Frequently a tablespoonful of slaked lime is added for bleaching. At the end of this long period of being cooked and resoaked the fish is ready for use. The cooking is the simplest part. The fish is dropped into salted boiling water, where it is cooked for from fifteen to twenty minutes. It is served with generous sprinklings of salt, pepper, and hot melted butter. Norwegians prefer the butter sauce, Swedes a white sauce.

Of course, when the church suppers are given, great quantities of fish must be prepared in advance, and to simplify the process barrels and tubs of fish already in the lye solution are imported from Minneapolis. Consequently, the work of the women of the church consists largely of giving the *lutefisk* its last cooking, boiling, preparing the trimmings, and serving the supper. The first supper starts at noon and ends about 2:30 in the afternoon. Then, after a period of recovery, when the dishes are washed, the tablecloths changed, and the church aired, the big supper commences; usually it continues from about 4:50 in the afternoon until after 8 at night. It is a gala affair. Pink-cheeked people have driven through the crisp air, often many cold miles, full of a hunger that comes from a self-imposed and epicurean asceticism. All day they have been preparing to gorge themselves, to eat as they eat only at *lutefisk* suppers. To appear with a small appetite is the grossest kind of *faux pas*; and to fail to stuff oneself to bursting is bad-mannered.

From noon to midnight the heavy odor of codfish hangs on the air outside the church; and from about 5:30 to 7:30 the crowds begin making their way through the damp pungency, up the church steps, to the door. At the door tickets are sold, and each ticket has a number on it indicating the order of the guest's appearance. The hungry guest must wait his turn; he must wait until there is space at a table in the crowded church basement; he must wait until he hears his number called out. And so he sits, sometimes for as long as two hours, in one of the pews of the steamy, fish-stuffy church. And yet he doesn't mind waiting very much; it is much like waiting to see the President or the Duke of Windsor. Half his fun is in the waiting, the anticipation, the consciousness of a growing hunger that he knows will be fully and deliciously assuaged.

Among those who wait there is a feeling of good fellowship. Sturdy Scandinavian farmers, businessmen, politicos, editors, housewives, children, and students of what America eats wait happily together for the basement tables to be cleared of the earlier eaters, for their own numbers to be called. And they joke about waiting, about hunger, about anticipation, and about their girths before and after. If a newcomer is present, a tyro in the special gastronomies of *lutefisk*, they will tell him, with an air of complacent knowledge, "You won't like it. Nobody likes *lutefisk* at first. You have to learn to like it. Better take meat balls." For Swedish meat balls are served to the uninitiated who have yet to grow to a liking of strong fish.

The church basement is filled with long tables, and as soon as people leave them the ladies of the church set new places. Great bowls of the pearl-colored fish are kept standing on the tables, and the diners help themselves. The ladies who serve are very eager to see that the fish does not get cold, that the bowls are refilled over and over again from the great kettles in the church kitchen, where new fish is continually being boiled. Pitchers of melted butter are emptied lavishly on the fish and replenished time and again.

There are certain inevitable accompaniments of *lutefisk* at the church supper. Boiled or steamed potatoes are served with it, a plain counterpoint to the fancier delicacy. Pickles are served, "to take the course off of all the butter you eat," as one church hostess said. A cabbage salad, usually cole slaw, is always served, and bright dishes full of red lingon-berry sauce pass up and down the tables. But the real Norwegian delicacy that accompanies *lutefisk* is *lefsa*, great piles of folded *lefsa*, looking like thin tannish paper napkins, heaped along the table in ever-diminishing and ever-replenished stacks. Before the *lefsa* is served, each crisp disk has been double-folded into a kind of triangle, thin and pliant. *Lefsa* is eaten in several ways: sometimes it is buttered, filled with white or brown sugar, and rolled cylinder-wise; sometimes it is buttered, stuffed with *lutefisk*, and rolled. At the *lutefisk* suppers cylinder after cylinder of *lefsa* is consumed, washed down by great quantities of coffee. If any *lefsa* remains, it is sold to those who wish to take it home with them.

The women of the church prepare the *lefsa* themselves, and there is great rivalry among the expert *lefsa*-makers, who vary the common recipe with a discrimination that comes from long experience. The following is a recipe from an excellent Norwegian cook: peel and boil enough potatoes to make two quarts then put through a ricer; add one tablespoon of lard or butter and a half a tablespoon of salt; add about three tablespoons of cream or milk (or simply use the liquid in the potatoes); add enough flour to make a dough of the right consistency for rolling, using one cupful of dough for each *lefsa*; roll the dough very thin with a grooved rolling pin; bake on both sides on the top of a wood range or on a cast-iron or steel top made for a gas stove; lay out the *lefsa* to cool; fold into triangular shapes; wrap in wax paper; and keep in a cool place.

When great quantities of *lutefisk*, boiled potatoes, and *lefsa* have been consumed, the *lutefisk*-supper habitué sits back, waits for ten or fifteen minutes, and then starts all over again. But at last, when he has been exhausted for a second or third time, he eats a piece of cake, has a last cup of coffee, and departs, to leave his seat to a new number that will be called upstairs. He drives home happily expansive both in body and soul. At breakfast the next morning he unfolds his newspaper, glances quickly at the war news, and then scans the minor columns for an announcement of the next *lutefisk* supper.

Norwegian Recipes from Minnesota

FLATBRØD

4 cups flour

2 tbsp. salt

1 cup corn meal

⅓ cup shortening

Boiling water

Add enough boiling water to the flour, corn meal and shortening to make a stiff dough, stirring constantly. Cool. Take portions the size of an egg and roll very thin into round sheets on a corn meal sprinkled canvas. Bake on top of stove, turning for even browning. Bake on both sides, using a stick to turn over.

LEFSA

    2 qts. hot boiled potatoes

    2 tbsp. lard

    ½ cup sweet cream

    1 heaping tbsp. salt

    Flour

Mash potatoes thoroughly. Cool. Heat lard and cream; add to cold potatoes. Knead in sufficient flour to roll very thin. Bake on top of stove.

NORWEGIAN MEAT BALLS

    2 lbs. ground beef

    ½ tsp. pepper

    1 cup bread crumbs

    ¼ tsp. nutmeg

    2 eggs, beaten

    1 small onion, chopped

    3 tsp. salt

    1 cup milk

Mix hamburger, bread crumbs, and seasonings. Add beaten eggs. Add milk, gradually, kneading well. Cool overnight. Roll into balls and fry. Remove meat balls from skillet; make gravy by browning flour, and adding equal parts of milk and water. Season to taste. Return meat balls to gravy; place in slow oven for about an hour.

FATTIGMAND

   10 egg yolks

   8 egg whites

   1 cup sugar

   1 cup whipping cream

   1½ tbsp. melted butter

   Enough flour to roll out

   2 tsp. cardamom

Beat egg whites and yolks with sugar for 20 minutes. Add cream, melted butter, and other ingredients. Roll thin; cut in diamonds, and fry in deep fat.

LUTEFISK

   Dry codfish

   Water

   Lye

The preparation of lutefisk by this method requires only fifteen days. Place the dry codfish in clean, cold water and let stand one week, changing water every morning. Then make lye solution; 1 tsp. lye to each 4 or 5 pounds of fish. Don't have the solution too strong, lest the fish soften too rapidly. Let stand four days, keeping in a cold place. Then pour off the lye solution and cover with clear, cold water. Soak another 4 days, changing water each morning, and continuing to keep in a cold place.

   When ready to cook, take the amount to be used and place in a cloth bag. Place in kettle and pour boiling water over it. Boil gently 5 to 10 minutes, until done. Add salt to taste. Carefully drain, skin, and bone. Put on a platter and serve with brown melted butter or cream sauce.

Indiana Pork Cake

FROM HAZEL M. NIXON,

40 NORTH GALESTON STREET, INDIANAPOLIS, INDIANA

1 pound of ground or finely chopped pork

1 cup of boiling water poured over pork

1 cup of molasses

2 cups of brown sugar

1 teaspoonful of soda

Stir in 1 pound of raisins, 1 pound of chopped dates (latter
    not necessary) and ½ pound of finely chopped citron

Add 4 cups of flour

1 teaspoonful of cloves

1 teaspoonful of cinnamon

1 teaspoonful of allspice

1 teaspoonful of nutmeg

Pork must be fresh and raw; fat preferred. Will keep two or three months, if wrapped in greased paper, then in dry paper. Don't bake too quickly.

Nebraska Lamb and Pig Fries

H. J. MOSS

O ften referred to as mountain oysters, lamb and pig fries are a much dramatized special food event. Being distinctly male in character it is associated more or less with stag parties or mere man get-to-gethers. Somehow the ladies just don't seem to fit into such affairs. Still they are sometimes present and take a keen interest in the menu, which of course is principally what the title of the banquet implies. Groups, such as the American Legion, hunting clubs, gun clubs, and so forth, go in for this sort of thing in Nebraska in a big way. Little publicity is necessary so the general public hears very little about such banquets or feeds.

Beer (or stronger) drinking is associated with these affairs and is probably the rule instead of the exception. Since the average lady cook has very little experience in cooking pig or lamb fries, a man cook, better versed, usually officiates at the stove. The fries are generally dipped in egg-batter and cracker crumbs and dropped into very hot, deep fat. Ordinarily most epicures like their fries done to a crisp. Rare fries are not looked upon with favor.

Fries are one article of food which seldom finds its way to the family table. It is definitely limited to male group meetings and is the theme of the entire program and the reason for its existence. It provides a subtle atmosphere of the carnal and unusual and its very character enhances the occasion in a sort of "forbidden fruit" or "a little of the devil" way.

These fries are quite popular in Nebraska and are more deliberate than they are spontaneous, since advance arrangements usually have to be made—the item generally not being available in the open market. Docking pigs and lambs is a sort of community activity and farmers often take advantage of the occasion to hold a fry as a fitting sequel to the activity itself. This food item is particularly rich and those who overeat are quite apt to be deviled with a splitting headache the following day, which malady often is blamed to the overindulgence in other refreshments more liquid in form.

FARMER EATS HAMBURGER AT CORN-
HUSKING CONTEST, MARSHALL COUNTY,
IOWA. (PHOTOGRAPH BY ARTHUR
ROTHSTEIN)

Kansas Beef Tour

WILLIAM LINDSAY WHITE

The reference to "Young Bill White" was because at this time he was largely known as the son of the newspaper editor William Allen White. Many of the people in Emporia, Kansas, thought that the younger Bill, William Lindsay White, was a bit too uppity. It was not just that he went to Harvard, but while there his Kansas accent seemed to have been replaced by something vaguely English that went with his new habit of wearing a monocle. For a time he was listed as one of the best-dressed men in America. His wife, Katherine, a friend of Bernard Baruch, Claire Booth Luce, and John O'Hara, was what was called in Emporia "a New York sophisticate." Baruch wrote that she was the most beautiful woman in New York. The Whites lived part-time in Kansas and part-time in their New York brownstone. White was a prominent war correspondent and worked with the legendary Edward R. Murrow at CBS. He wrote a number of successful books on World War II that were picked up by Hollywood, the most well known of which was the 1942 bestseller They Were Expendable.

But in 1944 his ailing father persuaded him to return to Kansas and take over the post of editor of the Emporia Gazette, *from which position he opposed urban renewal and championed Republican politicians. He played an important role in the launching of the career of U.S. Senator Bob Dole and was a friend and supporter of Richard Nixon. By coincidence, White died in 1973, at the height of his friend's Watergate scandal.*

The Lyon County Beef Tour and Barbecue, which has become an important annual event in the Flint Hills during the past few years, is described by W. L. "Young Bill" White, whose comments on the art of barbecue and other traditional dishes of the range will be interesting to the editors.

"The Beef Tour is a regular event in this part of the world, the annual feast day of the cow country. It is under the auspices of the county agent and this year there were several visiting dignitaries from the State Agricultural college and from the Department of Agriculture in Washington.

"It takes a whole day, and is routed through the best farms and ranches. At each stop the visitors range their cars in a huge half moon and stay in their seats so as not to frighten the cattle. Cowboys then drive the herd as close as possible, which is seldom closer than 50 yards from the line of windshields. Any nearer and the steers take fright and stampede, hightailing it off across the creek and over the hills on the horizon. But each cattleman has had a chance to judge them.

"He can study a 1,400 pound steer a city block away and tell you his weight within three pounds.

"Then the owner of the herd is called to the microphone attached to the big loudspeakers on top of the county agent's car, and he tells the other cowmen just what brand and breed his string is, how much they cost, how many pounds of feed per day they have eaten, what each kind cost, how much they have gained, when he expects to sell them, and what his profit is, as of the present market. The cattlemen listen attentively to these figures, each comparing it with the cost of his own string.

"At noon the caravan halts for chuck at the Eddie Jones ranch. The food, as you might guess, is beef, the barbecue hind quarters of a prime Lyon county steer specially ordered from the Kansas City stockyards for this discriminating audience. To make sure they got a good one the Verdigris Valley ladies who prepared it got Big Walter Jones to put in the order himself.

"Big Walter is the most important cattleman of the region. His pastures in Kansas and Texas, if put together, would make up a sizeable part of the State of Rhode Island. He ships thousands of cattle a year, judges the market shrewdly, and even the big packing companies jump when Big Walter speaks out. So Big Walter went to the phone, called the Morrell Packing Company in Kansas City and told them to send him down a hind quarter off one of that string of steers which Floyd Lowder had shipped to market last week. Big Walter, visiting Floyd, had seen that string munching out in Floyd's feeding corrals, and for 1,000 miles around there is no better judge of beef, either on the hoof or in the roaster, than Big Walter. You would agree if you could have seen the big chunks of it—each double the size of your head and beautifully roasted, set out on plank tables under the trees down by the creek on Eddie Jones' ranch, and watched the juicy tender slices curl away from the sharp edges of the butcher knives as the hot meat was doused with hot sauce and put into barbecue sandwiches.

"How much did it cost? Well, nobody knows exactly. But the Verdigris Valley ladies had prudently allowed a pound of beef apiece for everyone present. Then there was the bread and coffee and sugar and thick country cream—something less than $30 in all, and everyone in the county welcome to come and stuff himself with barbecue. So, to pay for it, after everyone had finished and was gossipin in the shade, a couple of the boys passed the hat. You dropped in what you liked, according to how much money you made this year or what you figured you had eaten—anything from a nickel to a silver dollar. It has been a good year for most cowmen, and when the big Stetson hat had gone halfway through that crowd it was so heavy the boys figured it must have at least $30 so they knocked off and didn't bother the rest of the folks.

"That's the way they do business out here in the cow country, where the descendants of Anxiety IV—$15,000,000 worth of them this year— are far away red dots in the big blue stem and buffalo-grass pastures of Kansas. Cowmen think it's a satisfactory way to do business when dealing with honest folks that you know—it's much quicker than double entry bookkeeping and you don't get your fingers all messed up with ink.

"The eastern visitor on vacation, driving west across the low mountains, heading down into the Mississippi valley and then beginning the slow climb toward the Rocky Mountains, is frequently mystified by the Barbecue Belt. He leaves the hot dog behind him as he crosses the Alleghenies. He enters the hamburger country at the Ohio valley. But as he nears the cattle country of the Southwest the barbecue stands displace the hamburger joints, and continue unbroken to the Pacific coast.

"If he samples Barbecue on the highway, he has eaten it at its worst. True Barbecue is seldom to be had, and is worth driving many miles to eat. In the strict definition of the term, Barbecue is any four footed animal—be it mouse or mastodon—whose dressed carcass is roasted whole. Occasionally it is a hog, often it is a fat sheep, but usually and at its best it is a fat steer, and it must be eaten within an hour of when it was cooked. For if ever the sun rises upon Barbecue its flavor vanishes like Cinderella's silks and it becomes cold baked beef—staler in the chill dawn than illicit love.

"This is why it can never be commercialized, for no roadside stand could cook and sell a whole steer in a day. This is why true Barbecue, like true love, cannot be bought but must always be given, and so is found only as a part of lavish hospitality in the cow country.

"Consider, for instance, how the Floyd Ranch at Sedan, Kansas, recently entertained several hundred visiting cowmen on the beef tour of Chautauqua county.

"The cowboys first cut out from the Floyds' herds a pair of the fattest 2-year-old steers. These were slaughtered, and the quartered carcasses hung in the cooler for proper aging. The day before the celebration a huge pit was dug, and in the early morning of the feast seasoned hickory logs were piled high in it and set ablaze. By mid afternoon it had burned down to a thick bed of red-hot coals. The two carcasses now come out of the cooler, the quarters are cut into 30 pound chunks and buried deep in the coals, which first sear the outside of the meat, sealing in the flavor, and then cook it slowly and succulently, the smell of baking beef and hickory smoke coming up through the coals and perfuming the country to attract discriminating eaters for miles around.

Thick pine planks set up on saw horses become serving tables. The big juicy chunks one by one are raked from the coals and carved on the tables with bits of charred hickory still clinging to their outsides, and the thick slices are slipped into buns. But first the meat is drenched in barbecue sauce, for which each ranch has its own recipe and about which there is much controversy. This sauce is as much part of the Latin heritage of the Southwest as are the crumbling Spanish Missions. Along the Rio Grande it is a dark crimson blend of tomatoes and chili peppers with the latter so hot and strong that a drop of it, spilled on the plank table, will leave a charred spot after it is wiped away. But as you come north the chili peppers weaken and finally disappear, until near the Canadian border they offer you nothing stronger than a watery scarlet store catsup.

"While Barbecue has covered half a continent, Son of a Bitch, its companion dish, has not, and I therefore offer its recipe for the benefit of the dainty city bride, who is constantly straining the resources of her apartment kitchen to tempt her husband with new plats du jour after a weary day in the office.

"First milady will take the entrails of two medium sized steers, but she will extract from them only the heart, liver, kidneys and intestines, which she will carefully clean. This done, she will cut them into chunks the size of her fist and toss them into a medium sized copper wash-boiler on her enameled stove. To this she will add a soupçon of potatoes (say a peck of peeled ones), about the same amount of unpeeled tomatoes and a quart can of hot green Mexican chili peppers. This is allowed to simmer for about three hours, without ever coming to a boil. After it has been thickened with a 5-pound sack of corn meal and salted to taste, then her Son of a Bitch is done and there will be enough for all, particularly if a dozen of her husband's old college chums, a company of U.S. Marines and a few taxi-drivers happen to drop in unexpectedly for dinner.

"While the recipe is substantially the same all along the north bank of the Rio Grande, the name occasionally varies, and in New Mexico the dish is called Prosecuting Attorney.

"The Old West has a fine tradition of freedom and a noble cuisine to back it up. So far this has stalwartly resisted the corrupting inroads of the dainty recipes of the ladies' magazines. As long as this cookery is maintained intact I have no fears for its political future. And yet there should be a note of warning: no race will spring to man the barricades with its stomach stuffed with Waldorf Salad nestled in a leaf of lettuce plus a dab of store-bought mayonnaise on top."

—W. L. White, in the *Emporia Gazette*, August 15, 16, 1939

Comments to Parker T. Van de Mark, November 4, 1941

Col. Edward N. Wentworth, Director
Armour's Livestock Bureau
Union Stock Yards, Chicago

Re: America Eats (Comments on Mr. Newsom's letter to Mr. Draper)

Colonel Wentworth reviewed the suggestions made in his letter to Mr. Van de Mark of October 31 (copy attached) and contributed some interesting sidelights on the matter of regional preferences in meat, principally in reply to questions raised by Mr. Newsom in his letter of October 16 to Mr. Norman Draper, Director, American Meat Institute, Chicago.

Steaks: *The South and West prefer the T-bone cut, while the East and North eat the sirloin, because the South and West, being farther from the supply of finished beef (Midwest corn-fattened), and therefore more dependent upon local animals (unfinished), require choicer cuts (the T-bone, containing more tenderloin, is in that respect superior to the sirloin).*

"New York cut" sirloins are presumably from prime beef.

Good steaks in the Cattle Country cost more than elsewhere because the Cattle Country is farther from the packers of finished beef than are other parts of the country; transportation costs increase the price.

A "Kansas City" steak is prized in the Southwest because it represents a steak from a finished animal. Kansas City was, and practically speaking still is, the nearest point to the Southwest dressing corn-finished beef. Also, Kansas City, on the main rail lines to the Southwest, was the source of supplies for Fred Harvey when he was developing his famed restaurants. Until recently, a Kansas City steak was the only good steak available in the Southwest. The name has stuck as a symbol of quality.

Regional Preferences: *Livers, hearts, brains, and sweetbreads are sold almost exclusively in the larger cities. The public taste elsewhere simply has not come to accept them, although the total sale is steadily increasing. Sweetbreads are sold principally to hotels. Colonel Wentworth suggests that it is possible to show that the consumption center for these items, formerly in New York, is moving steadily westward.*

Lamb and mutton, historically, are California meats, due to Spanish influence and to the fact that no good beef was available until recent years. Even today, California probably eats as much lamb and mutton as beef. Otherwise, New York is a principal center.

The Southeast probably consumes more chicken and pork than beef, lamb, and mutton because it is more readily available. Statistics, from the packers or from the American Meat Institute, would show interesting trends in meat consumption, Colonel Wentworth believes.

Colonel Wentworth had nothing to add to the suggestions in his letter, beyond the remark—decidedly off the record—that dietetics and cooking schools were responsible for the pitiful inability of the average housewife to prepare meat. No man would dream of doing more to a decent piece of meat than season it with a pinch of salt, but no modern woman can bring herself to serve a roast or steak until its natural flavor is completely destroyed by innumerable spices, herbs, and sauces. Also, few people, men or women, appreciate the fact that, given equal quality, the tenderest cuts are the least tasty; those that are most difficult to prepare satisfactorily are of the finest flavor.

Nebraska Eats Pheasants

H. J. MOSS

The pheasant is a bird so beautiful and delectable that it would seem that most anyone would want it, and that appears to be the case. It is a native of the Caucasus, what is now Georgia, but it spread throughout Asia. It was then transplanted to much of Europe. The Romans thought the plumage so beautiful that they stuck the feathers back in place before serving. The Roman gourmet Apicius offered a recipe for pheasant brains. This is all a bit too high-toned for 1940 Nebraska, and in fact some of the memos from Washington objected to America Eats *including pheasants at all.*

Exactly when and how it got to North America is not certain. In 1881 the American consul to Shanghai brought pheasants back with him to Oregon, and it is often claimed that this was when the birds were introduced to the United States, but they seem likely to have been brought here much earlier. They appear in mid-nineteenth-century recipe books. Seventeenth-century American colonists referred to eating pheasants but were actually talking about a bird correctly called the ruffed grouse. In 1785 Thomas Jefferson, in a letter to James Madison, wrote of stocking his estate with pheasants from France, along with grapes from all the great regions. It is not clear if he ever did, but four years later, in 1789, George Washington appears to have stocked Mount Vernon with the exotic birds.

Pheasant has long been at the center of a controversy over how long to age game. In the early nineteenth century Grimod

de La Reynière, a Frenchman who was the first food journal-
ist, wrote that a pheasant should be hung by its tail until the
bird was so rotten that it fell to the ground. That wouldn't fly
in Nebraska.

A quarter of a century ago, Nebraska was still prairie chicken minded, though in a rapidly diminishing way. Then came the Chinese pheasant, which made its appearance in the state in considerable numbers.

There is a certain allure attached to this now famous delicacy, which takes men, and even women, afield in great numbers and forms the theme of general conversation during the season, which is at its high point in October.

The pheasant, almost on a plane with peacocks and pea hens in beauty, is peculiarly relished as a food. It is all white meat and ordinarily very tender. Hunters, flushed with success, return by the hundreds bearing half a dozen or more of these birds. Acquired not, however, without considerable expense and effort.

The birds are usually still in the rough and require a careful picking, drawing and trimming. The feeds which follow are mostly family affairs but are also the theme of bigger get-to-gethers. The birds are often drawn before the hunters return and stuffed with hay, which seems to preserve their flavor but rarely are they picked. The new method is to dress them and pack with a small piece of dry ice. That is distinctly modern.

People work themselves into a general state of excitement at the mention of pheasants. When the triumphant hunter (if he is lucky) returns, the neighbors are called in and the spoils viewed with "ohs" and "ahs." Their value is strangely enhanced.

The feast is highly dramatized and everything takes on a glamorous atmosphere. Everyone exclaims at the delicious quality of the main entree. Whole organizations often call their members together for the big feed. Actually they eat mostly of mashed potatoes and trimmings, but yet pheasant is the main theme. Liquid refreshments in quantity often are another big feature but it is all in the name of pheasant. They may be chicken fried or baked or stewed but they remain in a class all their own. Outside of ducks and rabbits, pheasants are Nebraska's big wild game food event.

Nebraska Cooks Its Rabbits

H. J. MOSS

Other food game in Nebraska has come and gone. Many varieties have entirely disappeared from the plains and fields, but rabbits still abound in goodly numbers—some say that they are on the increase—and are delicious eating.

If anything, the evolution of rabbit cookery has led to a high degree of perfection, as opposed to earlier methods of preparation, which seemed to be perpetually in an experimental stage. Improved facilities for cooking have much to do with this, no doubt.

The pioneers and settlers of the nineteenth century used plenty of rabbits, but apparently many exercised little imagination in the handling and cooking. Some roasted the carcass over open fires, others used the kettle for plain stewing, and the frying pan was overworked. The latter process was the most popular, apparently, as fried rabbits came to be associated with fried chicken more and more.

While many were entirely satisfied with this method, others began to introduce some original ideas of their own. The trouble with just plain frying was that the meat, though well done on the outside, was underdone within and tended to be slimy.

Among other recipes, one in particular was much talked about in the

early 1900s. It was none other than soaking the dressed rabbit in vinegar and then flouring and frying. Baked rabbit was also given this treatment. The result was not bad, but sometimes a little sour, somewhat like
the rabbits that had fed too much on willow and other bark.

In the first decade of the twentieth century farm women paid a little
more attention to the matter of making rabbit meat more palatable. The
result was a more thorough investigation, by trial, of various methods in
bringing bunnies to the table in their most presentable and appetizing
form. It most certainly wasn't haphazard frying, but a combination of
stewing and frying or baking, preceded by a more elaborate preliminary
preparation.

This involved a thorough dressing process followed by a salt water
treatment and freezing. The actual cooking, itself, was not so complicated. The frozen rabbit carcass was articulated and thawed, then simmered in a mild solution of soda water, which was poured off. After
which fresh water was added with fat and the cuts of meat allowed to
stew for one hour to two hours, depending upon the age and size of rabbit. Thus the rabbit was stewed down in its own juices until only the
fatty liquid remained. This led to a complete browning in the pan by

either frying or baking. In
case of frying or baking the
lid of the cooking utensil was
eventually removed. The
result was a revelation—
tender, crisp-browned, separated chunks of meat. One
could by picking up, say, a leg
and giving it a jerk cause the

meat to drop away from the bone and be temptingly available to the
fork—or even fingers.

With the advent of steam pressure cookers, the cooking of rabbit is
even more simplified and the results more delightful. There is nothing
more delectable and satisfying than Nebraska corn-fed rabbit of the present day, captured in the prime during the months of November, December
and January, and prepared for the table as per the above process.

Minnesota Booya Picnic

The roof of the place where the booya is held is the blue Minnesota sky. Of course, the dish is obtainable in certain restaurants at certain times. It is a frequently advertised treat at taverns. But real booya lovers wait for summer and the special pleasure of a picnic booya.

These outdoor feasts begin in late June, and are particularly popular in communities where the population is largely German. Sometimes the American Legion acts as sponsor, sometimes the town fire department. But always it is a strictly male affair. Each community—whether it be village or city neighborhood—has its favorite booya cook, who takes great pride in his skill and is much in demand. To have a woman so much as peel a potato would be unthinkable. However, the women folks are not excluded from a share in the cook's savory creation after the cooking is finished. They and the children join the men at the site chosen for the outdoor festival, usually a grassy lakeside spot with plenty of shade trees.

The menu is simple: booya and crackers, with beer for the men and pop for the women and children. Some of the women drink beer, too, especially the older German women.

At the first hint of dawn, the preparations are under way. Oxtails, a meaty soup bone, veal and chicken are simmering in a huge vat, almost as high as the cook is tall, and as big around as three men. Several helpers are busy paring bushels of fresh vegetables, opening cans, putting allspice in a cheesecloth bag. The beans have been soaking since the previous afternoon. As soon as the meat is tender, it is removed from the bones, cut in small pieces and returned to the broth. The vegetables, cut very small, are added.

When the booya is ready to be eaten, the separate ingredients have lost their identity. It is neither soup nor stew, but something of both.

Around seven o'clock, a beer truck arrives, and a couple of husky drivers set up kegs, leaving a few in reserve. Bartenders tie on big white aprons and line up rows of steins. They pile bottles of pop in pails of cracked ice. Delectable odors are rising already.

About the time the beer is well chilled, the first customers start arriving. They stay a respectful distance from the chef who is seasoning, tasting, and seasoning some more, with critical intentness. The booya won't be ready to serve until about eleven.

Nobody minds waiting. They like having their appetites edged by good outdoor smells and cold amber beer. Little girls sit around primly, conscious of their ruffles, while their brothers wade in the lake or skip stones on the beach. The women cluster in chattering groups. Children quarrel over the comic sections of the Sunday papers.

The teasing odors grow stronger. Not until about a half hour before the first helping is dished out will the servers set out bowls, spoons, and plates of crackers.

As soon as the shout "Come and get it!" goes up, an eager crowd swarms around the table in front of the steaming kettle. There is much good-natured jostling. Some buy their tickets in advance, others pay a dime a bowl as they are served. The first bowl is considered merely an appetizer. Occasional cars pull up all afternoon. Their occupants carry away two-quart jars and pails of booya.

Many people remain all day. They eat, rest and visit a while, drink beer, then eat again. By evening the last dipper of booya is gone. Tired bartenders polish glasses, wash off tables, and count the profits. The cook and his helpers untie their stained and wrinkled aprons. In a short while the dishes have been packed away, the refuse collected and burned and everything set in order. The grove is left deserted in the darkness.

BOOYA

(Bouilli recipe for 60 gallons)

    30 lbs. oxtails, or 20 lbs. oxtails and 15 lbs. veal

    10 lb. beef soup bone

    4 fat hens

    ½ bu. tomatoes, or 2 gal. puree

1 peck onions

1 peck carrots

1 peck potatoes

1 peck kohlrabi

1 peck rutabagas

6 heads cabbage

12 stalks celery

6 cans corn

6 cans peas

2 quarts navy beans, soaked 12 hours

2 quarts string beans

1 peck barley

10 cans allspice (put in bag)

1½ oz. paprika

3 lbs. salt, or more if needed

Black pepper to taste

Boil meat and remove from bones; cut in small pieces; add vegetables cut in small pieces, and seasoning; have sufficient water to cover; add more if necessary. Cook until done.

Indiana Persimmon Pudding

Southern Indiana is a little far north to be persimmon country but their persimmons, Diospyros virginiana, *are indigenous. In 1863 an Indiana farmer named Logan Martin, destined to be nicknamed Persimmon Martin, took a gallon of local persimmons to market in nearby Louisville, Kentucky, and sold them for such a handsome profit that he decided to be a persimmon producer. In his southern Indiana town of Borden he produced more than two thousand gallons of persimmons every year for the next forty years.*

Borden, originally New Providence, was named after the city in Rhode Island, but always called Borden after the founder of the local college. The town—whose name was officially changed to Borden only in 1994—according to the last census has 818 inhabitants. A somewhat larger town with a few thousand residents in the next county, Mitchell, also a persimmon-producing town, has hosted an annual persimmon festival since 1947. The festival features a persimmon pudding contest. But this recipe, in which the author forgot to measure the milk, was collected earlier for America Eats.

1 cup of sugar
¼ cup of shortening
2 eggs
2 cups of flour
4 teaspoons of baking powder
½ teaspoon of salt

½ teaspoon of vanilla

½ teaspoon of cloves

2 teaspoons of cinnamon

1 teaspoon of nutmeg

2 teaspoons of butter

2 cups of seeded persimmons

Cream shortening, add sugar and beaten eggs, milk, flour, baking powder, salt; add persimmons after rubbing through a fine sieve, beat thoroughly and then add vanilla, cloves, cinnamon and nutmeg. Beat well, then pour in greased pudding mould, cover tightly and steam for two hours in an oven  300 degrees F., and serve with foamy sauce or whipped cream.

From Richard McCurry, 903 E. Hillside Drive, Bloomington, Indiana.

A Short History of the American Diet

NELSON ALGREN

Nelson Algren, from the Chicago office of the Illinois Writers' Project, was held up by the FWP as one of their best success stories. But it was not mutual. He seldom mentioned anything he had written for them and when he did it was usually disparagingly as just something he "did for the money." It was not much money. He was originally hired at a salary

*of $84 a month. Yet he was one of the few writers who stayed
in the project through to the last years. He periodically quit
or was fired but came back in search of the meager paycheck.
He liked to say that he learned "goldbricking" in the FWP
and liked to imply that he sneaked off to a bar whenever possible, but evidence points to the likelihood that his periodic
absences were because he was pursuing his own writing. And
toward the end of his life he said of the FWP, "Had it not been
for it, the suicide rate would have been much higher. It gave
new life to people who thought their life was over."*

*Born Nelson Algren Abraham in Detroit in 1909, he moved
to Chicago with his family at the age of three and settled in
the blue-collar immigrant South Side. His father, an auto
mechanic, was the son of a Swedish convert to Judaism and
his mother was a German Jew who ran a candy store. After
five years they moved up to the North Side.*

*Nelson graduated with a journalism degree from the Uni-
versity of Illinois in 1931 in a full-blown Depression that
offered few jobs to a young graduate. In search of a job, he
wandered to Texas, where in 1933 he wrote his first story,
"So Help Me." He was also caught stealing a typewriter and
served at least a month—he said four or five—in jail. The
fateful month is sometimes credited with his lifelong fascination with the marginal and down and out. But perhaps that
is just who he was, or else why did he steal the typewriter? In
any event, pimps, prostitutes, drug addicts, and petty crimi-
nals were the inhabitants of Algren's books.*

In 1935 his first novel, Somebody in Boots, *was the basis of
his standing as one of the seasoned professionals of the stellar
Chicago office of the Illinois Writers' Project. He was looked
up to by young upstarts such as Saul Bellow. But he did live
up to his promise, writing* Never Come Morning *while on the
project and publishing it in 1942, the year the project shut
down. In 1950 his novel* The Man with the Golden Arm *won
the first National Book Award. Simone de Beauvoir, with*

whom he had a much-publicized affair, once described him as "that classic American species: self-made leftist writer."

Algren, in addition to supervising, wrote for a number of FWP projects, some published, such as the Galena Guide, considered one of the best small-town guides in the series, and some never published, such as a series of folkloric industrial legends called A Tall Chance of Work. *In one of them a character modeled after Henry Ford rises after his death and turns to his six pallbearers and says, "You call this efficiency!"*

The following piece was to be the regional essay for the Middle West in America Eats. *A summing-up of the many submitted manuscripts, it is one of the few samples of how a finished* America Eats *might have been written. It was not without its failings, most notably attributing Dobos Torte, the pride of Budapest cooking, to Romania. But Algren was only the writer, not the researcher, working from the papers gathered from projects in the twelve-state region. Since the piece, like many in the* America Eats *collection, especially from the Midwest, is not signed, some have suggested that he was not even the writer, but, interviewed in 2006 for this book, Studs Terkel, who worked with Algren in the Chicago office, said he remembered him working on a food piece. The ninety-eight-page typed manuscript, collected and marked in pencil on a folder labeled "Nelson Algren" in the Library of Congress* America Eats *file, is also in the University of Iowa files and the Illinois FWP files as Nelson Algren's. Iowa got it from a personal friend of Algren's, Louis Szathmáry, who said he bought it in an auction of Algren's papers, and Algren himself identified it but characteristically dismissed it as something he just wrote for money when he was broke. The library at the University of Iowa identified the handwritten corrections in red pencil and blue ink as Algren's and said that it was typed on the same typewriter as the other manuscripts from the Illinois Writers' Project that are known to be Algren's.*

The copy in the Library of Congress contains a handwritten note from the Washington office expressing displeasure with the essay and comparing it unfavorably to the Montana Writers' Project's summary essay for the Far West.

The following is an excerpt.

The Buffalo Border

The Flowering Savannahs

If each, of all of the races of man which have subsisted in the vast Middlewest, could contribute one dish to one great Mid-western cauldron, it is certain that we'd have therein a most foreign, and most gigantic, stew:

> The grains that the French took over from the Indian, and the breads which the English brought later; hotly spiced Italian dishes and subtly seasoned Spanish ones; the sweet Swedish soups and the sour Polish ones; and all the old-world arts brought to the preparing of American beefsteak and hot mince pie.

Such a cauldron would contain more than many foods: it would be, at once, a symbol of many lands and a melting pot for many peoples.

Many peoples, yet one people; many lands, one land.

In the old French time the great inland plains were carpeted by a spiraling wild grass called bluestem. Between the bluestem grew the prairie wild flowers. It was a land of wild prairie flowers. In the fall the inland Indians set fire to the bluestem to provide pasturage for the buffalo in spring; the ranging shagskin herds that returned, with each returning spring, to the unstaked savannahs. To the spiraling bluestem of the flowering savannahs. By the time that the French came such fires had stripped three-fourths of the plains of trees.

In October, by the rivers of the wilderness and among the rushes of the swamps, the French adventurers watched Illiniwek braves harvesting knotted stalks of wild oats. The Indians passed, in canoes, among the overhanging stalks, to shake the wild grain down into the boats as they passed. The French saw that the Indians, as though taking on the autumn color of the bluestem country, wore blue-beaded moccasins and bright-blue head-feathers; and had the trick of turning autumn ears of yellow-brown corn into blue ears. With the wild oats they played no such tricks. They brought it back in the canoes, as brown as it grew, to their copper-brown women.

Cleaned of the chaff, the women dried the oats on a wooden lattice by sustaining a fire beneath it for several days. Then they put the oats in skin bags, forced it into holes in the ground, treaded out the grain, winnowed it, reduced it to meal, boiled it in water and seasoned it in bear grease. In the same fashion other Frenchmen watched the lean Menominees, in the Wisconsin country, harvesting wild rice.

On the shores of Lake Superior Frenchmen found Chippewas living largely on fish, fresh in summer, dried or smoked in winter; and Chippewa squaws feeding their babies fish soup. Fish heads seasoned with maple sugar were a Chippewa delicacy. And beaver-tails, because of their smooth fatness, were an especial treat.

Venison the Chippewas boiled with wild rice or sliced it, roasted it and pounded it out on a flat stone. Jerked and tenderized venison steaks they stored and packed in *makuks*, or birchbark boxes, the covers of which were sewn down with split spruce root. The fall-killed deer they dried in fire or wind, packed it in hide and jerked the meat against the bitter lake winters.

Sometimes they cut venison into yet smaller slices, spread it out on birchbark and stamped it into edibility. The braves were proud to do the stamping, for such work required strength and so was a brave's rightful task. Therefore the Chippewas called such meat, literally, "foot-trodden meat."

The squaws performed lesser labors. When meat was needed for a trek, they lined a hole in the ground with hide, skin side out, as for the wild oats, filled it with dried meat, and, with a stone for a pestle, pounded it until it was pulverized. When buffalo meat was used the result was

called "pemmican." Mixing it with fat or marrow, and sometimes pounding cherries into the meat, they sealed it by pouring melted fat over the
hide sacks. There it could keep for as long as three years. Such packs
commonly weighed between 100 and 300 pounds.

The French *engagés* brought steel knives to the Chippewa nation to use
instead of knives or ribs or bones of animals; clam shells were Chippewa
spoons. Pointed sticks were employed to take meat out of a kettle when
it was too hot to take with the fingers. Cups and all sorts of dishes were
fashioned by this people from birchbark. In freshly cut birchbark vessels
water could be heated before the bark was dry enough to catch fire.

The Chippewa customarily ate only once a day, usually about the
middle of the morning. But if food was abundant he ate as frequently
as his stomach would permit. He might go, in flush times, to as many
as seven feasts in a single day; and at each be expected to eat all that
was placed before him. When food was scarce, however, these, like other
tribes, suffered severely; for they possessed no methods for storing food
beyond the processing of pemmican.

Yet the explorer Coronado reported cultivated gardens and domesti-
cated turkeys among the Zunis. All the way east, across the sunburnt
mesas, he found Indian gardens. He came up the borders of old Nebraska
and on into dusty land: and found the Kansas Indians, in the sandy Kansas bottoms, gardening Indian corn. And growing a strange dark gourd
they called "askutasquash," the same that the French named "Pompon."

The gourd that we, today, call, simply, "squash."

And somewhere between Nebraska and Kansas Coronado reported
tribes to be existing on "maize whereof they have great store, and also
small white peas and venison, which by all likelihood they feed upon
(though they say not) for we found many skins of deer, of hares and
conies. They eat the best cakes that I ever saw and everybody generally
eats of them. They have the finest order and way to grind that we ever
saw in any place. And one Indian woman of the country will grind as
much as four women of Mexico."

It was from the Indian nations, of course, that the white man took
corn. They had expended hundreds of years in developing it out of a
seed-bearing grass. Centuries before Columbus, the Indian was culti-

vating this grass in both North and South America. Among some tribes Coronado reported not only blue, but also red, yellow, black and white ears colored for use in ceremonials. The secret of developing such colored ears has, to this date, eluded the white man.

Coronado also found the Kansas Indians to possess "most excellent salt kernal." But of the Sioux it is said that, as late as 1912, the older members of the tribe had never tasted salt. Yet, though the Sioux used neither salt nor pepper, they seasoned meat with wild ginger, and they brewed a sweet wilderness tea from wintergreen and raspberry leaves or little twigs of spruce. And in the long hot summers they refreshed themselves with cold water into which a little maple sugar had been dissolved.

Sioux living near the upper waters of the Minnesota River raised small patches of corn and beans, but their principal vegetable was *tipsinna* or "Dakota turnip," eaten raw or roasted or boiled with buffalo meat. Among the river rushes, or in the shallow inland creeks, they too harvested the wild rice. And, as with other Indian nations, roast dog was a delicacy reserved for feastdays. They cooked it indifferently, without removing claws or hair.

"They feed themselves with such meats as the soil affords," an early journal reports: ". . . their meat is very well sodden and they make broth very sweet and savory . . ."

Among this nation the French found beans, pumpkins, acorns and sunflowers, fresh and dried wild roots and bear fat and bulbs and oil of the wild sunflower's seeds. Bread was baked by fire or sun and flattened on warm stones. In season, berries were plentiful; papayas and persimmons and, with the first frost, hickory nuts and walnuts. But mostly the Sioux lived by the fish of the streams, the wild geese and the wild pigeon and all the game of the prairie groves.

Cornbread, still popular in both urban and rural sections of the Middlewest, does not derive from either the "journey-cakes" nor from the richer breads of Virginia, in the days of the Old Dominion. Midwestern cornbread is a direct descendant of the Indian ash-cake, mixed from cornmeal and water, fashioned into thick cakes and baked in the cinders and ashes of prairie camp fires.

In the years of the Buckskin Border this method of baking cornbread remained unmodified by the frontiersman. One legend has it that, on an occasion when an unusually long train of Conestoga wagons was crossing the plains of Kansas, it was found necessary to separate into two trains. With but one frying pan, and a single pot in the whole caravan, the division was accomplished by counting off those who preferred ash-cake to boiled dumplings. Those who preferred ash-cakes took the skillet; the ones who went for dumplings followed the pot.

Today cornbread and chicken, with dumplings, remains a favorite in Kansas. But an anonymous balladeer long ago warned all Nebraskans against the Kansas ash-cake:

> *Come, all young girls, pay attention to my noise*
> *Don't fall in love with the Kansas boys*
> *For if you do your portion it will be*
> *Ash-cake and antelope is all you'll see.*

And further deprecated Kansas:

> *When they get hungry and go to make bread*
> *They kindle a fire as high as your head*
> *Rake around the ashes and in they throw*
> *The name they give it is "doughboy's dough"*
> *When they go courting they take along a chair*
> *The first thing they say is, "Has your daddy killed a bear."*
> *The second thing they say when they sit down*
> *Is "Madam, your ash-cake is baking brown."*

In making bread, a thin sponge was made the night before, with yeast dissolved in lukewarm water, buckwheat flour, and enough additional water to make a thin paste. The batter bowl or crock was then covered with a lid and placed near the stove to rise overnight. If the night was quite cold, a piece of old blanket would be thrown over the crock just before going to bed, to keep the heat in. In the morning the batter, all bubbly from fermentation, would be stirred thoroughly with more buckwheat flour and water and seasoned. Sometimes milk was used as part of the liquid.

Baked on a cast-iron griddle, the cakes were small and not over an eighth of an inch thick, brown on top and crisp around the edges.

The residue of batter in the bowl was saved as a starter for the next morning's batch. After standing all day in the sun it was again well fermented and ready to be mixed into another thin sponge.

"When I was single,"

a married minstrel mourned,

"I eat biscuit an' pie.
Now I am married,
It's eat cornbread or die."

Such bread, like pemmican, would keep for a long time, and was easily transported by men who lived on their feet.

Broiling was accomplished by putting meat on the end of a pointed stick and holding it over a fire. When the hunter cut a smooth stick and thrust it through the body of the bird or animal he had killed, he could rest the two ends of the stick on stones and roast his meat over the coals.

The primitive Indian stick was replaced by a "spit" or iron rod to let the heat of the iron cook the inside of the roast. Finally, the cook learned to "baste" the meat with oil, water, or gravy collected in a dripping-pan set under the spit.

The barbecue was adapted by the white buffalo hunters from the Indian method of barbecuing. Even pemmican was sometimes barbecued by adding, to the jerked meat, ground corn and bacon, cooking the mess together in steaming bear fat.

The modifications effected by the Indian and frontiersmen upon each other's diet were reciprocal. The Indian taught the white man to exist in the wilderness, on the unstaked plains and across the endless desert passes; and, in turn, the frontiersmen instructed the Indian in the fastest known methods of getting blind drunk on barrel-whiskey.

For as little as one rabbit pelt a throw.

The frontiersmen did, however, stabilize the Indian diet by improving on and inventing methods of storage. He built timber silos for the stored grain, established himself in one place whereat he could alternate crops against the hard Midwestern winters. Though in all means of developing grain and providing against the future he was more thoughtful than the Indian, in the killing of wild game he was prodigal. Before the homesteaders had come, the great clouds of wild pigeons were gone, the buffalo were going, and the wilderness streams were fished dry. In killing he surpassed any savage. For he took to it imaginatively, as he might go dancing, for the anticipated pleasure and the relating of it after the slaughter was done; till the plains were littered with buffalo carcasses, touched only by the fingers of the wind.

He desolated the Indian lands, then went on to destroy the food of his own sons, making square-dance songs all the while:

> *Oh, the hawk shot the buzzard and the buzzard shot the crow*
> *And we'll rally 'round the canebrake to shoot the buffalo.*

It was not until the advent of the homesteaders, with all the caution that domestication brings, that some pause was put to the destruction. By that time the Indian was eating government rations from tins. And by the time of the War Between the States, the white had modified the Indian's natural diet in more ways than one. In fact, he had just about put a stop to it altogether.

Before the land was laced by the railroads, and the long fields bound by Sears-Roebuck fencing, the prairies yielded abundant game. Deer and wild turkey wandered the land. Bee trees gave such tubs of honey that every prairie grove sheltered sugar camps. Corn was cultivated for use in "johnny-cake," corn mush, "big hominy," ash-cake, corn whisky, corn pone; or the small loaves called "corn dodgers."

A corn-dodger carnival, in coonskin tatters, came through the Cumberland into Illinois. Hungry movers from the settled seaboard, flintlock vagrants looking for a home.

"I got a clock in my stomach, an' a watch in my head,"

one of them sang,

"But I'm getting superstitious 'bout my hog an' bread."

To many, the Illinois country looked like home. They built log cabins and exchanged their coonskins for wide farmer's straws and overalls. The flintlocks hung rusting on the cabin walls. The land was cleared and fields were sown. Rain came, sun came, the land was bounded.

Beside each cabin, in the squaw winters, they dug a pit, eight or ten feet long and about six feet deep, in which to store vegetables against the snow. Potatoes, cabbage, and turnips were covered with straw, and the entire pit covered with about three feet of earth, leaving a small opening near the center for the heat of the vegetables to escape. Sometimes, during extreme cold, one would have to start a fire to thaw out the frost so as to get at the food; this very seldom occurred as the heat of the vegetables kept the earth from freezing.

Cabin chairs were three or four-legged stools; tables had four legs but were made from puncheon; and the "silverware" consisted of jack knives or a butcher knife. Boarding house guests were frequently requested to bring their own cutlery. Plates and dishes were of tin or pewter, and often wooden bowls, known as noggins, served when metal containers were not available. Or sometimes even thin wooden shingles served for plates. Drinking cups made from gourds were common.

Corn-dodger days are occasionally recalled in Illinois by corn-dodger dinners; but in the early pioneer times they were the mainstay of the average man's diet. Six days a week the coonskin folk ate them. These were baked in a skillet to such a consistency that a wit of the era once observed that "you could knock down a Texas steer with a chunk of the stuff or split an end-board at forty-yards off-hand."

My clothes is all ragged, as my language is rough,

one tune complained,

My bread is corn-dodgers both solid and tough
But yet I am happy, and live at my ease
On sorghum molasses, bacon, and cheese.

Only on Sunday, if all the children had been good, was there any variation in this corn-dodger diet. The Lord's Day brought biscuit and preserves
to the righteous. And a casual visit by a circuit-riding preacher always
called for the best a homesteader could lay on the table. Perhaps it was
some such visit that inspired an anonymous hired-man, when requested
to say grace, to ad lib his own lines—with one eye on the table:

Oh Lord of Love who art above
Thy blessings have descended:
Biscuits and tea for supper I see,
When mush and milk was intended.

For mush and milk, like corn and salt-pork, were Illinois staples all year
around.

In winter selected kernels of corn were treated with lye, which
removed the hull, after which the grains were boiled or fried. This was
"big hominy" and was a wholesome, satisfying article of diet. Farmers
would save all their wood ashes until they had a sufficient quantity; then
would cover these with water till the combination formed the lye. The
lye water would then be filled with shelled white corn and left till the
grains swelled and popped open. The corn kernels were then scrubbed
over a washboard with the bare hands, to remove the hulls. Sometimes
a preliminary cooking was necessary to finish the removal of the hulls.
Then several more tubs of water were used to wash the corn to get the
heavy lye out. Much trouble was endured by the housewife to get this job
finished. Nowadays canned lye is used, but old timers say the hominy is
not so good.

"Hoe-cakes," originated by Virginians, were made by spreading a thin mixture of cornmeal over a hot iron plate, or on a board placed in front of the fire.

Wake up, Jacob, day's a-breakin'
Fryin' pan's on an' hoe-cake bakin'
Bacon in the pan, coffee in the pot
Git up now an' git it while it's hot.

The first inquiry a landlord of those years made of a guest at mealtime was, simply, "Well, stranger, what'll ye take, wheat-bread 'n chickenfixens, or corn-bread 'n common-doin's?" "Common-doin's" was corn-bread; just as corn-pone was, commonly, "knick-knacks." Of which it is told that, a settler, falling ill, called his best friend to his bedside and asked, "I want you to do one thing for me—take some corn to mill and get it ground, and make me some knick-knacks or I'll surely die."

A beverage popular with early Illinois settlers was a drink known as "stew," consisting of a mixture of water, sugar, whiskey, allspice and butter, served steaming hot. When pioneer schoolmasters followed the custom of celebrating the final day of the school term with parents and pupils, the oldest girl of the class was given the task of preparing the stew. Occasionally instructors partook too freely and became "stewed"—a phrase handed down to the present day.

Genuine tea was both difficult to obtain and very expensive; many substitute brews were used by the pioneers. Among the more popular substitutes were those made from sycamore chips and red-root leaves. In Mercer County the red-root leaves were first dried under a Dutch oven, and then pulverized by rolling between the hands. When brewed and sweetened with honey, this drink was called "grub hyson." Wheat parched and ground served for coffee. And early settlers agreed that the "hardest difficulty of all" was to teach Yankees to drink sour milk and to use honey for butter.

The homely wisdom of Illinois pioneers prescribed that children be passed through a hole in the trunk of a hollow tree to cure "short growth"; hogs must be slaughtered at certain times of the moon or the bacon would shrink; babies must be weaned at certain times of the zodiac; the "madstone," a small bone from the heart of a deer, was a valued antidote for hydrophobia or snake-bite; certain persons "blew the fire out of a burn," arrested hemorrhage or cured erysipelas by uttering mysterious charms; a pan of water under the bed was used to check night sweats; bleeding was the sovereign remedy for fits, loss of consciousness, fever, and many other ills; and in eruptive fevers, especially measles, where the eruption was delayed, a tea made of sheep's dung, popularly known as "nany tea," was a household remedy.

Illinoisans got their drinking water from springs. Those who came later dug wells, some of which failed to afford the needed supply of water for drinking, cooking and other purposes. After one or two such disappointments the property owner would sometimes call in the local "waterwitch." The waterwitch held a divining rod in his hands, which would be drawn down by some mysterious force when held over a vein of water. For this purpose a forked piece of witch hazel was usually selected. With a prong of this tightly grasped in each hand, his arms extended at full length, the point of the fork pointing upward, the waterwitch would slowly and gravely walk over a spot where it was desired to sink a well.

In the event water was found where the waterwitch directed, the discovery was heralded as proof of his powers.

Very few early settlers had cisterns, and rain water was obtained by catching it in a barrel into which the water from the eaves of the house was conveyed by a long slanting board. In warm weather, if this rain-water was not used soon, it would come to be filled with "wiggle-tails."

Following "winter diet" came "spring sickness." Nearly everybody used to be sick because of lack of green stuff to eat. In the spring the papers carried daily advertisements of sarsaparilla "to cure boils, sluggishness, thick blood, and other ailments resulting from heavy winter food."

"The matter in the blood is thoroughly vitiated," one journal advised its readers, and improving it must be a matter of time. Spring diet should do the work of medicine, largely. First in importance are salads of all sorts."

Hanging from the cabin rafters would be festoons of dried apples, dried pumpkins, dried peaches, peppers, bunches of sage for seasoning sausage; bunches of pennyroyal to "sweat" the sick and bunches of bone-set to "break the ager."

There's bread and cheese upon the shelf
If you want any, just help yourself.

A product strictly of the central prairies relished by Cavalier and Yankee alike was the vinegar pie. Early Illinoisans felt keenly the absence of native fruit. Along toward spring their systems developed a craving for something tart. To satisfy the craving ingenious housewives invented the vinegar pie—vinegar, molasses, water, a little nutmeg and flour enough to bring the mixture to the consistency of a custard. When baked in a pie tin the resulting product was much relished and remained a favorite springtime dessert until young orchards, coming into bearing, provided real fruit pies to take its place.

Going to mill was nearly always done on horseback. A sack of wheat or shelled corn would be put on a horse with the grain divided so there would be an equal amount in each end, and on this a boy would be mounted and started for the water-mill, which was never more than four or five miles away. Arrived there the miller would take the sack in the mill and pour its contents into the hopper, from which it ran in between the two millstones, one of which, connected with a water wheel in the stream beneath, revolved while the other was stationary. Both were sharply grooved properly to crush and grind the grain that passed between them. For this purpose the miller took toll, that is, a certain percentage of the grain, or as is usually said in this sense, the grist.

Land of Mighty Breakfasts

Following the Civil War, a considerable migration into the lumber country of Michigan occurred.

Houses were rudely built in these areas and settlement was transitory. Hundreds of small communities would spring up, only to disappear when the land was cut over and the saw-mills removed to new timber land. Such conditions did not encourage variation in diet; food monotony reached a new high in lumber operating sections of the state during the last three decades of the nineteenth century.

Paul Bunyan felt there were two kinds of Michigan lumber camp cooks, the Baking Powder Buns and the Sour-dough Stiffs. One Sour-dough Sam belonged to the latter school. He made everything but coffee out of sour-dough. He had only one arm and one leg, the other members having been lost when his sour-dough barrel blew up.

The hyperbole serves to emphasize a truth. The sour-dough pancake has always been a favorite food among lumberjacks everywhere. To the camp cook a continuous supply of sour-dough is an indispensable part of camp equipment, and he is never without his batch of "starter." The "starter" is a portion of dough reserved from previous mixtures and stored in the kind of barrel that proved disastrous to Sour-dough Sam. Zealously guarded, the "starter" can be kept for weeks in ordinary temperatures.

The night before the pancakes are to be fried, the cook assembles his batter, using the starter as a leavening agent. Flour and water are added to the starter, and the mixture is left near the stove to rise. By morning it is a light and frothy mass smelling pungently of fermentation. After reserving from the batch a starter for the next morning's pancakes, the cook adds salt, sugar, eggs, a little fat, and a pinch of soda. He pours large spoonsful of the batter on a huge, fire-blackened griddle, abundantly greased with smoking pork rind and very hot. Then, after the griddlecake has fried a few moments, he flips it expertly and it's as good as done.

In the old camps it was customary for the cook to install, near the door of the shanty, a crock containing sour-dough batter in various stages of fermentation. Into the crock went all left-over batter, and scraps of bread, doughnuts, cake, or pancakes, which quickly attained the semi-liquid consistency of the batter.

Standing in a box sled among steaming kettles of beans, beef stew and tea, the bull cook drove over a road to a central point in the woods, to blow his dinner horn. The call carried five miles through the snowy forest. Then he howled like an Irish wolf: "Ye-ow! 's goin' to waste." The men swarmed toward the box sled from every direction. Though they ate around a big fire of slash, the beans froze on their plates and the tea froze in their whiskers.

At night they came into camp stamping with cold and grim with hunger. In the cookhouse the long tables were loaded with food; smoking platters of fresh mush, bowls of mashed potatoes, piles of pancakes and pitchers of corn syrup, kettles of rich brown beans, pans of prunes, dried peaches, rice puddings, rows of apple pies. The big camps fed the men bountifully and well.

Run here, men, it's bilin' hot,
Sam 'n Dave's both eatin' out the pot
Old Uncle Jake says, "I'll be damn,
If I can't get a foreleg I'll take a ham."

The jacks ate silently, with great speed. If a greenhorn was tempted to make conversation, he was reminded by a placard on the wall: "No talking at the table."

The cook was the king bee of the camp. He was well paid and well worth his pay, handling prodigious quantities of food, baking, roasting, frying, stewing, for a hundred men who ate like horses, feeding them lavishly on an allowance of thirty cents a day per man.

The preparation of beans verged on ritual. A deep hole was dug on one side of the fire and filled with glowing embers. When the beans had been soaked for twenty-four hours they were taken out and scalded. With deliberation the cook now chose the right kind of an onion and placed it on the bottom of the pot. Then the beans were poured in until the pot was filled within six inches of the top. Slices of fat pork were laid across this, a sufficiency of molasses was poured upon the whole, and the pot sealed. The embers were now taken from the hole in the floor and the pot inserted. All space around the sides was filled and packed with hot coals and the bean hole covered up. The fire was made over it and kept burning twenty-four hours, when the cooking was complete. This made a rich and golden breakfast dish.

Beans and salt pork—generally "sow-belly"—were the substantialities of the menu, and fried cakes made the dessert. Upon this unadorned diet the men thrived, for there was little sickness among them.

Taken at random from a long list of meals served at small Michigan boarding houses, hotels and even in private homes, one that appears quite typical consisted of bread, fried salt pork, onions, home-grown lettuce and tea. This was for supper but breakfast was much the same, with the possible exception of onions. Those who carried a lunch to work took bread, pork, onions, and lettuce, and cooked dried beans in a tin pail. Such pails were more often than not of a 5-quart capacity and were filled to the brim. The tin dinner pail was the pivot point around which the day revolved—that and the water pail. The latter reposed on a bench near the school-house door with a tin dipper either in it or hanging from a near-by nail. Just above was a shelf for the dinner pails. The opening of the dinner pails in the country school, upon the very instant of dismissal, was an occasion for conjecture. Barter and trade ran high at the dinner hour, and those children whose mothers held the highest reputation in the culinary art were likely to go home at night in a state of hungry bitterness.

Released odors, as the tin tops were pried out of the pails, often gave out advance information regarding contents. That of sour pickles predominated, injudiciously mixed with the aroma of chocolate cake or fried cakes. Fresh bread, redbrown spice cake richly embedded with raisins, were fair plunder for the cunning speculator. Often, too, there would be an addition to the well packed pail—perhaps a small glass of jelly, with one of Grandmother's old silver spoons to eat it with. Or a little jar of baked beans with another of piccalilli or chilli sauce. The bread was of more than generous thickness, maybe a hunk of some kind of cold meat, a hard boiled egg, a piece of pie, a doughnut, and—for most—the inevitable pickle; if there was room for an apple it went in. Otherwise it went into a coat pocket.

Michigan house-raisings were conducted to the accompaniment of a great deal of liquor and in some quarters it was not considered proper to have a raising without it. When Indians were among those invited, special care had to be exercised in permitting them access to the barrel, as they had a tendency to drink almost as heavily as the whites.

Whisky by the barrel
Sugar by the pound
A great big bowl to put it in
And a spoon to stir it around.

It was a day of mighty breakfasts and Michigan was the state for it.

Come an' see what yo' got
On yo' breakfast table:
Ram, ham, chick'n 'n mutton
Ef yo' don't come now
You won't get nuttin.'

When the lumber boom died, Michigan lumber jacks packed up their axes and families and joined the great westward migrations of the sixties and seventies.

Remember beans before you start,

they were warned,

Likewise dried beef and ham
Beware of venison, damn the stuff,
It's oftener a ram.

Kitchens were accordingly huge in proportion to the ones which city-bred generations know. Much of rural family life was conducted in the country kitchens. Breakfast was generally served about 6 o'clock in the morning, and the meal was barely over before the women plunged into the business of preparing dinner. Dinners, too, were lusty affairs: From the cellar would come squash, rutabagas, cabbage and some canned fruit and pickles. There was fresh corn meal so recent from the mill that it had not yet become infested with weasels. A roaring wood fire in a stove that stood high on four legs, with an apron as a resting place for an iron spider, was the axis around which revolved the kitchen program.

Donation parties were interesting events in the lives of Michigan people who lived at widely separated distances from each other. Everybody
brought something. Competition ran in a manner much the same as at a
county fair; because all articles were open and labeled with the name of
the donor. It was about the only time each person had the opportunity to
estimate the contents of the other fellow's cellar and smokehouse. Great
hams, huge slabs of bacon, sow bellies, and sausages of various kinds
were strewn here and there on a long table.

Potatoes in huge sacks, apples in rough board barrels, dry beans by
the peck and other items from the cellar under the house or the root-
cellar—cabbage, turnips, parsnips, and squash. The women came in
for their share of attention by presenting handiwork. Jellies and jams,
applebutter, pickles, and large jars of canned fruits were exhibited before
critical neighbors, who knew from experience just how a pickle should be
placed in a jar to avoid display of a white spot, and who knew how to
select a cucumber in order to bring out its best qualities. Such neighbors
also knew how to counteract the ultimate appearance of wrinkles that
enlarge the warts on a pickle or the magnifying effect of glass on the
fuzz of pickled peaches.

The men took this occasion to show off the results of their husbandry.
Well selected potatoes—not a little one in an entire sack—carefully
graded apples, corn, both dry for stock feed or ground into meal, the
biggest squashes he grew the summer before, and a variety of other commodities that would excite the envy of a modern storekeeper, were all
there—and on exhibition for the information and edification of their
neighbors.

This spirit of friendly rivalry was not only an outlet for these people,
but incidentally, provided the minister with what it takes.

Michigan farmers years ago used to meet for a turkey shoot, held by
another farmer who had a yard full of turkeys to sell and devised this
method of disposing of them: A pit was dug from which to fire, and a turkey was placed in a box with only the head sticking out. The object was
to shoot the head off at a range of eighty rods, with a price of twenty-five
cents for ten shots, on the average. Expert hunters who had proved their
marksmanship on previous shoots were restricted to five shots for the

same price, but even then they were often good enough with the use of their guns to bag half a wagon load of birds.

At these meets, when it became too dark for further shooting, cold roast turkey, pumpkin pie and cider made a grand supper for farmers to be followed by dancing to the tune of hornpipes and fiddle.

Sugar in the gourd
Honey in the horn
Balance to your partners
Honey in the horn.

THE
FAR WEST EATS

MONTANA—*responsible for the region*

WYOMING

IDAHO

COLORADO

UTAH

NEVADA

NORTHERN CALIFORNIA

OREGON

WASHINGTON

The Far West

The Far West region, though it was made up of only nine Writers' Projects from eight and a half states, including Northern California, represents about a third of the area of the forty-eight states that were the country at the time of *America Eats*. It bundles together two very different cuisines, that of the Rocky Mountains and that of the Pacific Northwest and Northern California.

From San Francisco to Washington State are rich valleys providing some of the best agricultural products in the country and a sea coast whose bounty, while considered not up to the standards of New England, still offered tremendous varieties of fish and shellfish. In fact, the assumption of inferiority to the North Atlantic meant that while New England was already showing early signs of abuse, Pacific catches were still plentiful. Abalone, which is endangered today, was commonly eaten, and Pacific salmon, a threatened luxury today, was sold for a few cents a pound. This was then and remains today one of the better eating areas of the country.

Kenneth Rexroth, like many Californians, was born in Indiana. He was enormously influential in defining the literary role of San Francisco. He was the material of literary legends, supposedly frequenting hobo camps, earning money as a wrestler, and serving jail time for being part owner of a brothel. He moved to San Francisco in the 1920s, wrote original poetry that was a forerunner of Beat, and attracted others who have influenced the city's writing to this day. He led the Northern California Writers' Project and was so dominant that after he resigned in 1939 it rapidly failed to function and made no contribution to *America Eats*.

Rocky Mountain cuisine has always been a bit wild and eccentric when interesting at all. It is still the place to eat elk and other game, and entrées such as wildcat, beaver tail, wild duck, and foraged foods in Montana still typify the region. Edward B. Reynolds and Michael Kennedy of the Montana Project, who wrote the long regional essay for the Far West, said of the mountain region: "Here you will find no lacy frills to catch the eye, or subtle nuances of taste and smell to goad the appetite of the jaded and world-weary gastronome."

This was the view from Montana, not from the coast. Michael Kennedy, a writer of sports and Western stories, was the supervisor of the Montana Writers' Project for which Edward B. Reynolds (1894–1983) also worked. It is not known why they were selected to write the Far West section, but it doubtless was related to the fact that all the more prominent figures in the region, such as Rexroth and Vardis Fisher of Idaho, had left the FWP.

In any event, the Washington staff seemed extremely pleased with their essay and even told Nelson Algren to look at it to see what was wrong with his own contribution. Kennedy and Reynolds did incorporate the diverse material submitted into a single voice of charm and fluidity. The essay was full of broad observations about the West, such as, "The life of these people is not entirely one monotonous round of fried beans, baked beans, boiled beans, and just beans, varied only by an occasional jack rabbit or two. Not as long as the creative ability of these Western people holds forth. . . . And until you've tasted jack rabbit mincemeat pie you have never appreciated the true brilliance of creative ability." And, "As a result of this tradition of masculine cookery, a man who dons an apron and enters a kitchen or approaches an outdoor fire is not looked upon with scorn in the West."

To the indigenous peoples of the Northwest, salmon has always been a food staple, a constant cultural image in carvings, paintings, and dance, a symbol of fertility. Barbecued salmon, planked salmon, most of the recipes for cooking salmon on a direct fire, as well as preserving the fish through drying, smoking, or pressing, were Indian traditions.

The first white traders to arrive in the Pacific Northwest marveled at the quantity of salmon. In 1805 the Lewis and Clark expedition struggled to move their boats in the salmon-clogged Columbia River. But the first to commercialize these fish were the Russians, which is why the biological names for all the salmon species of the Pacific Northwest are Russian. The leading species are *O. tshawytscha*, or chinook or king, which are the largest, and *O. nerka*, or sockeye salmon. At the time of *America Eats* salmon were still plentiful, and whether based on earnest gastronomic judgment or just regional snobbery, Atlantic salmon from the more influential Northeast was generally considered of higher quality, and so the Pacific Northwest was still clogged with cheap salmon.

But salmon is highly vulnerable to overfishing because it is at its most desirable as it heads back toward the river of its birth, which is to say, just before spawning—the ones Clark found clogging the Columbia had probably just finished spawning, which is the least toothsome phase. Salmon is also extremely vulnerable to pollution and its life cycle is stopped by the damming or otherwise blocking of spawning rivers. The result is that today salmon has become a luxury item. Atlantic salmon is almost extinct in North America and attempts to farm it have produced an incomparably inferior product. Salmon from the Pacific Northwest have become one of the most high-priced fish in America. In 2008 severe restrictions were placed on fishing Pacific salmon in the hopes of replenishing seriously depleted stocks.

Oregon Salmon Barbecue

JOSEPH McLAUGHLIN

One day at Yachats we were preparing a huge salmon barbecue, and our local "character" Dunkhorst requested the privilege of preparing the salmon. He said that he had a method that came from Germany and he had never seen it used in this country. Naturally we allowed him the "privilege" he desired because it meant less work for the rest of us. But we all watched the procedure.

First the salmon (five of them) were cleaned. Then "Dunk" dissolved a lot of brown sugar in a big tub of water. The salmon were then "dunked" (in more ways than one) in the sweetened solution. After about half an hour they were removed and placed in the barbecue pit and covered with ferns and grass.

The result of this treatment was a dish that was hard to beat. The salmon retained all its rich salmon flavor but had lost its "fishy" taste. A further result is that all Yachats housewives now wash their salmon in water sweetened with brown sugar before they cook it.

Puget Sound
Indian Salmon Feasts

The Indians of the Northwest Puget Sound country prepare salmon in a unique way which makes it a very delicious and appetizing meal. In August 1941, the district 4H Leader's Council held their semi-annual meeting at the Tulalip Indian Reservation where the 4H members and their leaders among the Indians acted as hosts. After the morning session the various delegates visited the Indian council house, a large log and shake structure on the shores of Tulalip Bay, where the Indian women were preparing the salmon. This council house has a dirt floor on which a fire had been built in a rectangular shape; about 8 feet by 4 feet. Around the fire were long strips of salmon on sticks stuck in the ground. The Indian women, in their native dress, were tending the salmon and turning the sticks from side to side so that a slow smoked bake was achieved. We were told by some of the older Indians that this method of cooking salmon had been used by the Indians long before the coming of the White Man.

From the council house the delegates were invited into a very modern community hall, a few feet distant, where long tables were very attractively set up and where they were served with the salmon prepared in the tribal fashion but disguised with the usual modern strip of lemon, leaf of lettuce, dab of potato salad, hot biscuits, coffee and apple pie, all served by Indian girls dressed as any other American High School girl.

—*Written for* America Eats *by James L. Earl, December 11, 1941*

The late Wm. Shelton, called "chief" Shelton by the whites and acknowledged as chief by most of the Indians, made an annual affair of the salmon bake, usually in August or September when 15 or 20 prominent people, among whom was always included Professor Edmund Meany of the University of Washington, were invited for the occasion.

—Everett Daily Herald, *August 5, 1933, page 2*

ANNUAL SALMON DAY TO BE IN SEPTEMBER. . . .

September 10th has been set as annual salmon day at the home of (Chief William Shelton at Tulalip). Each year a group of old friends gather at the home of one of the Northwest's foremost Indians, Chief Shelton, and partake of a salmon dinner, cooked in the Indian style.

About fifteen men from all parts of the state are expected this year, including Professor Meany of the University of Washington and Professor Fish of the Stats Normal School at Ellensburg. Indian women of the reservation will cook and serve the fish in the real old potlatch method.

—Everett Daily Herald, *Saturday, August 5, 1933, page 2*

Washington's Geoduck Clams

Like maple syrup, only stranger, geoducks appear to be a food that is eaten abroad but only produced in the United States and Canada. A geoduck, one of nature's ugliest comestible creatures, is North America's largest clam, with an oval shell four to six inches wide from which extends a thick hose more than a foot long. There really is no polite way to effectively describe them. They look like a large clam that has bitten an even larger penis. When you pick one out of the water the long phallic neck squirts water and then sadly falls flacid. If that alone does not make them hard to sell, the name is pronounced "gooey duck." The

*earliest published record of the name is 1883 and it is believed
to originate with the word for "digging deep" in the language
of the Nisqualli Indians. Since they can bury their bodies as
deep as four feet in the sand, this seems more plausible than the
other explanation—that it was named after a John F. Gowey,
who accidentally shot a clam while duck hunting. Geoducks are
dug for, and it takes some tugging to yank them out of the sand.
The obscene foot is strong and tenacious. They are found on the
beach at low tide, their necks barely visible out of the sand spout-
ing water. You have to dig fast because they try to go deeper.*

In the nineteenth century an attempt to transplant geoducks
to the Atlantic coast failed. At the time of America Eats *geoducks were a local delicacy in Washington State, British Columbia, and lower Alaska, but today there are geoduck farms that
hope to commercialize these clams broadly as was done with
oysters. So far they have only become popular in Japan. We'll
have to wait and see. Geoducks are patient—they live about 150
years—but as of yet they don't seem to be catching on. They don't
sell well in Seattle's popular waterfront Pike Street market. One
fish merchant said, in his New Jersey accent, "We stopped carrying the ducks." A lot of people have moved to Seattle, and it's
getting hard to find a native here. The complaint at Pike Street
was that everyone wanted to see a geoduck, but nobody wanted
to buy one. At another market they said they would only special order them. The problem is that they are large (five pounds
or more today, though this* America Eats *article says they are
smaller) and you have to be willing to buy a whole clam. They
sell for about $18 a pound, so at the least it would cost $90.*

But if geoducks are rare and expensive, Asians will buy
them, especially the Japanese. At the Uwajimaya market,
Seattle's eighty-year-old Asian market, they sell geoducks live
from a tank. They will clean them for the customer, throwing
out the belly and skinning the neck. Some people use the clams
for chowder, but as the man cleaning them in the market said,
for $18 a pound, "If you cook it you lose your money."

Sushi restaurants serve geoduck raw as sushi or sashimi or sometimes sautéed with mushrooms. Raw, it tastes like clam, but a tough clam.

It is not entirely true, as the following essay claims, that geoducks do not swim. Like many other bivalves, they have a free-swimming youth until they go on to settle down in the mud.

The humble Geoduck has been much publicized throughout the nation on various quiz programs during the past year. This interesting animal known to science as *Glycimeris generosa* neither flies nor swims but in common with other bivalves carries its house on its back and buries itself in the sand. They average about 1½ to 2½ pounds and at one time were very numerous in the northern Puget Sound area. Of late, however, it has been found necessary to place them under the protection of the Fish and Game Law. In 1931 the State Legislature made it unlawful for any person to take more than 3 geoducks in any one day. They also made it unlawful for anyone to can or sell any geoducks and specified the manner in which the bivalves should be taken that no tools other than "fork, pick or shovel, operated by hand by one person for personal use" should be used and that no person should, "at any time, maim or injure any geoduck or thrust any stick or other instrument through the neck or body of such geoduck before digging."

—*L. 1931, p. 147, sec. 1; Pierces Code 1939, sec. 2510–6*

Following is a narrative account of a geoduck hunt in Snohomish County in 1935.

Two families of us went clam digging on the beach about a mile south of Mukilteo. The tide was extremely low and while walking along the beach we spotted a geoduck's head just about level with the sand or a little above. One of the men took two or three quick shovels of sand, then they grabbed it by the neck and started to shovel sand as quickly as they could, as the geoduck draws his neck in when disturbed. This one was about 2½ or 3 feet deep and owing to the fact that the sand kept caving in and that care had to be taken to avoid injuring the geoduck's neck, it took us about an hour to dig him out. The tide started to come in and we thought we would have to give up as the hole kept filling up. By the time the geoduck was loosened enough so that we could pull him out of the sand and water, I was mired down to the knees and had to be pulled out as there was quite a suction in the sand and the tide was coming in pretty fast.

—*Written for* America Eats *by Mrs. Emma Olsen, December 11, 1941*

The Puget Sound Indians used a fish hook on a pole to snag the geoduck's head and as the geoduck pulled his neck in he drew the pole after him and the Indians followed the pole down with their digging instruments until they found the geoduck.

—*Information supplied by Mrs. Emma Olsen, December 11, 1941*

Another system used by the Puget Sound settlers was to push a section of stove pipe down over the bivalve's neck and digging around the base of the pipe.

—*Information obtained from Carl Bartlett,*
December 4, 1941, by James L. Earl

The geoduck is seldom prepared at clam bakes or for outdoor suppers but is usually made into chowder. An authority on local sea food gives these directions for preparing the geoduck: "scald, remove entrails, cut up the neck, chop up body and use for chowder." He also states, "They are planted by the State as they are very rare."

—*Information received from Mr. Trafton, Sea Food Market, Pier 5,*
Everett, Washington, December 4, 1941, by Minerva Stongel

FORTY-FOUR SACKS OF CLAMS FOR EAGLE'S PICNIC

Forty-four sacks of clams will be consumed at Eagle's picnic to be held at Mukilteo. At least that many clams will be prepared for the picnickers, baked and steamed.

—Everett News, *Saturday, August 25, 1923, p. 8.*

A Washington Community
Smelt Fry

CARROLL KENNEDY

An annual event which is finding favor with thousands of tourists as well as residents of nearby counties is the huge smelt fry held on the banks of the Cowlitz River at Longview, Washington, in March of each year.

Authoritative sources state that there are several types of the smelt family, but the one type under discussion here is native to the waters of the Pacific Northwest. It is allied to the salmon family and its usual habitat is the salt water channels near the spot where the Columbia River empties into the sea. Between August of each year and May of the succeeding year, the smelt leave their briny home in schools, going upstream into fresh waters to spawn and then return to their native waters.

It is during this hegira that the fish are entrapped in the Columbia River and its tributaries, one of the largest of which is the Cowlitz River. The peak of the "run" at this point occurs in late February or early March, when millions of the little silvery fellows can be seen and caught on their way upstream.

State statutes prohibit the taking of more than 20 pounds of the fish per person a day, but with the entire family engaged in the pursuit during the run, sufficient quantities are taken by the household to provide several meals of this nutritious sea food. Ranging in size from 4 to 8 inches in length, the smelt is probably the least troublesome of all fish to prepare for the table. In most instances neither the head nor tail is removed; one quick slit with a sharp knife lengthwise removes the viscera and backbone and after a thorough cleansing in cold water this morsel of fish is ready for the cracker-meal in which it is rolled before being placed in the frying pan.

At the most recent annual affair glorifying the lowly smelt in Longview, over 3,000 persons gathered on the banks of the Cowlitz River to enjoy a breakfast of the freshly ensnared smelt. Fishing gear of every description had been employed to catch the fish; bird's cages, laundry baskets, perforated boxes, colanders, and fishing nets were all brought into use to land the ton or more fish to be cooked.

To whet the appetite as well as to furnish the publicity which goes with such an event, a 10 foot skillet was placed over a blazing Presto Log fire. Greasing the huge pan was accomplished by tying bacon rind to the feet of two girls who skated and danced around in the sizzling utensil. Hundreds of pounds of the fish were then dumped into the pan and seasoned with salt and pepper from huge containers. Flour, or some facsimile, was sprinkled over the mass of fish, while the chef vigorously turned the contents of the pan with the aid of a large garden rake.

After the contents of the pan had attained a well-browned color, the entire production was dumped into the Cowlitz River, thereby allaying the fears of the thousands who had accepted the invitation to have a smelt breakfast that maybe after all they were expected to eat what was being prepared. Instead, a coterie of beautiful girls appeared in the crowd bearing large trays of crispy, corn-meal rolled smelt, freshly fried, which had been prepared earlier at a nearby hotel for the occasion. After satisfying the inner man, the thousands of guests departed, each content that a good performance had been given and that a most worthy member of the fish family had been eulogized.

Montana Fried Beaver Tail

EDWARD B. REYNOLDS

Among the rare foods of the west, rare because of trapping restrictions, but still a delicacy in the Rocky Mountain area, is fried beaver's tail. In the early days, before conservation, it was much more common.

The tail of the beaver is held over a fire by means of a stick, pincers, or even the hand. When the fat softens the skin is peeled off like a banana skin. Any other method is exceedingly difficult because the skin is tough as shoe leather and hard to separate from the flesh by means of a knife.

When the fat is trimmed away, the tail may be rolled in flour and fried. When boiled, it is best pickled in vinegar in a manner similar to preparing pigs' feet.

Oregon Wild Duck

JOSEPH McLAUGHLIN

Many of Oregon's hunters have a special way of cooking duck and other wild game birds. The birds are bled and cleaned, but not plucked. The bird, feathers and all, is then rolled in a clean clay so that it is completely covered to a thickness of about ¼ inch. Next a bed of hot coals is prepared and the birds are placed upon it and covered with a thick coat of green leaves or ferns. Since it is virtually impossible to burn the bird by this method, it may be left in its open-air oven until the men are ready to eat it. As a rule this isn't very long after preparations have begun. When the cooked bird is removed from the fire, the clay, which now holds fast all the feathers, is broken off and the bird is ready to eat—so are the men. The clay coating seals in all the juices of the meat. A better flavored or more tender bird is impossible by any other method.

Utah Salmi of Wild Duck

WILLIAM H. MEAL

Four ducks—clean thoroughly, not neglecting to remove the oil glands.

Soak three hours in salt water; this partially removes the fishy flavor.

Roast 30 minutes in hot oven or until quite brown. Do not use the liquid left from roasting.

Cut ducks up, four pieces to the duck; cut first in two length-wise, then cut in two crosswise, making four pieces.

Place in good sized stew kettle.

Add:

  1 pint consommé or bouillon
  2 large ripe tomatoes or the equivalent of canned tomatoes
  1 large carrot, diced ½ inch
  1 medium sized parsnip, diced
  5 outside celery stalks, cut into ½ inch lengths
  1 large onion, cut into quite small pieces
  2 medium sized pimentos
  4 or 5 chile tepenis
  1 clove garlic
  1 level teaspoon black pepper
  7 or 8 whole cloves
  Spoonful ground thyme
  1 level spoon curry powder

Salt to taste
1 tablespoon Worcestershire sauce

Cook gently not less than three hours.
    Thicken slightly with scorched flour.

Before serving add:

    Large can of shredded mushrooms with the juice
    Several dozen small stuffed olives
    1 wine glass sherry

When serving use the entire sauce at the same time.

Washington Wildcat Parties

CARROLL KENNEDY

According to a news item appearing in a Longview, Washington, newspaper several years ago, the city firefighters of a sister city, Kelso, had been guests the previous night at a banquet whereupon the "pièce de résistance" of the meal served was—perish the thought—wildcat meat!

That the main dish of this dinner tasted a "little like veal," but stronger in odor, was all that the participants could remember or cared to release for publication. But this incident was the impetus for the recollections of other days long passed, when "cougar meat" was consumed by some of the residents of the same community.

The consumption of cougar meat at these repasts was impelled more from a standpoint of "reprisals" than from a cultivated appetite for the animal. As the story is related, "A woman by the name of Minnie (Christian name unimportant) was attacked and partially devoured by one of these

deadly prowlers of the woods. The surviving relatives of the family, even to the third and fourth generation, have vowed to relentlessly track down all the future offspring and descendants of the offending cougar and to give vent to their wrath by eating the prey when trapped."

As cougars are not too plentiful now-a-days even in the wooded country of Cowlitz County, it is quite doubtful that the family is able to provide such an animal often enough for them to become tired of the fare. But when they do enjoy such a repast, 'tis said the family always refer to the meal as "eating Aunt Minnie."

It is unlikely that cougar meat will become a standardized article on the menus of the rest of the populace in the state, particularly in those families which do not have or ever have had an aunt with such an unfortunate surname.

Foraging in Montana

EDWARD B. REYNOLDS

Mushrooms, water cress, pig weeds and lambs quarters as well as dandelion leaves supplement the vegetable and salad dishes of Westerners who continue to take advantage of native foods, although to lesser extent today than did the pioneers.

Chokecherries and dandelion blossoms are made into wine, while wild berries form the base of sauces, pies, jellies and jams.

Montana Dulce

EDWARD B. REYNOLDS

Dulce, dried seaweed, is good for what ails you.

That's the opinion of both the Irish and the New Englanders who have been transplanted to the mining districts of the west. And they conquer their ailments by eating the leathery, reddish-brown weed like candy, relishing its salty taste and confident that it will prevent such things as goiter.

The Irish receive their dulce from the coastal counties of Ireland in letters or parcels; it also is shipped in from Maine and sold in the stores. In both Maine and Ireland, where it is fresh, it is sometimes cooked like spinach. But in the Rocky Mountains it serves as a "nibbler" to be put in the pocket and munched whenever the desire arises.

Washington Aplets and Cotlets

*One of my clearest memories of trips to the dark and rough
waterfront town of Seattle when I was a child was those
sugar-dusted squares that are known in America as "Turkish
delight" and in the Arab-speaking world as* lokum, *but were
and still are known to everyone in Washington State as aplets
and cotlets, the local candy. They are still produced by Liberty
Orchards with Washington State apples. Washington is the
leading apple-producing state in America.*

Liberty Orchards Company
Cashmere, Washington

December 13, 1941
Mr. Glenn H. Lathrop,
State Supervisor,
Washington Historical Records Survey,
Work Projects Administration,
819 Western Avenue,
Seattle, Washington

Dear Sir:

*We are in receipt of a letter from Viola Lawton, Area Supervisor
of District No. 1, in Spokane, requesting that we furnish your office
with data on Aplets, as a food product peculiar to our state. Not
knowing just what type of data you desire makes it rather difficult
for us to determine just what to give you in this letter.*

*Aplets were first put on the market in late 1919 and early 1920, by
two naturalized citizens of Armenian parentage, Mr. M. S. Balaban
and Mr. A. L. Tertsagian, brothers-in-law, who for a few years previous*

to that time had been putting out evaporated apples in a small plant located in Cashmere, Washington. When the new confection caught the public fancy, this evaporating business was discontinued and the factory given over to the manufacture of the candy alone. In 1923, a larger and more convenient factory was built adjoining the old frame building in which the industry was started. This new factory was damaged by fire in 1928, and rebuilt after the fire, with an office addition built on at that time.

Aplets are based on apple juice extracted from the lower grades of the fruit grown so abundantly in the Wenatchee Valley, sugar, the finest quality of California and Oregon walnut meats, and other ingredients of correspondingly high grade. In 1932 another fruit-nut confection, called Cotlets, because it contains sun-dried apricots, and apricot pulp, was added to the line, and is also becoming most popular with the buying public. Both products meet the high quality demanded by the Pure Food and Drug Act, and are healthful, satisfying sweets for all ages and classes.

We trust this is the information desired, and are

Very truly yours,

Liberty Orchards Co.,
By: Blanche Wood

"The Unique Fruit-Nut Confections of the Golden West"

Colorado Superstitions

Every state has numerous folklore traditions that have been handed down from generation to generation. Colorado is no exception. Many of these traditions and superstitions were brought here by our pioneer ancestors and probably were products of another environment. Among the more commonly known superstitions are these:

1. If apple butter is made in the dark of the moon, it will not splash in cooking.
2. In stirring butter or in churning butter, the motions must be sunwise. Reversing the direction will invite bad luck.
3. Do not burn bread crust in the kitchen fire, or bad luck will come to that household.
4. In killing meat of any kind, it should be done near the full of the moon, and the meat will not shrink up when cooked.
5. Always make vinegar in the full of the moon.
6. Make sauerkraut in the sign of the feet, and it will always cook tender and remain sweet.
7. Set the home so that the chickens come out in the full of the moon.
8. Potatoes planted in the "light" of the moon run to stalk. Those placed in the "dark" of the moon will make better potatoes.
9. A Ute Indian superstition is: "Plant all root plants, like beets, potatoes, onions in the dark of the moon, and all plants like spinach, lettuce and corn in the light of the moon. If you plant these vegetables in the light of the moon, they will be all tops."
10. In moving to another house, take a loaf of bread and a small bag of salt to the house first; hide these articles somewhere in the house. Privation and want will never enter that house.

11. Vegetables or fruit that produce above the ground should be planted on the increase of the moon. Roots and vegetables that produce in the earth should be planted on the decrease of the new moon.

12. You will receive mail from the direction in which your pie is pointing, when it is set down at your place at the table.

13. A piece of pie set with the point toward you meant a letter; with point to one side, a package; if directly away from you, it means nothing.

14. If a piece of silver falls to the floor from the dining table, it means that someone is coming hungry.

15. A long thin tea-leaf in a cup of tea means a stranger is coming to see you. If you put it on the back of your hand and stamp it with your other fist for each day of the week, you can tell when he is coming (by the day at which the leaf adheres to the fist).

16. Salt spilled toward a person is a lucky omen.

17. Thirteen guests at a dinner-table means a betrayal.

18. If you spill something on the stove, put salt on it to keep from having a fuss.

LUMBERJACK EATS LUNCH, LONG BELL LUMBER COMPANY, COWLITZ COUNTY, WASHINGTON. (PHOTO-GRAPH BY RUSSELL LEE)

19. Cook black-eyed peas on New Year's Day and you will be blessed with plenty all the year.

20. If you put a piece of wedding-cake under your pillow for seven successive nights, on the seventh you will dream of your future husband.

21. If a dandelion (or buttercup) placed under your chin throws a yellow light, you "love butter."

Washington State Hot School Lunches

Prior to 1936, in Snohomish County and rural districts of other counties in the Puget Sound Northwest, there was no original plan for "Hot Lunches" for school children. During the early depression period, 1929–36, many plans were tried at the various schools for supplying additional food to undernourished children.

In School District #6, Snohomish County (Mukilteo), the custom was instituted in 1930 of having the families take turns in supplying a hot dish for the entire school. The Parent Teachers Association purchased kettles and small electric hot plates to be used for the school lunch purpose and the hot dish generally consisted of one of the following: boiled beans, macaroni and cheese, spaghetti and tomatoes, various kinds of soups, or hot cocoa. No attempt was made at a balanced diet, the main object being to supply undernourished children with at least one hot dish per day.

Families living close to the school building delivered the dish hot at noon time, while those living further away sent the prepared food on the school bus and it was warmed up on the school hot plates by the teacher at lunch time.

This system was adopted by other school districts with variations in manner of handling. At Silver Lake, in 1932, the hot dish was prepared by volunteers of the Unemployed Citizens League, who also solicited foods to be used and served to the children without charge. In other districts the program was sponsored by community clubs, granges, and unemployed groups.

The School Lunch Program, under the Works Progress Administration since 1936, has grown from a few school districts cooperating until in October 1941, 32 separate school lunch projects were operating in second and third class districts throughout Snohomish County, serving an average of 4,112 hot lunches daily at an average cost of 2¢ per lunch. The cooks and helpers are supplied by the Work Projects Administration [the WPA name changed to Work Projects Administration in 1939] and a certain amount of food is supplied by the Surplus Commodities; all other finances are taken care of by the district sponsoring the program, either by per dish charge, weekly or monthly contributions by parents, or donations of foods.

The Basques of the Boise Valley

RAYMOND THOMPSON

The Basques, the oldest European culture, a people who live in a small coastal region of the western Pyrenees between France and Spain, speak an ancient language unrelated to any other known tongue, and have long been at the vortex of whirling controversies over linguistics, anthropology, and politics. But they are largely known in the American West as shepherds or, as they say in the West, sheepherders.

The American West—eastern California, Oregon, Washington, Southern Idaho, and Nevada—has suffered a shortage of sheepherders since the mid-nineteenth century. Sheep will graze and flourish in land too rugged for cattle. But sheep are much more work than cattle because they must be moved from one slope to another to find food. It was and still is a hard and lonely job, working long hours alone in the mountains, living in a crude trailer with only hard-working sheep dogs for companions.

At first the owners recruited Scots for the work, but by the late nineteenth century through to the time of America Eats

*they recruited Basques who had grown up on farms where they
looked after a few sheep. Many such farms were on the French
side, which is not losing its Basque character as the following article suggested, but more were from the Spanish side.
It is also not true, as this Idaho Writers' Project article suggests, that they came to the United States because they were
from an ancient line of shepherds. There were few full-time
shepherds in the Basque provinces. The recruits were simply farm people in need of work. Nor is it true, as Thompson
states, that they were drawn to the West because it resembled
their native land. Basque land—with its velvet green slopes
on mountains on the scale of the Adirondacks, though more
rugged, and never far from the Atlantic Ocean, a central part
of Basque history—is very different from the giant, arid landscape of the landlocked Rocky Mountains.*

*At home their family may have owned a few sheep or even a
large flock of several hundred. But in the American West they
were left in charge of many thousands of valuable sheep. A flock
could be worth hundreds of thousands of dollars. Today a single
sheep is worth about one hundred dollars. A sheepherder had
to be both skilled and responsible. The western range, unlike
their native European farms, included thousands of miles.
Some Basques did not know exactly what they were doing. One
Basque, who said he came because he didn't like the jobs he was
finding at home, said, "The only thing I knew about sheep was
that they know where they are going. So I followed them."*

*The Basques, both in their native Europe and in the West,
are widely appreciated for their food and cooking ability.
Some of the dishes mentioned here are typically Basque, but
many are Spanish. The anisette mentioned is not at all a
Basque drink.*

*The Basque tendency to assimilate in Idaho seems true
because today, while they still maintain traditional festivals
with Basque music and dance and an entire block of downtown Boise is devoted to Basque culture, few Idaho Basques*

speak the ancient language. The second, third, and fourth generations are not shepherds but doctors, lawyers, bankers, politicians, building contractors, and, of course, a few restaurateurs. And while they are still appreciated for their culinary abilities, Idaho Basques have evolved their own cuisine, which seldom includes the salt cod, baby eels, or other seafood that typifies Basque cuisine. Instead it is a cuisine largely based on lamb. While lamb is part of the Basque tradition, nowhere is it as central as it is to today's Idaho Basques. This in turn is a little surprising because in general Americans now eat far less lamb than in the days of America Eats. At the time of America Eats there were literally more sheep than people in Idaho, but today the sheep population is about one tenth of its pre–World War II population. Before the war so much lamb and mutton was produced in the West that the U.S. Army bought massive amounts, especially of mutton, and froze it, producing such awful meals for World War II G.I.s that many came home vowing never to eat lamb again. The market for lamb rapidly declined after the war, except in New York City, which has always been known for its love of lamb. After the war New York consumed more than half the lamb eaten in America.

With Basques too affluent in Europe to emigrate and herd sheep, today the Western sheep owners represented by the Western Range Association recruit Peruvians and a few Mexicans and an occasional Mongolian. They are allowed to bring these people in, as they were the Basques and Scots before them, because of the claim that there is no one in America willing and qualified to do the job. To prove the claim the Western Range Association periodically runs ads looking for American shepherds, but no qualified applicants ever turn up.

J ust as the Swedes hold forth with their Smorgasbords and other banquets in north Idaho, so the annual Sheepherders Ball of the Basques in south Idaho has attracted much attention.

Classified as a linguistic and social, rather than a racial group, the Basques formerly occupied the western Pyrenees on both French and Spanish sides but in later years seem to be linked more with the Spanish alone.

The native tongue, the Euskara, has puzzled philologists to the extent that its origin seems safely lost in obscurity. In search of a land whose topographical and climate conditions closely resembled the native country, the Basques came to Idaho and Oregon in the 1880s, chiefly to follow their ancient occupation of sheepherding.

They took small bands into the hills and stayed with them for years, until they finally had many large flocks.

Following the First World War, many Basques came to this country. The usual practice was for a brother to send for his nearest male kin, until whole clans followed.

"Bosco," a colloquial name for themselves and their tongue, is spoken universally. Yet most of them also speak Spanish and English fluently.

They play cards but rarely gamble, drink but do not become boisterous or vulgar.

At the annual Sheepherders Ball, where dress clothes are prohibited and denim overalls quite the thing, the feasting is attended with dancing their own folk numbers, as well as American and Spanish dances. The men wear bright sashes.

Lamb and turkey auctions are held in December usually, and are the occasion for additional feasting, dancing and singing.

Although the Basques have assimilated many of the Americanisms, and are intensely loyal to the country of their adoption, it seems safe to say they will retain and hand down many old traditions, among which are various ways of preparing foods.

Their famous "chorizos," or sausages, are made from pork cut into small pieces seasoned with salt, red pepper, a touch of garlic, and preserved in shortening.

Another characteristic dish is the "garbanzos," a yellow bean about the size of a middle-sized pea. When boiled and properly seasoned, it becomes larger than ordinary hominy and real tasty.

The Basques are fond of coffee, which they drink in huge cups. A half cup of boiled milk is poured in first and then the cup is filled with coffee.

Annual picnics held in summer have become decidedly American; principal items on the menu are hot dogs, beans and beer.

The holiday season starts December 24th and continues to January 6th. Shortly after this, the men must get back to their flocks, as there is much work to be done in preparing for the lambing season. However, during the two weeks they celebrate gloriously, going from home to home for parties which include both feasting and dancing. Christmas Eve is kept for family reunions.

January 6th is "Three Kings Day" with the Basques, to commemorate the arrival of the Three Wise Men at Bethlehem. In their home country, it is the day they give and receive gifts, but in America, they hold Christmas as we do.

TYPICAL BASQUE HOLIDAY MENUS

Whoever wrote up this menu clearly had little knowledge of the Spanish language.

Before breakfast—a liquor of their own, called Anisette

Breakfast—served with wine

Tortilla de Chorizo (Spanish sausage omelet)
or Bacalao Frito con Vino (dry codfish seared or toasted on hot coals)

Lunch—served with wine

Sopa de Pollo (chicken soup)
Ensalada Bejitabeles (vegetable salad)
Potaje de Garbanzo (chick peas or chick beans from Mexico)
Lengua on Salsa de Pimento (tongue in red pepper sauce)
Tortilla de Eiskillas (shrimp in omelet)
Callos a La Viscaina (tripe)

Dessert

Compote de Peras con Vino (pears cooked in wine)
Colinets (rum cake or cake made with rum or Sherry wine)
Coffee Completo (Coffee Royal)

Second Lunch, around 4:00 p.m.

Chocolate con Churros (fritters)
Morcilas Frilos con Vino o Cervesa (Blood sausages with wine or beer)

Dinner

Sopa de Chirlas (clam soup)
Mexcla de Ensalada (mixture of salad—tuna, eggs, lettuce, etc., with
   vinegar and oil, never mayonnaise)
Angulas on Aceita (Brood of Eel, imported)
Eel eggs
Arroz con Pollo (Spanish rice with chicken)
Calemaros Rellenos on Su Tints (stuffed squid or ink fish—a special
   Christmas dish)
Chuletas de Ternera con Pimentos Lorrenes (veal cutlets in pimento sauce)
Patas de Cerdero en Salada de Chili (pigs' feet in chili sauce)
Caracoles (snails)
Pollo (chicken)

Dessert

Salada de— Nueces (nut dessert)

Flan Casero (Basque custard)

Turron Nougat (almond paste cookies shaped like rabbits, or other animals, or even snakes)

Coffee Completo (Coffee Royal rest of the night, with dancing and singing)

The Basque dinner starts about 8 P.M. and lasts 4 hours, with an extra one thrown in for coffee drinking. They eat slowly because they believe in lots of loud joyous conversation. They are by nature a happy people.

Western Revolving Tables

EDWARD B. REYNOLDS

The old-timer's revolving table typifies the lusty eating habits of Westerners. Although today it is but occasionally found in isolated ranch houses, the idea is carried out in copious platters and dishes of food placed close to diners who do their own "reaching" and whose hosts and hostesses make a fetish of huge appetites and measure a feast by the quantity of food involved.

The old time revolving table was usually a home-made, circular affair with a smaller table in the center, placed about eight inches above the main table. This smaller table revolved and was loaded with food. When spun by the diners it created a miniature cafeteria of succulent roasts, rich gravies, brightly colored jellies, fruits, vegetables, breads, and whatnot. It was the epitome of lavish hospitality.

Oregon Pioneer Memories

SARA WRENN

*This interview by Sara Wrenn of the Oregon Writers' Project
is in the tradition of FWP oral histories.*

Draw Up an' Eat

The annual pioneer dinner! Well, I ought to know somethin' about it.
Haven't I been going to those pioneer reunions and dinners for well nigh
seventy years? They started way back in '75. November it was. Later on
they changed the time to June. Guess they thought there was more good
things to eat in June, so now we've been having the reunion in June
for years and years. My—my—how time flies: But, there, you want to
know about the dinner. When a body gets to be ninety years old there's
so much to remember it's hard to stick to one thing.

Yes, it was in 1875 when we had the first dinner. I mind me well the
time, 'cause that was the first year of the Pioneer Reunion, that took
place at Butteville. We had the reunion, with a program and speeches
an' everything, an' after that was all over an' everybody was good and
hungry, then we had the dinner. Only them who crossed the plains could
belong to the Pioneers' Association, as they named it. They was the only
ones who could wear the badges, so they wouldn't be a lot of newcom-
ers edgin' in. Oh, of course the sons an' daughters could come, but they
wasn't pioneers. All they could do was to take charge of the tables an'
wait on the rest of us—an' nobody else could do that but the sons an'
daughters either, an' we've always kept it that way, clear down to now.

In them early days the reunion took place sometimes at Oregon City
and sometimes at the State Fair Grounds at Salem. Only about the last

forty years they've had it all the time in Portland. 'Course them first dinners was cooked an' brought by the wives an' mothers, and while they was preparin' it, all the men did was smoke an' talk an' make speeches. But maybe the men was tired, drivin' from far an' near—sometimes as much as a hundred miles or more. There was only one railroad in Oregon in '75, and anyway railroad travel cost money for a whole family, so they drove mostly, some in hacks an' some in wagons. Sometimes the roads, they was awful, what with chuckholes an' dust. But they managed to get there. Lordy, what crowds we used to have. I mind me one year there was close to a thousand set down at the tables, with sixty to seventy to a table. That was in the Industrial Fair pavilion at Portland—the place where they hold the big industrial fair every year. It was a wooden building that must of covered more'n a block, and it sure made a big fire when it burned, back 'bout 1911, I think it was. After that we met in the City Armory till the World War came along an' we couldn't use the armory any more. 'Most ever since then we've had our gatherin' in the city auditorium, where the Oregon Historical Society is, you know.

There—there, if I ain't getting off on something else again. Well, if I do say so, them pioneer dinners is just about the best dinners in the world. First they had mostly boiled ham an' roast chicken, but lots of the folks they come from inland an' they liked salmon. By salmon I don't mean just any old salmon. I mean our Columbia River salmon, nice an' firm an' red-meated. There ain't any better fish anywhere—maybe I'd better say there ain't as good fish anywhere as our Columbia River Chinook. Whenever us Oregonians want to do something specially nice for anybody, like the President of the United States, or some other bigwig, we give him one of them grand fish. Of course we still have some ham an' chicken, but, as I was sayin', the salmon's the big thing—bigger'n more ways than one. Baked whole, with nice strips of bacon laid across it so it won't stick to the roastin' pan—'course I mean after it's cleaned and the scales scraped good with a sharp knife—them baked salmon sure is a pretty sight. The waiters—sons and daughters, mind you— carry them in a procession 'round the tables for everybody to see. Used to be there was a long procession of 'em, all of 'em with a salmon maybe three feet long, crisp and shinin' an' decorated with parsley. Then, after everybody had a look, they'd take the salmon to one of the booths, where it was dished out in portions, with the best hot cream-and-egg sauce you ever tasted. Then there's the potato salad. That's the kind of salad we've stuck to year in an' year out. It's good too. As to how they make it, it's the same receipt I use I guess. Leastwise it tastes the same. I take nice, firm potatoes, an' I boil an' skin 'em an' cut 'em up in little squares. After that I add just the right amount of onion cut up in little pieces too—but not too much, so the breath gets smelly. After that, if I have any, I put in some shredded parsley, an' then I mix it all with a boiled dressing. It's the dressing that really makes the salad after all, an' here's the receipt for that, if you want it. For a little bit, like for a family, I take half a cup o' vinegar, a cup o' water, a teaspoon each of dry mustard and sugar, a half teaspoon of salt, two tablespoons flour or cornstarch, an' butter the size of a walnut. Mix everything, 'xcept the butter, an' let it boil 'bout five minutes, stirring all the time, an' just at the last drop the butter in an' stir good till it melts. When you get through you've got a thick paste that ought to be thinned with cream. When that's mixed well with the potatoes an' onions, an' then hard-boiled eggs sliced and laid over the top—well, you got something then that it ain't no wonder all the pioneers come back for a second helpin' of.

Of course we have all kinds of pickles and jams with bread an' butter. Used to be we always had hot biscuit. For years an' years just one lady made them biscuits—hundreds an' hundreds of 'em she made, but she isn't so young now herself, so we don't have 'em any more. That's one thing—baker's bread—that's a big savin' of time and maybe just as good as our homemade bread too, with no worry over the batter sourin' like in old times.

Yes, of course, there's coffee and tea—plenty, with all the cream an' sugar anybody wants. But, next to the salmon, the big part of the dinner is ice-cream an' cake. Used to be ice-cream wasn't so easy to get as nowadays, an' even today there's plenty of pioneers that don't have it so often it ain't a big treat. Anyway if they do have it at home it ain't the same as at the reunion, where they're thinkin' an' talkin' about old times. There's always lots of ice-cream an' everybody can have all they want. 'Most everybody takes two dishes. I recollect once when a man sent his dish back four times. That means five dishes o' ice-cream that he ate. An' he didn't care a mite when we laughed at him. Said if he had room he'd eat some more, but his belly was plum ready to bust—that's just what he said.

Maybe I forgot to tell you that we've always had the dinner followin' the speeches and singin' an' everything, today just like in the beginning. The tables always look so pretty, all decorated in flowers, and the young folks—daughters an' granddaughters doin' everything to make it nice for us, with some of the young menfolks to do the heavy work. There ain't so many tables nowadays o' course, but a good many of what are left still have the family name that they started with. That's nice, don't you think, carryin' on the name? Several of the old families have been decoratin' their tables with the same flowers every year. One, I mind me, uses calla lillies, an' another always has sweetpeas. Of course a lot of 'em have roses, for roses is the flower that most of us love best here in Oregon. Once we all get set down at the tables we sure do keep them young folks busy carryin' the food from the booths all around. Every booth and every table has its lady in charge, an' she has her helpers, an' just as I was tellin' you they all got to be of pioneer families. No outsiders ain't allowed at our pioneer dinner. When everybody gets up from the tables, and afore they get started on their yarn-spinning at what they call their campfire, the flowers are given all 'round to anybody that wants 'em— the pioneers, I mean.

Yes, we're thinnin' out. I don't calculate I'll be at many more pioneer dinners. We're goin' pretty fast into that West beyond the sunset. What a grand time they must be havin'—talkin' about early times. But, you know, I bet they miss our Chinook salmon!

Two Recipes from the Bohemia District of Oregon

JOSEPH McLAUGHLIN

The Bohemia district, in western Oregon, is a mining region. The inhabitants exchange their favorite recipes. Today, you will find everyone cooking more or less the same dishes. Two of the best are as follows:

Mock Baked Potatoes. Since baking takes a long time—and lots of firewood, potatoes are frequently boiled in water in which 6, 7, or 8 tablespoons of salt (rook salt, if available) have been dissolved. The increased heat of the boiling water due to the presence of the salt cooks the potatoes as if they had been baked except that the skins are thinner. If placed in a hot oven for two or three minutes, they cannot be distinguished from true baked potatoes. Try it sometime yourself.

India Pickle. (Not to be confused with India Relish.) The product of this recipe may be used to make Thousand Island Dressing, as the filler for Spanish Omelette, as a sandwich spread, as a sauce for meat loaves or in the loaf itself. It is also good with baked beans. It wouldn't surprise me if it was used as a mustard plaster or as an axle grease for the farm machinery. Here it is: "12 apples, 10 ripe tomatoes, 9 medium onions, 3 cups vinegar. When this comes to a boil add 3 cups sugar, ¼ cup salt, ½ teaspoon cinnamon, ½ teaspoon cloves, ½ teaspoon black pepper. Cook till tender and seal."

An Oregon Protest Against Mashed Potatoes

CLAIRE WARNER CHURCHILL

Claire Warner Churchill, a native of Portland, Oregon, born in 1898, was a field supervisor for the Oregon Writers' Project. She wrote on Oregon history, often from an Indian perspective, and was published locally. Slave Wives of Nehalem, *a novel with an Oregon Indian setting, was published in 1933.* South of the Sunset, *a novel about Sacajawea, an Indian woman who aided the Lewis and Clark expedition, was published in 1936. The FWP afforded Churchill an opportunity to further study Oregon history at a time when the last few survivors of the Oregon Trail were still alive. She died in 1956. Apparently, she was particular about her mashed potatoes.*

There ought to be a law, that's what there ought, a law against mashed potatoes being served in restaurants. There ought to be a law against even the use of the words on menus. Somebody ought to sue someone for libel. Libel on mashed potatoes. Think of it. Tomorrow a million men, even ten million men, will sit down at tables and order merchant lunches. Whereupon there will appear ten million plates bearing what chefs will declare to be mashed potatoes. Mashed potatoes indeed! If grandma ever got to thinking what a reflection upon her cooking restaurant mashed potatoes are I tremble for the culinary locals responsible for serving them. Mashed potatoes! The beatings, the maulings, and the ultimate degradation to which an honest Irish potato must submit tomorrow turn me sad-eyed from my plate (Merchant plate, 65¢).

No, I am not to be fooled by your whipped potatoes, your fluffed potatoes, your watered pastes that pass in many restaurants for honest to God mashed potatoes. I know them for what they are: horrible travesties upon a self-respecting dish of mashed, and I mean mashed, not macerated potatoes.

I've eaten in places where they even thin them down, whip them up, or by some diabolical process known to and understood by only the restaurant trade, make them suitable for squeezing through a pastry tube. Believe it or not they squirt them around a wafery slice of prime rib au jus in an anemic looking ruffle or worse yet drop them off in disgusting rosettes around a sliver of ham. Even on the hoof ham would never recognize a spud in such a condition. Imagine how the potato must feel. A good old earth apple, once prized for its alleged aphrodisiac qualities, peeled, boiled, bruised, whipped, and squirted out of all semblance to its once lusty self. Come to think of it, what's the matter with a potato in its original size and shape? Is anything tastier than a spud boiled in its own jacket or baked in its skin? But let that pass. Such tubers require no defense. I was speaking of mashed potatoes.

Never have I learned the secret of the three o'clock or so-called blue gray mashed potatoes. In some restaurants along toward the shank of the afternoon late lunchers often encounter this variety. It is not a true gray nor yet a veritable blue, but a suspicious looking color somewhere between the two. These gems it is said can be prepared in not less than three hours. The chef starts about eleven, plopping an unconscionable lot of peeled potatoes into boiling water. Somewhere near twelve it is said that he mashes them, and at one he pops whatever is left onto a steam table. When time permits or the spirit moves him he stirs them. Three hours of this treatment, or lack of treatment as the case may be, will remove every semblance of mashed potatoes, destroy the texture, ruin whatever flavor nature provided, and reduce the spuds to a nasty paste, but by golly, it will give you color. What color, even the chefs cannot predict, but color you'll get—pied blue, pinto gray or pale saffron. The paste, however, is said to be useful in paper-hanging, or mixed with gesso is excellent for molding small figurines for your mantel. Of course, if it is flavor and texture you want, why, eat at twelve or order French fries. But heck, they even pre-fry French fries now-a-days. What chance has a potato?

Another restaurant mystery is the manner in which chefs inject lumps into mashed potatoes. Try as you may you can invest a given amount of mashed potatoes with just so many lumps. A chef knows no such limitations. He can get more lumps to the cubic inch of mashed potatoes than a Swiss can holes in cheese. There's no limit to his ingenuity. He begins, perversely enough, by selecting the wrong kind of spuds. This requires nice discrimination, I've heard, only those grown in watery or badly drained soil being suitable for lumping, and culls being preferred.

With an experienced hand and a practiced eye an expert in this kind of mashing can predict almost to the dozen the number of lumps possible in one serving. Never have I learned the exact formula for this kind of cooking and mashing, but I do know the two fundamentals are the buying of the wrong kind of potatoes and their removal from the fire before they are done. From then on each chef permits his inventiveness to run hog-wild. Whether or not you want them you'll get lumps. Lumps cunningly concealed in a thin coating of mashed potatoes and destined to take a grievous toll of disillusionment among diners.

To my notion the most insulting treatment ever accorded an underground rhizome (potato to you) in the name of mashed potatoes is that process known among tea room operators as whipped or fluffed potatoes. Their sole virtue is their snowy whiteness. In this respect they at least resemble mashed potatoes. Alas, here the likeness ends. Plunge your fork into a heap, a ring, a dab of whipped potatoes and what do you find? Nothing. Exactly nothing. Except for a complete lack of flavor you might as well be eating spun sugar candy like that sold on a stick at county fairs.

Whipped potatoes, thank heaven, are seldom encountered except in places catering to women. Eschew the Orange Lanterns, the Green Gates, the Blue Ducks; flee as from the fiend all cute signs and exotic nomenclature and you may be pretty certain of avoiding whipped potatoes. For completely frustrating a male I recommend nothing better than subjecting him to a ruffle of whipped potatoes around a heap of spinach. If the atmosphere of the place does not completely befuddle him the potatoes will. Thereafter he is your man. You may do with him as you will.

When I think what grandpa would have done if grandma had served him whipped potatoes in a frill—he'd have scooped up a handful and rubbed them into her pompadour, that's what he'd have done. But grandma knew better. You'd never have caught her tempting grandpa or providence by doing anything to a potato but *mashing* it. Of course grandma had sense enough not to try to serve mashed potatoes the year round, something no restaurant chef appears to recognize as impossible.

There are some months in which a spud, understanding its destiny far better than modern cooks do, refuses to be mashed. If you attempt to mash a potato in late May or early June it rebels and despite your most artful efforts it will become a translucent paste. No person except him who would defy nature and the last judgment should try to mash a potato after June first.

Passionately opposed to being mashed in this verdant season it will submit, even will cooperate in French or cottage fries and escalloped dishes. Never have I witnessed a finer friendship than that exhibited between old potatoes and ham when they are tucked into a casserole of cream, sprinkled with pepper, salt, and parsley, and permitted the intimacy of a hot oven for fifty minutes or an hour.

During the summer months potatoes, wisely enough, defy all kitchen legerdemain. No cook, thank God, has ever yet devised a way of mashing new potatoes. If they are served they must be boiled whole. Having boiled them grandma introduced them to thickened cream made savory with butter, salt, and considerable pepper, or rolled them in melted butter and served with a garnish of fresh green pepper grass.

Grandma would have been shocked if anyone had ever intimated that a mashed potato could be served before autumn. She preferred October or even November for introducing to the table the first snowy mound. About the time hogs were killed and their pink carcasses hung out in the freezing air, or say, when the headcheese was in the making and a few pork chines were clamoring to be roasted to provide the makings for gravy, then grandma considered the season appropriate for making public the secret affinity of mashed potatoes and gravy.

She selected only upland spuds, raised in loamy soil and arrogant as to size. There was no fol-de-rol about cooking them. Sometime between peeling the carrots and pouring the syrup over the baking apples and near the time she mixed the dry ingredients for the biscuit dough she caught up a pan of potatoes, zipped of a thin layer of skin, popped them into a modicum of boiling salted water, and settled the kettle lid firmly into place. When I hear modern cooks talk about pouring the water off the potatoes I have to laugh. When grandma boiled the spuds there wasn't any water left to pour off.

She went about her business for the length of time it takes to baste the roast just once more, to roll out the biscuit dough and slip it into the oven, to remove the glazed and reddening apples to a platter, to lift the roast and make the gravy and—well, then she just lifted the lid off the potatoes and there they lay, almost dry, their mealy hearts bursting and begging for a drink of cream. A few resounding thumps with the battered old wooden masher and it was discarded for a hickory spoon. You had to feel a mashed potato to be sure it was right, grandma said, as she tossed in the cream and butter and whisked the snowy heap onto a dish, cuddled a lump of butter on the crest and dusted it with pepper. Not paprika. God forbid. But coarse black pepper so fresh from the spice mill that it set us all to sniffing.

The memory betrays me. I find myself bursting into nostalgic tears. Tears of pity for myself, tears for our lost generation of restaurant diners who never will know the truth about mashed potatoes, for whom spuds are fluffed, whipped, paddled, pounded, beaten, bruised, crushed, flounced and shaken, but never—oh the pity of it—never mashed.

The Potatoes of Kow Kanyon, Oregon

JOSEPH McLAUGHLIN

A few years ago there lived in Yachats a retired blacksmith. His name was Dunkhorst, but was known to all as just plain "Dunk." If he had a first name, no one knew what it was. Now Dunk fancied himself quite a poet and still a better cook. As a matter of fact he didn't rate very high as either. He did have, however, one special dish that he was frequently called upon to prepare for community gatherings. He called it simply "Kow Kanyon" and claimed he invented it while camping in Cow Canyon, Eastern Oregon. It went like this: "For 40 people, prepare 25 pounds of spuds, 4 pounds of onions, 1½ pounds of cheese, 8 eggs, 6 pounds of bacon, ¼ pound of butter, and one large can of milk. Boil and mash spuds. Grind bacon and fry with onions. Melt cheese. Add bacon, onions, cheese, eggs, butter and milk to the mashed potatoes and bake." This dish never failed to bring praise to its creator, and surprisingly it did taste much better than it sounds.

Depression Cake

MICHAEL KENNEDY AND EDWARD B. REYNOLDS

This is from the Far West Eats regional essay. It is the story of the creation of Depression Cake, an eggless, butterless concoction born out of necessity by a young woman preparing for a July 4 "picnic, rodeo, and general get-together."

Eggs! She had none. The few hens she possessed were either burdened with the responsibility of baby chicks, or setting on eggs, dispositions ruined and cross-eyed with chagrin over confinement and hot weather.

Butter and milk! Ye Gods! Old Stubby had taken a leave of absence and followed a herd of whitefaces that were grazing over the West Fork, having observed a fine gentleman among them who appealed to her fickle heart. Ethel must remember to have Nick go after her right after the Fourth.

Ethel looked at the pan of raisins stewing on the stove. An idea entered her mind: it was worth trying, and she could experiment on her husband and brother. Necessity was the mother of invention.

When the raisins had partially cooled, she carefully measured a cup of the juice and poured them into a mixing bowl, adding a teaspoon of soda, a half a teaspoonful of cinnamon and nutmeg, a pinch of cloves, ginger and allspice. A heaping tablespoon of bacon drippings went next, and she watched the mixture bubble and froth, wondering if the stuff would explode. She sifted one and three fourths cups of common flour and a cup of sugar, a pinch of salt and a teaspoonful of baking powder, added them to the volcanic mass in her mixing bowl. After a moment of hesitation, she put in a teaspoonful of flavoring. What was it? A cake or pudding? She did not know.

After greasing and flouring a loaf cake tin, she spread the batter in the pan. And closing her eyes, prayed fervently as she closed the oven door. Spices—no odor from the old world ever smelled more delicious. The cake—for by all the Gods it was a cake—had risen, round, light, brown, shrinking away from the pan, proclaiming to the world that it was sufficiently baked.

No modern chef ever carried a brainchild more carefully or more proudly than Ethel when she placed the cake to cool. Her creation appeared beautiful, but how would it taste?

When the men came in weary and hungry from work, they were greeted at the door with the odor of that cake, which held the place of honor in the center of the table.

"How?" asked the man of the house, well aware of the lack of provisions.

"Eat it first," answered Ethel. "I'm afraid to talk."

After the cake had been eaten to the last crumb, the brother inquired cautiously, "Gosh, Ethel. Do you reckon you can do it again?"

Ethel nodded assent. The Fourth of July celebration was a success, and that's how "Depression Cake" came into being.

Oregon Blue Ruin

ANDREW SHERBERT

E ven before 1844—and Oregon did not become a state until 1859—
Oregonians were game to test the ability of their stomachs to
handle alcoholic drinks of strange and ferocious character. In 1844 one
James Conner, with the help of one Dick McCrary and one Hi Straight,
set up a makeshift distillery consisting of a large kettle with a metal
horn condenser. The finished liquor was drawn off through a wooden
spigot and was guaranteed lethal by its enterprising makers who called
it "blue ruin." The stuff was made from shorts, wheat, and black-strap
molasses and the first snifter was said to glaze the eye, palsy the hand,
and confuse the feet of the intrepid drinker.

In Portland, Oregon, prototypes of the early take-a-chance drinker
have persisted ever since, coming to full flower during the prohibition
era, when sterling citizens drank bath-tub gin, and many of the not so
sterling citizens courted the blind staggers imbibing potations founded
on wood alcohol, or redistilled radiator anti-freeze. A type of drinker
evolved from the "noble experiment" was the "canned heat" addict. These
drinkers were many—usually a tatterdemalion lot who "cooked" the alcohol from the soapy vehicle in which it came, at "jungle" fires on the river's
edge beneath Portland's Burnside, Morrison, Madison, or "Steel" bridges.
To lend variety and vary the monotony of their drinking bouts, the
"canned heaters" frequently swung to denatured alcohol for a jolt. Denatured alcohol (industrial alcohol) was ethyl, or grain alcohol tinctured
with a poisonous ingredient rendering it unfit for beverage purposes, or
so it was intended, but this deterred the canned heater not at all. He
gulped it down with a "here's how" and thumbed his nose at the sinister

skull and cross-bones on the bottle. In the waning days of prohibition an unethical Portland druggist dispensed one day a particularly poisonous mess of alcohol to his "skid-road" clientele and, tough as they were, they couldn't take it. That day, and the day or two following, some thirty sorry victims found release from mortal agony on cool marble slabs at the city morgue; and the druggist went to the penitentiary for manslaughter.

Coming up to the present, a new genus of drinker takes a bow. He is known as the "wine-o," the appellation arising from the fact that he keeps in a continual state of inebriation through imbibing "fortified" wine. Fortified wine, if properly used, is a grateful and salutary beverage. The vintners intend, and sane usage demands, that these types of wine be drunk in moderation. They are heavy wines to be served sparingly with meat or dessert courses, and are termed "fortified" because they are "natural" wines whose low alcohol content has been elevated eight or ten percent by the addition of brandy, cognac, or rectified spirits. Abundance of wine fruits and berries, competition, and relatively low tax rates combine to place these wines on the retail market at extremely low prices, two-bits being the current price asked for a pint of the sort of wine the wine-o goes for.

The wine-o doubtless would prefer whiskey to wine, but the state of Oregon controls the price and sale of hard liquors and a pint bottle of even the poorest whiskey stocked by the state liquor stores is far beyond reach of the wine-o, who toils not, neither does he spin, nor does he clutter any industrial pay-roll. Beer joints are not more than a spit and jump apart in Portland, but beer—considering the amount necessary to give the wine-o the alcoholic shock required to bring him to a state of physical and mental numbness—is expensive even at ten cents a glass.

Fortified wine addicts are gregarious sots who run in cliques or packs. Members of the clan comb Portland streets between Third Street and the river at all hours of the day and night, "mooching" nickels from soft passersby with a plaintive "spare a nickel for a cuppa cawfee?" It disturbs a mooching wine-o not at all to be told that he has a breath like the dreggy bottom of a wine vat and that you just KNOW he intends to apply your nickel on a mickey of wine. He doesn't bother to deny the accusation but, giving you a bleary grin, repeats his request, "just a measly nickel for a cuppa cawfee." When he gets hold of a nickel he quickly rejoins his mooching comrades and their nickels are pooled and a bottle purchased, whereupon the group shambles up the street to drink furtively in a shadowy doorway.

Promising to make the wine-o and "blue ruin" drinker look like a sissy, a new type of tippler now tops all predecessors in drinking bravado, according to Portland police. His drink is a mixture of gasoline and evaporated milk, and he gets just as "high" on this automotive high-ball as does the wealthy nabob on Portland Heights with tall, cool, horses necks made of Haig and Haig. Theory is that the evaporated milk forms a temporary protective lining for the stomach while the gasoline, which after all is a chemical step-brother to the potent though highly respectable grain alcohol, volatilizes and permeates the tissues bringing on the same sensory reaction one gets from drinking Four (or more) Roses. It would seem that to smoke while on a milk and gasoline bender would be fraught with more or less danger. And might not an addict explode of spontaneous combustion as did a gin-soaked character in Dickens' *Bleak House*? The drink is too new to have gathered a name like the "blue ruin" of early Oregon, or the "Jick" of a decade ago. A name suggested, and here given gratis, is "Milkoline"—and may its drinkers get more miles to the gallon.

THE
SOUTHWEST EATS

ARIZONA—*responsible for the region*

NEW MEXICO

OKLAHOMA

TEXAS

SOUTHERN CALIFORNIA

The Southwest

This is the region that has changed the most. At the time of *America Eats* Arizona had been a state for less than thirty years and there were still many people in the Southwest who remembered the frontier days. Migration to the Southwest, without air conditioning, was on a small scale, except for Los Angeles. There were only two decades between 1870 and 1940 when the population of Los Angeles did not increase by at least 25 percent and some decades as much as 50 percent. According to the 1940 census 1,496,792 people lived in Los Angeles, and the speed limit in both business and residential areas was 25 miles per hour. The overwhelming majority of the population was not born there and the majority of the transplants came from the Midwest. The WPA Guide Book to Los Angeles said, "People who have lived here a dozen years are likely to regard themselves as old timers." But the first two essays show a Los Angeles not that different from today. Not surprising for a city of people reinventing themselves, Los Angeles had an obsession for what is new and what is hip. Today both geographically and demographically much larger, it is still that way.

At the time of *America Eats* the Southwest had its own cuisine. It was the only place in America with Mexican food, but it was a uniquely American Chicano variation of the food known in Mexico as Norteño, the food of the northern Mexican states. At the time of *America Eats* such food was not widespread because tortillas were made at home by women through a laborious process that began with hand-grinding corn on stones. In the 1940s and '50s, one of the first widespread uses of small gas engines and electric motors was to power wet grain grinders for making the corn dough for tortillas. Even then the tortilla was patted into shape by hand or fashioned on a hand press. Tortilla-making machines were not developed until the 1960s, with the result of inferior tortillas. But because of these machines food such as tacos became well known first among the non-Spanish population of the Southwest and then across the country.

Iowa Picnic in Los Angeles

JOHN MOSTE

Back in his native state, the average Iowan takes his picnics in stride. But once he has moved to the shores of the Pacific, he falls easy victim to that greatest of all western lures—the southern California picnic. For although most state societies in southern California hold one annual picnic, the Iowans hold two—a summer and a winter picnic. In addition to these festivities, they also hold a dinner on December 28 (unless it falls on a Sunday) to commemorate their native state's admission to the Union. This dinner takes place at some Los Angeles hotel.

The Iowa winter picnic, which occurs on the last Saturday in February, is staged at Lincoln Park, Mission Road and Alhambra Avenue, in the eastern part of Los Angeles. About fifteen of the park's forty-six acres—a thickly carpeted greensward lying between the lake and the conservatory—are used as the picnic grounds.

Here a considerable number of benches and tables are set up for the purpose, but as a rule these are insufficient in number to accommodate the usually heavy attendance, with the result that countless picnickers serve their lunches on robes and blankets spread upon the lawn. Attendance at this seasonal outing, according to C. H. Parsons, secretary of the Iowa State Association, has amounted to no less than 150,000 on occasions before the depression cut down the hegira of Iowans to the Golden State.

The Iowa summer picnic is held in the 10.12-acre Bixby Park, Long Beach. This park faces Ocean Boulevard at Cherry Street, and its spreading cypresses and stately eucalyptus trees are so huge and its lawns so inviting that it is considered one of the most beautiful parks in southern California. An all-time high of 100,000 attendants was claimed for the Iowa summer picnic in 1929.

Both picnics, following a practice established long ago within the borders of the state "where the tall corn grows," are much alike in their general characteristics. And lest old acquaintances be forgot—or fail to be renewed—stakes topped with placards, naming the various Iowa counties, are placed here and there about the picnic grounds to indicate where the respective groups from "back home" are forgathering. This enables many individuals and families to quickly find or relocate friends and relatives.

Bright and early on either day of these gala occasions, there is an unwonted stir in all Iowa households—an eager lift and buoyancy that is not altogether due to California's clear-blue skies and sun-kissed landscapes. There is cheerfulness, expectancy—perhaps it's the bright and radiant countenances of all—that bespeak an event out of the ordinary. For reflected in this spirit of eager anticipation there are to be found old and fond memories of other delightful occasions—of friendly intercourse, of sweetness in the cup, of gustatory delights shared together over savory viands done to a brown turn, the likes of which only "mother used to make."

Well before the sun reaches the zenith, thousands of Iowa picnickers filter into the park. By auto, streetcar, bicycle, and on foot, they come from city, town, and hamlet. Waving banners, blaring bands, ballyhoo—this is the scene; everyone is gaily bedecked and hospitable. A picnic indeed: It's more than that, really—it's an Iowa picnic; and the moment you enter the park you begin to feel something of that infectious spirit of goodfellowship which is but one of the many delightful characteristics of this gay and colorful occasion.

There are greetings and the resounding laughter and the shouts of carefree youngsters; then yarns—those famous tall tales—are swapped by the oldsters. But the climax is reached when countless baskets, boxes, and hampers disclose their sundry dishes. Chicken fried, baked, and stewed; hams boiled and baked; great roasts of beef; breads and buns and biscuits in large variety; deep bowls of salad—potato salad especially made from recipes handed down from past generations—together with pickles galore: mustard, sweet, dill, and homemade bread-and-butter pickles that lend color and add zest to the appetite. No, sir, one can't go wrong—dietetically speaking—in attending an Iowa picnic feast.

Each item of food, to be sure, has been carefully prepared and seasoned, for Iowa cooks are highly competitive when it comes to displaying their skill in picnic cookery. Most of the recipes are time-tested by generations of these Midwestern folk, but occasionally some one more adventurous than the others will experiment with spices and condiments alien to Iowa.

At length, after everyone has had his fill, the coffee and cakes are served. There are plain and fancy cakes, devil's food and angel food cakes, walnut, spice, and banana cakes. And lest cake alone should fail to appease the crowd's sweet tooth, there are all kinds of pies. These fall into three classifications: Open face, crisscross, and "hunter's case," their tasty fillings limited only by the whims of their makers. These consist of pumpkin, gooseberry, loganberry, lemon, cream, banana, and cherry.

Following the repast, the picnickers stroll away to engage in one activity or another; some resume their interested chats, many spend their time visiting, while others make their way to the speakers' stand to take part in the afternoon program. Here C. H. Parsons, before introducing the speaker of the day, goes through the ritual of detailing his experiences as a regular attendant of every Iowa picnic since the first one was held in the Raymond Hills of Pasadena in 1900. Further entertainment for the picnickers is provided by bands, singers, and cowboy minstrels.

Later on, when the first shadows of evening begin to fall across the greensward, hampers and other food containers are again brought forth for one last snack before the picnickers call it a glorious day and wend their way homeward.

Approved by C. H. Parsons, Secy. Iowa State Assoc., 12-31-41

Food à la Concentrate
in Los Angeles

DON DOLAN

There was a day when every diet-conscious person chanted "calories." . . . "Ya gotta watch your calories." Today the litany is "vitamins and minerals," a creed gaining more adherents every day. In the robust manner in which Americans accept the new, a principle of real dietary value has ballooned into that fabled panacea, the Elixir of Life.

Nowhere is this so evident as in the Los Angeles area, the most important center for all Health Food activity.

From here, thirty firms grind and pack capsules and tablets of pulverized vegetable mixtures, and ship these out in a constant stream to treat the ungastronomic tongues of the nation. Here numerous retail stores, unofficial consultants on your bodily needs, greet you with the hushed cheer of a mortician, help you to select your herb tea, your nonsugar candies, your powdered vegetable mixture most suited to your particular form of astigmatism or gout or midafternoon slump. Here many restaurants cater to the intent determination of the teeming dietists, all of whom have become health authorities from a two-week wishful reading of advertising pamphlets.

Despite the exaggerated fervor in search of the optimum in food content, much good already has developed. A thiamin (Vitamin B_1) deficiency in the body results in nervousness, and people with no pep can not put forth their best efforts in national defense. It was found that our bread lacks the thiamin it should contain, because the refining of the flour milled out this priceless ingredient. Bakers now offer us "enriched" bread: loaves to which have been added a proper proportion of chemically produced thiamin. So that even though, in the traditional humorless manner of American big business, artificial Vitamin B_1 must be added to replace the natural Vitamin B_1 which had once been there, still the result is an improvement in national diet.

Knowledge that foods could satisfy the appetite without satisfying the bodily needs took place long ago in the British Navy. Seamen got a sufficient quota of salt pork and bully beef and potatoes and hardtack—but they still developed scurvy. The addition of lime juice to their diet prevented this, leaving these "limeys" more alert. The principle had been proved: foods can lack oomph.

Chicago Dr. J. W. Wigelsworth in 1920 got tired of preaching to his patients: "Eat more vegetables—lots and lots of them." They would agree that vegetables probably were good for them, but they would not bother to eat them. So the doctor started some experiments, to the dismay of the clean-kitchen instincts of his household. For days he kept the oven full of chopped vegetables. Then, when the water content had evaporated, he laboriously mashed the residues with mortar and pestle. The result was something pretty tasteless and lacking in that fine eye appeal; but a spoonful of it was the equivalent of a bale of the raw product. Of course, eaten even with a liberal sluicing of water, it went down hard and tended to gag. But when poked into a gelatin capsule, the doctor's patients would swallow it faithfully. After all, they were accustomed to having their medicines in pellets. And the stuff helped them: Through the course of his clinical experiments, Dr. Wigelsworth evolved the formulae for several combinations of vegetables which seemed particularly effective in the treatment of particular maladies of his patients.

With more knowledge of engineering and promotion, his brother constructed an arrangement of ovens by which the drying-out process could be accomplished for a lot of vegetables at once. The result was the Anabolic Food Products, Inc., with a factory in Glendale and sales offices in Los Angeles, Chicago, and New York.

The possible combinations of foods applicable to specific human ills have grown to number forty-three items that are now prepared and marketed by Anabolic. Aware of the flagrant misuse to which any remedy often is put, Anabolic furnishes its preparations only through the medical profession, acting somewhat in the capacity of a doctor to doctors.

Would you like a pretty pill of endive, Cape Cod cranberries, Irish kelp, and garlic: Anabolic probably has it. Of course, it will not look like anything but a capsule of brown powder, but it has guts. When did an eye for nutrition ever have to be also the lyric eye of a Brillat-Savarin?

Beneath the professional reticence common in the field of medicine, one gathers that Anabolic sees too much enthusiasm with too little common sense of health applied in the general field of health foods.

Not long since, an eastern doctor stopped at a Central Market stand selling vegetable juice extractors. In the pure whine of a barker, the clinically clad attendant "proved" that his juicer was best, because "See this vegetable? See the vitamins crawling all over the skin? Put through an ordinary juicer, all these vitamins are thrown away. I have seen it. Now watch! When I put it in this juicer, all the vitamins go right into the juice, where you have them to drink to get healthy and young again."

In the health-food restaurants, tables are supplied with nothing as ruinous as sugar, salt, pepper. There will be a bowl of raw sugar, which looks like brown sugar caught in the damp. The two shakers will contain 1) alfalfa dust, and 2) sodium glutaurate, which gives color to your food. A popular dish is a vegetable salad sprayed with a dressing of mixed lemon juice and honey. A wheat-germ porridge is another favorite. This being southern California, there will be a health version of a Spanish omelet. For dessert, you may have your choice of carrot ice cream or ice cream with pollenless honey. You will drink a soy concoction which looks like boiled-down roily water off a red clay-bottomed brook—and tastes like just plain mud—and probably have a side order of soy beans prepared in parched form.

These restaurants are almost all cafeterias. One reason for this may be so that the diner can select what dishes he wants so as to balance his own meals unless it is that he would not possibly choose such dishes by their truthfully unappetizing names, so that they must be seen to be believed and picked. Another reason probably is that steamable style is more informal, promotes more friendliness among the patrons, most of whom are there partially to find a group sympathetic to their own habits of eating and vitamin-chart existence.

The health-food cult has developed a language all its own. Until you are initiated into the mysteries of the mineral and the vitamin, you are apt to blink at a restaurant listing its offerings as "live" or "raw" foods. Involved words to describe other phases of the field are built up from obscure Greek or Latin roots, suggesting the mythology from which they spring.

But, filtering out the candor from the cant, there emerge hygienic truths in the health-food business. And nutritional satisfaction need not mean gustatory grief. Much food value that had been discarded from carelessness now begins to make an appearance in the dishes we eat; and tastes lose no pleasure from joining hands with dietary satisfaction. Food specialists today are giving serious consideration to the advantage of dehydration to reduce awkward bulk in both army rations and civilian fare.

Los Angeles! Where religion turns into thousands of obscure cults; where by street dress men and women merge into a common sex; and where the fine art of eating becomes a pseudo scientific search for a lost vitality hidden in the juice of a raw carrot.

Sources: Dr. Fowler, Anabolic Food Products, Inc., Glendale, California, and personal observation.

A Los Angeles Sandwich Called a Taco

DON DOLAN

Naturally, the Mexican influence pervades southern California sandwiches. Given the Mexican *tortilla*—the plate-sized wafer of powdered corn—along with beans and chili, and you have the ingredients for a sandwich called a *taco*: a *tortilla* fluttered through hot grease, folded around shrimp, sausage, and chili stew, garnished with shredded lettuces and grated cheese. A finger-size *taco* from Olvera Street bears the baby name of *taquito*.

Another variety, the *tostadita*, results when a small *tortilla* is toasted deep brown, edges crimped in a ridge around the filling, arranged on the plate with shredded lettuce and sliced radishes, and served steaming hot.

Chalupa means a canoe for two . . . soft night—rippling water—a man and a maid. But even love feels the pangs of hunger, so a *chalupa* becomes a curled-edge *tortilla* fresh from sizzling fat, filled with beans, avocado, green chili, minced onions, chili stew, and sprayed with a piquant tomato sauce. Romance thrives on that.

The *burrito*, simplest Mexican sandwich, calls for a *tortilla* wrapped like a jelly roll around beans. Or, more elaborately, it takes the form of a club sandwich filled with avocado and the white meat of chicken.

Los Angeles—American edition—retains the art of the sandwich; in so doing, it is guilty on at least three counts of providing the piece de resistance of an eat-and-run meal.

Of these, two came from restaurateur De Forest, whose colorful business name evolved from the jests of customers. It metamorphosed from "T. N. De Forest" through "Female Tommy" to "Texas Female Tommy's Ptomaine Tabernacle," whence it crystallized into the unforgettable "Ptomaine Tommy's."

"Size" was the happy thought born of hunger in Ptomaine Tommy. Proprietor of a lunch wagon in 1915, on the North Broadway fringe of Mexican town, he of necessity provided his own board—and became very tired tasting the few available dishes. In a need of pure experiment he strewed chili and beans over a hamburger steak, and covered the whole with chopped onions.

Curious customers saw it, asked for it, liked it, and then demanded it. They would order, from the degree of their hunger, according to how big a cake they wished of the ground beef which forms the basis of the dish. Thus, "hamburger size" or "steak size." The name generally settled to "size," with the larger version becoming an "oversize," and the Ptomaine Tommy sprinkling of chopped onions on it, called a "shower." "Size" remains the chef-d'oeuvre of the new restaurant to which it gave birth, and has been widely copied.

Trial and error also produced the Ptomaine Tommy specialty of "Egg Royal Decorated." A butter-fried mixture of egg and ground beef—seemingly known as Denver or Western sandwich—is "decorated" with chili beans.

From Los Angeles comes the "French-dipped" sandwich, a quick lunch developed to satisfy the appetites of hard-working factory hands. Two Italian brothers named Martin, who in 1921 operated a day-and-night sawdust-floored delicatessen-counter restaurant under the French name of "Philippe's," were the creators. From an *au jus* base they concocted a sauce from a secret Philippe formula. Generous slices of good roast meat are spread on half a fresh-baked French (longish, crusty) roll, the cover half being dipped liberally in the sauce.

The French-dip sandwich has spread to lunchrooms all over the country, gustatory proof of its appeal; and to the original Philippe's—still in its lowly warehouse district home—comes a continuous and popular pilgrimage of sandwich connoisseurs.

CONSTRUCTION WORKERS EATING LUNCH AT THE SHASTA DAM. SHASTA COUNTY, CALIFORNIA. (PHOTOGRAPH BY RUSSELL LEE)

A California Grunion Fry

CHARLES J. SULLIVAN

California grunion, a specific species known in science as Leuresthes tenuis, *are sardine-sized silver fish. At mating*

time the females come up on the beach and dig their tails into
the sand to lay their eggs. A male then curls around the female
to deposit his sperm. The grunion eggs remain hidden in the
sand until the eggs hatch at high tide and the young grunion
are washed out to sea.

Among California's "unusuals" is the Grunion Fry, an annual fishing festival peculiar to the beaches of the Golden State—a hilarious sport and picnic in which no tackle of any kind is used, and each inning lasts less than thirty seconds. Nevertheless, the "hunt" is a strenuous one during this fleeting interval.

The grunion itself, 3 to 6 inches in length, is a succulent relative of the smelt, but differing from the species and other fish in the manner of its spawning—a natural phenomenon which prompts thousands of men, women, and children to congregate at California's beaches on certain specified nights of each year to feast upon these clever, but luckless little fellows. That they make a tasty morsel goes without saying. Even the epicureans agree that there are few sea foods equal to them when fried in deep fat on the ocean beach soon after they are caught.

It is a motley gathering of determined souls who find their way to the scene of these grunion hunts, and they arrive in various stages of dress and dishabille—for grunion wait for no man!—some in beach pajamas or shorts, many in gay swimsuits, while others, drawn by idle curiosity, incongruously appear in their spotless evening clothes. Seen in the half-light of moon and stars—gathered around their driftwood fires, or parading the shadowy sands like sentinels on watch against an invading host—here is a strange carnival of sport!

One can't be sure about these silvery little fellows—there is no exact science available to save the fisherman time and patience; and even though the grunion run is prognosticated by experts in coast newspapers, or over the radio, or sometimes even by the technically thorough weatherman—their scheduled appearance often is a matter of uncertainty.

The grunion—as learned from observation covering a long period of years—do their courting out at sea on the first night of the maximum high tide which occurs between March and August. Then, on the second, third, and fourth nights, literally millions of these tiny fish mount the highest comber and ride gaily landward. The same instinct which leads them to select the highest wave for a safe landing, also guides them from the threatening reefs and dangerous shores to the more pacific beaches of democratic Santa Monica, Redondo, Long Beach, or exclusive Malibu. As each great grunion-laden wave booms upon the sand, the males—peculiarly upright in the water—come "dancing in on their tails" a half second ahead of their consorts. Then, at the proper instant, the brides arrive and immediately wriggle into the sand where they deposit their eggs. The grooms immediately squirm over the deposits, fertilizing the eggs, whereupon each couple, with surprising agility, begins wriggling back into the ebbing backwash—the whole procedure consummating less than half a minute.

During this half minute, the long stretch of beach becomes a scene of feverish activity. This is the moment for which everyone has been waiting, and the word spreads quickly. "Grunion! The grunion are running!" The question that has been uppermost in the minds of everyone now has been answered. As each wave deposits numberless thousands of the wriggling, silvery creatures upon the sand, the waiting hosts of excited fishermen, not to be denied, swoop upon them, filling pails, pockets, hats, shirt-fronts—in fact, any available receptacle which might serve as a container while their nimble fingers do their work. The State Fish and Game Commission does not permit the use of gunny-sacks, shovels, box-nets, or other contrivances as was formerly the case; all grunion, the law now reads, must be caught with the bare hands. Therefore the "catch" calls for a certain amount of nimbleness and skill, for the tiny fish are slippery; although thousands of the grunion are caught, many more thousands escape to find their way back into the briny deep.

When the run is over, weary but exultant fishermen carry their catch further back upon the beach where the cooks and fire-watchers take charge. Having set things in order during this foray on the grunion—tending kettles of deep fat, preparing accompanying side-dishes and watching over refreshing beverages—they now quickly prepare the fish and drop them into the sizzling fat. Soon the zestful aroma of golden-crisp grunion fills the air. Afterwards, if there are any grunion left, they will probably constitute tomorrow's appetizing breakfast for the fishermen, or for those who did not attend the gala catch.

What is the scientific explanation of the grunion run? No one seems to know, much less care, and authorities on marine life—outside their knowledge of the times and conditions of these mating and spawning periods—are rather vague on the subject. However, it is no secret that back at the water's edge, a vast number of eggs are left buried in the sand despite the fate which overtakes so many of the parent grunion, and that in a short time the progeny comes to life, rides out to sea on an ebbing tide, and so lives to repeat the performance of its forebears the following year.

La Merienda in New Mexico

A delightful custom that prevails in rural sections of New Mexico is a lunch eaten in the middle of the afternoon at the scene of whatever task is being performed. For the most part, the lunch consists of the same dishes that made up the noon meal; but under the open sky everyday dishes take on added interest, especially when eaten with coffee brewed on the spot.

It is a welcome interlude, when the slanting sun rides in the west, to lay down sickle or hoe for the grateful shade of a tree or the bank of an arroyo. The younger members of the family seem to know when *la merienda* is due, and as the hour approaches cast anxious eyes in the direction from which the mother and the sisters and younger brothers will come. When they are seen, the young workers are first to slacken hold on hoe or whatever implement they are wielding and hasten to meet the mother who comes with a dishpan filled with jars and dishes deftly balanced on her head. Her erect figure is heightened by the burden she holds securely with one hand and the snow-white cloth that tops it and protects it from the summer dust.

A plume of smoke guides her to where the husband has selected a spot for *la merienda*, and soon water is placed in a pot and put over raked out coals to boil. The reclining husband and father watches his wife as she brings forth the various bowls and jars which contain the lunch. The cloth that covered them now serves as spread on which the meal is laid.

The beans served at noon have undergone a slight change and are now *frijoles refritos* (fried beans), which makes them carried more easily and in no way detracts from their delectable flavor; instead, it adds. Cold tortillas and oven-baked bread are served with roast ribs of *cabrito* (kid) as well as other portions of this savory meat. Perhaps a cheese is added, with a jar of homemade jelly or jam to eat with it. Cold, boiled goat's milk, with a little salt added for flavor, has been brought for the children; and for dessert there is pumpkin pie, still warm—not the pumpkin pie that is known elsewhere in America, but a flat pastry with a line of sweet pumpkin showing between two contrastingly thick crusts and known as *pastel de raymta* (line pie). This is in humorous allusion to the thin strip of filling showing between the crusts.

No sooner is the meal ready than all fall to with appetites sharpened by work in the open air. The man eats more slowly while his eyes wander over the work done and notes what remains to be done. His wife follows with hers, but says nothing until he directs her attention with his pointing finger, then dutifully praises what has been accomplished. Then she says: "Gabriel died an hour before we set out. Did you not hear the bell tolling?" "*Sí,*" he answers; "God rest his soul. I knew it must have been Gabriel; no one else was ill."

She pours another cup of coffee as he rolls cigarettes for both of them. The children have rushed away to seize a few minutes' play, each with a piece of jam-spread cheese clutched in his hand. The oldest boy remains with his parents, joining in the talk about tomorrow's work. He is getting to be a man now and is conscious of his approaching responsibilities. His father will be going away in the fall to work in the sheep camps in Wyoming—adding thus to the family income—and the boy will be entrusted with the work of gathering in the crops.

The conversation comes to a halt as the father stands and calls to the children playing by the little stream. Work must be resumed. *La merienda* is over. The oldest girl returns with the younger ones in tow, then helps her mother put away the empty dishes, after which they return to the house.

Choctaw Indian Dishes

PETER J. HUDSON, CHOCTAW

The Choctaw were originally from Louisiana, Mississippi, and Alabama, but in the 1830s a large number were forced to relocate to Oklahoma. A peaceful people, they played a form of stickball as a substitute for warfare. Since 2002 they have prospered as casino operators.

The process of preparing corn for *Tash-labona* and *Ta-fula* is about the same.

For *Tash-labona*, soak the corn for a short time or until the hull is loosened, and then beat it in a mortar until the hull has slipped off, leaving the grain of corn as whole as possible. Then take the corn out and fan it in a basket (*ufko*) to separate the hulls from the grain of corn. This basket, or *ufko*, is made of stripped cane. It is about 3 feet long and 18 inches wide. One half of this basket is flat, having no sides, but starting from the center of the length, sides gradually rise from a fraction of an inch to five inches, one end being five inches in height. The corn is fanned and the grains all go to the end with the sides while the hulls are blown off the flat end. After the hulls are all disposed of, put the corn in a kettle with lots of water, salt and pieces of fresh pork and boil it down until it is thick. When it is done you have *Tash-labona*, which is very rich. Don't eat too much *Tash-labona*, as it will make you sick.

With *Ta-fula*, the same process is followed as with *Tash-labona*, only the corn is beaten until the grains of corn are broken into three or four pieces, then take it out into the basket and separate the hulls from the grains. It can then be cooked with beans, with wood ashes or in any other way you wish. Meat is not cooked with *Ta-fula*. Use plenty of water and boil it down until there is a lot of juice. You can eat all the *Ta-fula* you want as it contains no grease.

For Bread or *Banaha* or, in English, Shuck Bread, soak the corn a long time, maybe all night, then beat it in a mortar until the hulls are off and then put in the basket and separate the hulls from the grains, after which put it back in the mortar and beat it into meal. Then sift it. That meal is as fine as wheat flour. Of course there will be some grits left that cannot go through the sieve.

In making Sour Bread, the grits are mixed with the dough. The dough is made the night before and allowed to sour and then it is cooked.

In making *Banaha* the meal is made into dough and then rolled out into lengths of Hot Tamales but about four or five times bigger around than Hot Tamales, and each one covered with corn shucks and tied in the middle with a corn shuck string. The middle is smaller than the ends when tied up. It is then boiled in water until done and the shucks taken off when ready to eat. When *Banaha* is to be carried on a trip the shucks should be left on.

Another bread is made with this meal by wrapping the dough in green fodder and boiling. It is very fine. Sometimes the hulls of peas are burned and the ashes put in this dough, which makes it a brownish color.

Walakshi is another Choctaw dish made on special occasions. Wild grapes are gathered in the fall and put away on stem to dry to be used when wanted. To cook, the grapes are boiled and then strained through a sack, only the juice being used. Then dumplings are made of the corn flour described above and dropped in the grape juice and cooked until done. Of course more or less grape juice is absorbed by the dumpling and the remainder of the juice is thickened. *Walakshi* was always furnished by the bride's relatives at weddings, while the bridegroom's relatives furnished the venison.

Bota-Kapvasa is a cold meal made of parched corn. The grains of corn are poured into a kettle; a fire is built under it and hot ashes are poured in the kettle with the corn. The corn is stirred continually until it is parched brown and then it is taken out and put in the basket described above to be fanned, the ashes being separated from the corn. Then the parched corn is put into the mortar and the hulls loosened from the grain of corn and then it is put back in the basket again to be fanned, separating the hulls from the grain of corn. Then it is again put in the mortar and pounded until it becomes a fine meal. This is *Bota-Kapvasa* and is very nourishing. The Indian hunters and warriors used to take a small sack of it on their journeys and when they became hungry or thirsty, a small amount was put in a cup of water and upon drinking it, the thirst as well as the hunger was satisfied.

At roasting ear time, roasting ears were gathered, a fire in a long string was built and a pole laid over the fire, then the roasting ears were laid against the pole in front of the fire and the ears turned every few minutes so that they will cook evenly and also to keep them from burning. When they are all cooked, the corn is shelled from the ear and dried in the sun, and then sacked and put away for winter use. It is cooked in water and because it swells a great deal, a little corn will make a big meal. It is good for invalids.

In making Choctaw dishes, flint corn is preferable, but if flint corn cannot be obtained any corn can be used. Horses will not eat flint corn. Flint corn is called by the Choctaws *Tanchi Hlimimpa*. It is the only kind of corn the Choctaw Indians in Mississippi had when the white people found them.

In making Hickory *Ta-fulla*, the hickory nuts are gathered and put in a sack over the fire place to dry for a month at least. Then when ready to make Hickory *Ta-fulla*, the nuts are cracked real fine, shells and kernels together, then put in a sack and water poured over the nuts to drain. After this water is drained, it looks like milk. This hickory nut water is then poured into the *Ta-fulla* and cooked. This makes a very rich dish.

When pumpkins are gathered in the fall, they are peeled and cut into narrow strips and dried for winter use.

Funeral Cry Feast of the Choctaws

O ne of the most ancient customs of the Choctaw Indians and one that is to some extent followed to this day, is the funeral cry. When a member of the family dies, he is quietly buried with some or all of his personal belongings, at which time the stoicism of the Indian is apparent for it is not often that any tears are shed at the burial service.

On the day of the burial the head of the family cuts and trims nicely twenty-eight little sticks, which he lays up in the cracks of the log cabin as representing the twenty-eight days of the moon month. Every morning he takes down one of these sticks until there are seven remaining, then he hands out invitations to his kinsmen and friends to come to the funeral cry, which is to be on the day the last stick is taken down. The kinsmen and guests are required to bring with them a specific amount of foods or provisions. One is allotted so much meal, another so much flour, and another so much beef, etc. This request is strictly complied with.

The congregation of relatives, friends, and even the strangers meet at the grave or near the grave of the late deceased, where a circular place has been cleaned of all shrubs and grass, in the midst of which a table is spread for the immediate family. At intervals around this center table are tables arranged for all other kinsmen and still outside of these are tables for friends and visitors.

Before the feast is spread, some relative of the deceased rises and begins an oration, telling of the good qualities of the deceased, of his courage and prowess, and as he proceeds he grows more and more eloquent and impassioned. When the cry starts then begins a copious flow of tears, something of which the Indian is very sparing, accompanied by low wailing and moaning that forces the onlooker to join in the cry.

When the cry has gone on for some time the feast is spread, and certain ones of the deceased's relatives are appointed to wait upon the inner table and others are selected to wait on the other tables.

The alternate ceremony of feasting, crying and wailing is kept up for two or three days. The intrusion and curiosity of the white people has tended to lessen the frequency and publicity of the funeral cry as well as many other ancient customs and ceremonies of the Choctaw Indians. Many people regard the funeral cry of the Indian as a relic of barbarism, but really it is like a ceremony of some of the Christian denominations except that the latter confine themselves to fasting and prayers for the dead, leaving off the feasting and wailing.

If it is not convenient, or if weather conditions are not such that the cry can be held at the grave of the deceased, the relatives and friends go to the church, where the feast is spread and candles are lighted around, which they assemble in prayer and weeping; dividing their time between the candles and the festive board and local oratory.

Ref: *Indians & Pioneers*, Vol. 78, pp. 131–133 [a collection of interviews obtained by the Okla. WPA].

Arizona Out-of-Doors Cookery

EDWARD PARRISH WARE

Edward Parrish Ware was born in Harrisburg, Pennsylvania, in 1884 but lived most of his life in Prescott, Arizona. He was a prolific author of detective stories in the 1920s, '30s, and '40s for such magazines as Real Detective Tales and Mystery Stories, Flynn's Weekly Detective Fiction, Thrilling Detective, *and* Detective Action Stories. *He also wrote Westerns for such magazines as* West, The Frontier, *and* Zane Grey's Western Magazine.

The old-timers and the Indians of the Southwest usually had good luck with out-of-doors cooking. They knew that it required skillful fingers and good judgment to construct a satisfactory cooking-fire. They knew that the spot selected should be cleared of all grass, leaves, twigs, and should be of considerable circumference. They knew better than to build a cooking-fire against a down log or the trunk of a tree, and the soil selected would be of gravel or clay if such could be had.

They knew, too, that evergreen wood—cedar, piñon, spruce—is a soft wood and good for kindling, but unfit for a lasting fire. Evergreen wood burns too quickly. Wood from leaf-bearing trees—oak, ironwood, mesquite, ash—burns slowly and provides good hot coals. Many cooking-fires in the Southwest have been laid far from mountainous or hilly country where hardwood is to be had, and quick-burning woods—the pines, cottonwoods, poplar and willow—just naturally had to be used. Corncobs, dried cow-dung, sagebrush and even cactus stalks have provided fuel in the Southwest for more fires than a man could count in a hundred years. But, since good coals are always best for a cooking-fire, hard or leaf-wood is naturally favored. Steaks, game, fowl, stews, corn-on-the-cob, eggs, for instance, can be cooked perfectly only when good red coals are beneath them.

Feast of the Christening

The Feast of the Christening is a colorful ceremony of the Hopi Indians of Arizona. On the 20th day of the baby's life, up to which time the sun is not supposed to have shone upon it, the infant is washed in yucca-root water by its paternal grandmother and rubbed all over with cornmeal and the pollen of flowers. Wrapped firmly on its cradle-board, it is then carried to the edge of a mesa, with the mother in her bridal clothing and carrying an ear of corn in her hand. There, with the sun shining full upon it, the baby is touched with the ear of corn in christening, and the officiating high-priest gives it its chosen names. Then the friends of the parents, and there will always be many, also touch the infant with the ear of corn, each in turn bestowing upon the baby such names as they wish it to bear. Thus it is that a newly christened baby may have fifty or even a hundred names.

The christening over, the entire procession marches to the home of the parents for the Christening Feast. And such a feast is truly a great event. It is, in fact, a feast no Hopi family would even think of passing up.

The principal dish at the feast—and all foods are cooked out-of-doors—is mutton, roasted or stewed with corn and beans. Rich cornmeal pudding, filled with peach-seed kernels and bits of mutton-fat, baked in wrappers of cornhusks, is always a part of the feast. In season, green corn, beans, tomatoes, fruit and melons are served. While the guests eat, they make wishes for the baby and each person gives presents of food.

Piki bread in gay colors surrounds the feasters.

The Piki Bread of the Hopis

Piki bread was being made by the Hopi Indians as far back as 1540, and time has not materially changed the bread or the methods of its making. Colored corn is dried in the sun and shelled. Then the grain is broken in a rough metate, passed on to a finer stone for thorough pounding, and then into a stone bin where it is thoroughly pulverized. Then it is placed in a big earthen mixing-bowl and thinned to a batter with water.

In the meantime a big stone two feet long by one foot wide has been heating over a wood-fire. The top of this baking-stone, rubbed to a satin smoothness, is greased with mutton-tallow. When it is smoking hot the baker dips her fingers into the batter and with one swift sweep spreads a layer entirely over the hot surface, where it cooks almost instantly. With another swift jerk she removes the thin sheet from the stone and smears another over it. The sheets are rolled into cylinders about the size of an ear of corn.

No Hopi dance or christening is considered complete without a feast to follow, and the serving of piki bread is so usual it might well be called a ritual.

Superstitions About Foods

The Navajo Indians have taboos in regard to certain foods.

During the Eagle Chant, a religious ceremonial, the participants must not eat eggs of any kind, turkey, chicken, or the flesh of any fowl whatsoever.

Duck or bear meat is never at any time even tasted by the Navajos.

Food being cooked in a skillet or kettle must not be stirred with a knife.

If a knife-point is thrust first into a melon or other food, the food must not be eaten, as it carries with it the curse of lightning stroke.

During the month of July, beef cooked with corn may not be eaten, as the two foods are thought to quarrel with each other in digestion.

An Indian boy who has not attained the stature of a full brave may not eat of the entrails of any animal, such choice viands being reserved solely for the men who do the fighting. Considered strong meat, a boy's stomach would decay should he partake of it before he has reached a certain age.

Typical Cow-Boy Breakfast in Arizona

A bunch of cowboys in camp make no bones about "joshing" the range boss, the wagon boss and each other, but the cook is invariably treated with all the fine courtesy noticeable in the conduct of a bunch of freshmen toward their professors. The camp-cook doesn't have to take "sass" from anybody, and he knows it.

Dane Coolidge, in *Texas Cowboys*, tells of one such cook who was widely known to Southwestern cattlemen in general and to cow-camps in Arizona particularly.

Sam Elkins, the cook referred to, was hiding out from the Tucson law when Mr. Coolidge first made his acquaintance. It appears that Sam, according to his own story, had been set upon by a drunken bully wielding a large butcher-knife, greatly hampering Sam in his free use of the streets of Tucson while in pursuit of such happiness as might otherwise have been found. Sam retired to a wagon-yard in the outskirts of town, hoping thereby to throw the aforesaid bully off the trail, but the bully declined to be thrown. He discovered Sam—and met his own waterloo.

Armed with the butcher-knife, the bully chased Sam around and around a wagon, threatening to slit the cook's throat and then perform on his gizzard as a sort of post mortem good measure, so frightening Sam (still according to Sam) that he in desperation seized a wagon-yoke and caved the bully's skull quite some. Later, an unsympathetic judge had sentenced Sam to two weeks in jail, while giving the bully the same. So Sam, fearing that should he remain in Tucson until the bully's release he might up and take the bully's life, high-tailed it to the cactus and sagebrush rather than serve his time.

Be that as may be, Sam Elkins was cooking for a Three C's roundup crew when Mr. Coolidge first came across him. Sam was a first class camp-cook, but he had many habits which irked punchers to an irritating degree. For instance, Sam would roll into his blankets at night, set his alarm clock for four in the morning, place the clock on a dish-pan turned bottom upward beside him, then go to sleep. When that clock went off in the morning it would, reinforced by the hollow sounding-board which was in daytime an ordinary dish-pan, make racket enough to wake the dead. No amount of argument or protest ever got Sam to discard the dish-pan, although the lesser racket of the clock by itself would have made alarm a-plenty.

Having alarmed himself and everybody else into a state of complete wakefulness, Sam would roll out and proceed with his breakfast preparations.

First he would rake the dead ashes from his banked cooking-fire, then take from the chuck box a chunk of fat pine and from the "possum belly" or "cooney" beneath the chuck-wagon a supply of dry wood, or maybe cow-chips. He would whittle pine shaving from the chunk directly upon the live coals of the fire, then add dry wood and cow-chips to the ensuing blaze. Soon a good fire would be lighting up the circumference of the entire camp.

Coffee-water in a huge boiler would then be set on the fire, the chuck-box lid lowered and the actual business of breakfast would proceed.

Sam's sourdough biscuits, Dutch-oven baked, were always large, light and plentiful, the beef-steak, chicken-fried, invariably brown, fluffy, tender—and likewise plentiful. Black-strap molasses, commonly called "lick," served invariably as a breakfast dessert, and the triple extract of coffee, hot and plentiful, served always to wipe out any and all resentment on the part of the hands anent the alarm-clock-dishpan contraption.

With very little variation, the above set-up constituted the breakfast generally favored by cowboys on roundup in the Southwest.

Some Things the Spanish-Americans Eat

No matter how humble the hut, the Spanish family there residing will have its countless *ristras* (strings or chains) of scarlet chiles hung like red icicles from its roof beams, and somewhere at hand its store of *piñones*.

Early in September every member of a Spanish family goes into the fields to pick the shining green pepper-pods from the long rows of chiles. They are heaped in a dark store-room until the green shows splotches of orange. Then Mamacita and the children leave the fields and sit on the floor all day and into the night to tie the pods, three at a twist, onto a ten-foot cord. The work goes swiftly. Soon the cords are full and tied together at the ends. Then they are hung over the roof or from the roof-poles to dry, always high above the reach of straying *bestias*—for goats, sheep, burros and the like have a keen appetite for the red delicacies, regardless that they are super-hot. After six weeks in the sunshine the pods are thoroughly cured and are then stored for winter use.

There is usually another arresting red line to be seen picked out against the drab walls of a Spanish home. It consists of meat, cut in strips, and hung up to dry in the sun. A cow or a goat has been butchered on the rack back of the house, and why waste the surplus meat when it will be so good to eat in the winter time? It goes well in a jerked beef or goat-meat stew and may even, at a pinch, form the *carne* in chile.

But the Spanish folk will tell you that the *piñon* crop is the true gift of God. It is manna succoring the children in the wilderness. Cabeza de Vaca was saved from starvation by living on *piñones* for three days (Note: Ruth Laughlin Barker in *Caballeros*, D. Appleton & Co. New York—London, 1931), and many a sheepherder depends upon these rich piney nuts to supply the fat in his diet.

The *piñon* shrubs, seldom more than twice as high as a man's stature, dot the red foothills like a thick sprinkling of black pepper. As soon as frost turns the aspens to gold and opens the resin-coated cones, whole families go to the hills to camp and pick *piñones* before the first snow turns them rancid. At home the *piñones* are roasted like the coffee beans they resemble (although not nearly so large), for eating much as Americans eat roasted peanuts, but they are used largely in the preparation of countless Spanish food favorites.

Piñones add a high nutritive value to the simple native diet. All of the oil and sweetness of the pine are concentrated in the small white kernel. Old Spanish recipes call for *piñones* for stuffing wild turkey and chicken, for fried pies and for that great favorite brown sugar dulce, *piñonate*. The uses in cookery for the little brown nut are legion, and no Spanish family is ever without a goodly store.

Spanish cooking, whether one's Nordically inhibited stomach quarrels with it or not, offers a savory variety. It is never a simple matter of broiling a beefsteak and sprinkling on a pinch of salt. It is far more than that. It is an art. Verily, it is indeed a high art.

There is always a suggestion of dried mint leaves, a glass of Sherry, a hint of *sabrosa española*, a nuance of oregano, a bit of olives and olive oil, two or three chile pods, a stain of tomato, a reminder of minced onion, *and the dead certainty of garlic*—one or all in every Spanish dish.

Spanish suppers usually begin with *albondigas*, force-meat balls rolled in blue cornmeal and boiled until the soup is thick and the tender balls are still as round as marbles. For entrees there are enchiladas, the blue cornmeal pancakes spread between with chopped raw onions and melted cheese, the stack swamped with chile sauce, and two fried eggs on top staring out like drowning yellow eyes. Then *chiles rellenos* which are called, and deservedly so from the epicurean point of view, angel's dreams. They are green peppers stuffed with chicken and cheese, dipped in batter and crisped to a golden brown in sizzling fat.

Along comes *posole*, the Spanish for "hog and hominy." The corn kernels have been soaked in lye water until the tough outer skin peels off. The hominy simmers all day with rounds of fresh ham hock until the meat falls to pieces and the bracelets of rind and fat form that delectable tidbit, *cueritos*.

Many, many times there is chili—and always, with all meals, there are frijoles. These brown beans are to Bernardo what potatoes are to Paddy. They are more of a staple than daily bread and fully as nourishing. They may be cooked with or without meat or seasoning, and the longer they cook the better they are.

For vegetables, there are tender spring greens, called *quelites*, and known to the non-Spanish person as sheep-sorrel and pig-weed. These "greens" are cooked like spinach, dried and fried with minced onion, and sometimes with the addition of the almost ever-present little *piñones* helped the deliciousness by the addition of raisins and hard-boiled eggs.

During the winter Mamacita cooks rounds of dried yellow squash and pumpkin. *Chicos* are a favorite dish with the summertime flavor of fresh corn. The cobs are boiled when the corn first ripens and then dried, to be cooked during the long winter. Sliced dried cucumbers are a Lenten delicacy, along with other dried vegetables and eggs cooked in almost countless ways. Beets and carrots, cabbage and celery make *ensaladas* with a piquant vinegar and oil salad dressing.

After these numerous meat dishes, fruit and a pat of goat's milk cheese are sufficient desserts. But for *fiestas* there will be *sopa*, a bread pudding with layers of apples, butter and sugar, cheese browned on top, dusted with cinnamon and served with a wine sauce. Or there will be *empanadas*, those fried pies shaped in a triangle and stuffed with tongue, currants, *piñones*, spices and wine. Or *sopapillas*, sweet hollow pincushions of puff pastry, fried like doughnuts and eaten with hot, homemade syrup. Sometimes a glorified rice pudding, called *arroz con leche*. Or *biscochitos*, shortbread cut in fancy shapes, flavored with anise seeds and glazed with sugar.

Hot thick chocolate is often served in the afternoon with the *sopapillas*. A dash of cinnamon has been added to it and the whole beaten to a froth with a wooden chocolate pestle. Strong black coffee simmers on the stove all day long. Wine goes with all meals. Water is used as a chaser, if at all, after the meal is over.

Bread? Anybody who has never eaten the round, crisp loaves baked in an *estufa*—a hive-shaped oven of thick mud-walls set out-of-doors—certainly does not know just how good bread can be.

Throughout Arizona and New Mexico, in the cities as well as the villages and rural settlements, those outside bread-ovens will be found wherever Spanish peoples dwell—and they dwell pretty much all over. And, lastly, there is the indispensable *tortilla*. (Pronounced tor-tea-a.) They are simply large thin pancakes, made without baking-powder, and browned on a hot griddle.

A lifetime might well be spent in telling of the good things the Spanish peoples in America eat, but the foods described herein are typical. They are greatly in favor wherever Spanish people eat—and they do seem to be eating most of the time.

This writer has at various times partaken of the dishes described herein, but the most succulent and satisfying feast he can recall was upon the occasion of an annual fall barbecue spread at the headquarters ranch of the San Simon outfit in the San Simon Valley of southern Arizona. It was typical of all such after-the-roundup barbecue foods served in that locality, and it was a little bit better than good.

Early on the morning preceding the day of the feast, certain old-timers among the menfolk of the locality gathered at the ranchhouse. Some of them scattered to the brush to cut leaf-wood poles to form the "grid" to be placed across the top of the barbecue pit. These poles were about the thickness of a large man's forearm and were uniformly about six feet in length. Other men rode out for the purpose of dragging up at rope-end logs and chunks of good hardwood, wherever it might be found. Still others remained at home to attend to the digging of the pit.

This barbecue pit was, as I recall, about twenty-five feet long, four feet across and three feet deep. Each end was scooped out and left open so that red-hot coals might be heaved in, and at certain spots along the grid itself a pole or two would be omitted for the accommodation of other hot coals. For coals only were used in the pit. Any blaze that might show up would be promptly doused with a handful of earth.

When the pole cutters returned with their loads, the men proceeded to lay the poles across the pit from end to end. Being of hardwood and green with sap, they would char but not burn. Then the wood for the fire was given attention. This great fire was built at some distance from the pit, its sole purpose being to reduce the wood to coals for the pit. The pit and its grid prepared, the wood-heap fired, the meat itself was then brought up. This part of the preparations occurred in late afternoon.

There were two fat beeves, ribs and quarters, fore and aft, four shoats, four sheep and two goats. This party was to be a large one, everybody who wanted to attend was welcome, and direct invitations were dispensed with.

The heavier parts of the beeves were placed on the grid, lying lengthwise of the pit, after a thick layer of red coals had been thrown in throughout the needed length. There were fire-tenders, basters and turners. The basters were equipped with long green poles to which clean flour-sacks had been fixed in a sort of sponge-like assembly. With these "sops" the basting fluid, or barbecue sauce, was applied (vinegar, butter, salt, pepper, bay-leaves). Salt and pepper would be sprinkled over the meat when it should be about half-way cooked, but the basters began applying their "sops" after the first turning of the meats.

Half a dozen men, working in pairs, equipped with three-tined hay-forks, attended to the turning. Over and over that meat would be turned by the simple method of two hay-forks driven into each piece from opposite sides of the pit—the rest being strength and awkwardness, plus considerable coordination. After each turning the meat would be browner—until at length it would acquire, when thoroughly cooked, a crisp, almost black crust. Later during the night the hogs, sheep and goats were laid out on the grid and treated in precisely the same manner.

During the night the attendants refreshed themselves from bottles, jugs, fruit-jars, or what-did-you-bring-it-in? And the womenfolk from the house served hot food whenever it was wanted.

While all this was going on there were men laying boards across carpenter's horses and whatever other supports the ranch afforded, and thus setting up long tables at which the meats were to be served. It was notable that while there were a few chairs intended for the older folk among the women, there was no such accommodation set out for the younger women, or for any men at all. They were expected to sit, stand or squat.

I was greatly surprised when in early morning of the big day the feasters began to arrive. Not so much because of the fact that the entire terrain surrounding the ranchhouse appeared to be a-crawl, so far as the eye could see, with people. They came horseback, in buckboards, buggies, roadwagons, flivvers—every conceivable way except afoot. Nobody, of course, walked. What surprised me was not the numbers or the manner of arrival, but what each family or lone individual brought along to add to the festivities.

There were hams baked and boiled, roasted turkeys and chickens, and more than one haunch of baked (and at that season illegal) venison. Cucumber pickles, sweet peach-pickles, pickled chiles, piccalillis, jellies, preserves arrived in all kinds and sizes of containers. There were scores and scores of loaves of brown bread, layer-cakes, plain cakes, cookies, gingerbread. Fruits, cabbage-slaw, potato salad, salmon salad, shrimp salad—all kinds of cold salads in amounts which staggered this beholder, and almost staggered those who carried the delectable provisions.

When all these eatables were spread out over the long tables, men brought on the barbecued meats. A dozen women took over the carving and many more presided over the four fifty-gallon lard cans which, filled to the brim with strong black coffee, simmered on adjacent fires. There were other liquids for drinking, but, as is almost always the case in the Southwest, coffee, strong, hot and plentiful, was preferred with the eats. Afterwards—but that is another story.

The dancing began early and lasted all night long, but there were many of us who were just naturally too full of good grub, and likewise good cheer, to give the minor entertainment much mind. Dancing may be all right on an empty stomach, or on one only moderately filled, but after a stuffing like that one—not!

Notes on Oklahoma
Pioneer Eating

Notes on pioneer eating in Oklahoma, from "Indiana and Pioneers," a collection of interviews obtained by the Oklahoma WPA.

There were no flies in those days and we could kill a beef and cover it with a cloth to keep dirt away and hang it on the north side of house and it would not spoil even in the hottest weather."

"When we killed beef we drew the meat to the top of a 25-ft. pole and the flies wouldn't bother it. It would keep some time there even if weather was not cold."

"We kept butter. Made into balls and wrapped in clean soft cloths, in kegs of brine: when used, it was soaked in clean water to extract the salt."

In November 3 or 4 families went to the timber to kill hogs, beef, deer. Salt down best 10 days, then take out and scald in solution of vinegar, brown sugar, black and red pepper and water: hang in dry place and smoke with hickory for 3 days: then pack in box with corn hucks, charcoal and wood ashes. Meat so treated would keep for a year."

"Dried venison was wrapped in the deer's hide and brought in."

"We had nothing but kaffir corn pancakes for days. We flailed and winnowed it by hand and had it ground. . . . Mother put the meal in a pitcher, added salt, and filled the pitcher almost full of water. This set all night. In the morning, she added soda. She greased the griddle with salt pork stuck on a fork, then fried the cakes. In that period, we ate 'em 3 times a day—no butter, no syrup—and at times as a snack between meals."

"The 2nd year we had a good crop of sweet potatoes and sorghum cane. We children helped strip the cane for the sorghum—and such sorghum? One barrel, 31 gallons, was black strap and when we wanted some we went to the barrel with a big spoon and wound and wound until the sorghum's own weight separated it from the spoon and it fell into our container. Another barrel went in sugar—for company. I was nearly grown before I knew pumpkin pies could be sweetened with anything but sorghum."

"A potato pumpkin cut in two and baked in the oven is as good as sweet potato."

"Wild grapes and plums, and a citrus melon called pie melon were plentiful, and I made lots of both sour and sweet pickles out of this wild pie melon."

"We brought religion to the country. My husband was a Primitive Baptist preacher . . . we had our foot washings once every year. The ladies washed each others' feet, and the men theirs . . . In our 3-day meetings we always had our dinner on the ground where we had our preaching . . . I always killed a calf and most generally roasted a hind quarter for the meeting . . . and pies and preserves according to how the Lord had blessed us."

An Arizona Menudo Party

J. DEL CASTILLO

Asense of family responsibility has taken hold of Mike Grijalva and he decided to give a party at his house. This year Mike had his first child baptized and made his first *compadre*. Of course, he had several other compadres, but in making them he had stood the godfather of the children of his friends. This Christmas Mike was going to invite his friends, his relatives and his compadres and their families to his house for a menudo party soon after the Midnight Mass of *Misa de Gallo*. In the past his mother used to give the party, before he himself had a family. His mother now is living with him, and he earns the family keep.

Menudo is good, wholesome and nourishing, his mother often said. To feed so many relatives and friends menudo would provide a delightful meal at comparatively less cost. Besides, who is the Mexican who does not relish menudo? When Mike's family wants to eat menudo, there's always the problem of buying the entire tripe of a beef. It weighs from fifteen pounds or more. It comes already cleaned and dressed for cooking from the slaughter-house. In the old days a Mexican family killed their own beef, that was at a special fiesta or celebration. So when a Mexican family wants to eat the delicious menudo it was best to get all the relatives together and all the friends.

On the afternoon of the twenty-fourth, Mike brought home the tripe, the whole entrails of a beef, including the intestines. They were white and cleaned. His mother and his wife washed the tripe over to be sure it was thoroughly clean. Mike's wife has heard that if you soaked it in salt-water it would be cleaner. The mother agreed, although she explained the menudo would taste better with full flavor of the tripe in it. When they were satisfied the tripe was well cleaned, they chopped it up in small pieces, piling it over in a large basin.

Before they had their supper, they had already started boiling the tripe in a huge kettle or cauldron. The tripe has to boil at least four hours. Sometimes when it has been boiling long enough they pour in corn (hominy) and flavor it with pepper and salt to taste. By midnight the menudo would be tender and tasty enough to eat. The hominy would then be so steeped in the juice of the tripe and the tripe cooked in the corn that both make a complete and appetizing meal.

Mike took his wife and mother to the Midnight Mass. His mother always takes her Communion, and the three of them took Communion on this important holiday. When the Mass was over, the air had become chilly. It was good to hurry home. On the way they met some of their friends and they went home together. Aunts and uncles with the children and in-laws began coming, coming from the Mass. They exchanged felicitations.

On the table were set glasses and wine and tequila or brandy. Mike began filling the glasses up and distributing drinks around. Many preferred wine, and more wine. Port, said one of Mike's uncles, is also good for the health. But what the entire party was interested most in was the hot menudo, which they could smell—mealy and brothy.

Mike's wife, assisted by her friends, dished the menudo in wide bowls. It was steaming hot. It is best to eat menudo while it is hot, when you could get the full goodness and flavor of it. Among the tripe bits, curled and tender, swam bursting corn kernels, swollen with the rich soup of the tripe. The soup glistened with globules of fat and substance boiled out of the tripe. One could hardly wait for it to cool before one sipped it. Ah! sighed Mike's uncle, there's nothing like menudo for a good meal of a chilly evening. You can feel it warm inside you and feel its strength nourishing your body. It peps you up.

But one of Mike's aunts stared at her bowl with an air that did not agree with Mike's uncle. She had in her bowl mostly soup and drifts of corn. She wanted to tell Mike's uncle that no wonder he appreciated his bowl of menudo so much—he had a bowlful of the tripe itself. But she remembered her manners and kept her peace. However, it would break no etiquette to accept a second bowl and one could suggest that she could do with a lot of tripe. It is always understood that everybody relishes menudo, and one could eat all one can.

When one eats menudo, one seasons it with crushed herb seasoning and chile. The herb seasoning may be enough for those who could not stand the stinging hotness of chili sauce. Mike shook chili sauce in his bowl until it turned deep pink. When he ate it, his face flamed up very red, water starting in his eyes. One may season his menudo to his individual taste—and capacity for endurance. Bread was served with the menudo for anyone who wanted it and [was] not satisfied with eating the bready hominy in the soup. Coffee and dessert came next.

Tucson's Menudo Party

To celebrate the world's premiere of the movie *Arizona*, filmed in Tucson, the town held a public menudo party after the first show. For fifty cents, one could eat all he wanted of menudo. But on the night of the menudo party, they served bowls of menudo to whoever came and wanted to eat. Tucson intends to hold menudo parties during the town's festivals and during the Rodeo day—menudo at night and barbecue at day time. The movie personalities and the excitement of the first world premiere the town ever had so dazzled the midnight menudo party that it is hard to draw a balanced perspective of the actual menudo eating part of the party. It seemed that the public was too excited to appreciate the flavor and appetizing values of the menudo. The menudo party was better reading at the time the publicity releases were published. From corners of the nation requests were made for the menudo recipe.

When John Walton Became
Governor of Oklahoma

From: *High Lights in the Life of John (Jack) Galloway Walton*, by F. A. Ruth:

"Jack Walton was elected Governor of Oklahoma by the largest majority ever given a candidate up to that time. His inauguration was featured by the famous Jack Walton barbecue, Jan. 8, 1923, the largest event of its kind ever held in the world's history. It lasted for three days, during which time square dancing, fiddlers' contest, and free amusements of all kinds were had. For the barbecue, there were built there 10,000 gallon coffee pots that required the steam from six steam fire engines to keep them boiling. Three carloads of coffee were used, and 300,000 tin cups were distributed in the crowds. More than a mile of trenches were dug for barbecuing the meat, which consisted of one carload of Alaskan reindeer, one train load of cattle, chickens, rabbits, and buffalo. One carload of pepper [!] and one carload of salt were used for seasoning. Two hundred and fifty thousand buns were used. The official checkers counted over 250,000 guests who participated."

From: Okla. City *Daily Oklahoman*, Jan. 10, 1923:

"When I am elected governor, there will not be any inaugural ball, and there will not be a 'tea dansant.' I am going to give an old-fashioned square dance and barbecue; it will be a party for all the people, and I want you all to come!"

That statement was repeated in each of the 400 campaign speeches of J. G. (Jack) Walton, the candidate. Tuesday [Jan. 8, 1923], his second day in office, Walton, the Governor, had fulfilled that pledge to the utmost and one of the greatest crowds [100,000 or more] ever assembled in Oklahoma [at the State Fair Grounds] stood by to see him make good the first of his campaign pledges . . .

War Dance Staged

At the fair grounds there was color aplenty. Dick Light, soloist with the Walton campaign party, sang "Old Pal, Old Pal," at the request of the "Bryan County 5,000." An Indian war dance was staged in front of the grand stand, with Zack Mulhall whirling about on a sweat-streaked steed. Eugene Naple, the 10-year-old orator from Grandfield, delivered a eulogy to the new governor. Senator Robert L. Owen, through the loud speaker, expressed the "greatest hope, the greatest faith, in the success of Jack Walton . . ."

More than 60,000 are fed by:

Barbecue Meat

Streaming endlessly through the fifteen serving units, rich man, poor man, women with sealskin coats and diamonds, farm wives and children, swelled the total fed at the barbecue to approximately 60,000 at sundown, according to John R. Boardman, chairman of the serving committee. Fifteen lines of humanity were still surging through the openings and passing the little windows where barbecued beef, bear, deer, rabbit, turkey, chicken and reindeer were being passed out on paper plates with buns, pickles, onions and sugar at dark.

Meat Served All Night

"They will be fed as long as it lasts. Another shift of workers is going on and we will continue serving all night," Boardman said.

The first rush started at 12:30 o'clock and for thirty minutes the mammoth crowd, without guidance, "swamped" the 165 busy workers who were filling plates for the hungry. In thirty minutes the National Guardsmen were thrown in to control the tidal wave of humanity which was soon formed into the fifteen lines which continued pouring through the serving units until late Tuesday night.

"Hot Dawg, some barbecue!" declared a youth . . .

Fifteen Plates a Minute

Fifteen plates a minute at each unit were passed out to the visitors, Boardman said. Arrangements were made to serve a plate a second, but the meat could not be sliced fast enough and brought in huge army trucks to the serving units. However, fifteen is a conservative estimate and probably 80,000 persons will be fed before the night is over, Boardman thinks.

Eight girls, two men and a captain at each unit, marshalled by Mrs. Will Owens, sliced pickles and onions, filled plates and passed them out the little windows provided at the fronts of stock sheds.

Mother Earth Serves as Table

Baby was robbed of his blanket, overcoats, papers and most anything available were used by the guests who broke the bread of Oklahoma's governor to sit on the ground and consume the feast. The large basin on the east end of the grounds was black with people who used "Mother earth" as a festive board for the meat and the tin cup as a goblet for the drink [coffee from a battery of 10,000-gallon metal tanks] provided to celebrate the inaugural.

Oklahoma Scrambled Eggs and Wild Onions

In the eastern, Indian, section of Oklahoma housekeepers watch eagerly for the appearance, in late February or early March, of Indian wild onion gatherers. Their neatly tied bundles are chopped, cooked briefly, then mixed in the skillet with enough eggs to make a family feast. To be invited to such a dinner is an experience not soon forgotten.

MEXICAN LABOR CONTRACTOR IN CENTER WITH TWO CARROT WORK-
ERS EATING "SECOND BREAKFAST" NEAR SANTA MARIA, TEXAS.
(PHOTOGRAPH BY RUSSELL LEE)

Texas Chuck Wagon

Wherever, throughout the ranching areas of the Southwest, there is a reunion of cattlemen, ex-cowboys, or old trail drives, a feature of the gathering is almost certain to be a meal that centers around an old-time chuck wagon.

It had no other name, this essential of the cattle industry in range days—a field kitchen that accompanied the cow-waddies on their chores of rounding up, branding, driving, and otherwise conditioning cattle for the market. It went with the men and their herds, even on the epic treks of the trail drives to northern markets. Of roads there were few or none. The chuck wagon moved from day to day over every kind of terrain across which a cowboy could ride a horse or drive a steer.

In this modified prairie schooner the cook was a monarch. His domain included a circle around his stronghold, a radius of about sixty feet, but varying with cooks and local customs. At the back of the wagon was a let-down shelf from which the hungry cowboy took his eating tools and such foods as the cook saw fit to hand out there. He then went over to the fire and helped himself to whatever else had been concocted or brewed for his sustenance.

Except for rare feasts, generally before round-ups, the meals were plain and monotonous—beans, salt pork (usually "side-meat," modernly called bacon), fresh unfattened beef from the range, and sourdough biscuits. Various criteria were used in judging chuck-wagon cooks, but it is generally agreed that in the evaluation of these always important personages, good sourdough biscuits would cover a multitude of other sins, for sourdough biscuits were the bread of life of the Texas plains.

Into their construction the competent range cook put time and loving care. He started, usually, with a potato, some sugar, and a little flour. These—the potato being grated—were worked together until smooth and set in a warm place to ferment—often, under range conditions, being wrapped in a blanket and placed near the fire. When the dough had risen, more water and flour were kneaded in, together with salt, soda, and sugar if required. The mixture having reached the proper smoothness, pieces were pinched off and moulded in the hollow of the hand. Dutch ovens were preferred for baking. Shoved into hot ashes and covered with ashes and coals, they became hot and held their heat, and the bread could be baked in them without danger of burning.

Surrounded as he was by the great open spaces and without much companionship—the men that he served appeared from their range labors only at mealtimes, and he seldom saw anyone else—the genius who reigned at the chuck wagon sometimes felt the urge to let his visions roam beyond the dull routine of his daily vocation, to dream artistically of menu complexities that might be accomplished within the limitations of his normal materials. Such an artist evolved a dish that today, in one of several similar forms, is the main feature of every chuck-wagon banquet.

Precisely how and why it gained its original name has been lost in the mists of antiquity, and that name, in the interest of politeness, has long since been amended. Except by the older cattle set—and by them only on rare and wholly masculine occasions—it is now called son-of-a-gun stew.

The dish—at first a general preparation designed to use appetizingly the best parts of a freshly killed calf—developed specialists with varying recipes. Aging men with slightly bowed legs and handle-bar mustaches still argue, and will until they die, as to the relative merits of what these super-cooks worked out. John Snyder, of Amarillo in the Texas Panhandle, who is nationally famous as a barbecue artist, is also held in high esteem for his son-of-a-gun, and this is his recipe:

"You kill and dress the fattest calf that can be found. Then you take parts of the liver, heart, sweetbreads, narrowgut, tongue, and some of the tenderloin, and choice bits of flank steak. You start the cooking by putting some bits of suet in the round-up kettle, to be frying while you cut the ingredients into small pieces. You add the pieces, cover well with warm water, and add hot water from time to time, as needed. Season with salt, pepper, and a little onion. Last of all, you add the brains. Cook until tender, which will take about two hours." He and all the other experts seem to agree that the result can never be satisfactory unless the cooking begins at the earliest possible moment after the killing of the calf.

Many a one-time cowboy will maintain that there positively is no other dish on land or sea with which this can be compared. Driven to it, he may admit that you can get a mild and altogether imperfect idea of how it tastes by thinking of the best chicken giblets and gravy you ever ate. Serious offense could be given in the old days by claiming that any part of the concoction was better than any other, and it was not etiquette to be in the slightest degree choosey. When it was served from beside the chuck wagon the cook was wont to announce: "Come and get it! Get all you want—but don't pick!"

John Arnot, also of the Texas Panhandle and a former president of the T Anchor cowboy reunion, who ate his first son-of-a-gun at a Cimarron River cow camp in 1884, observed through the years the reactions of womenfolk to the dish, and was quoted on the subject by the *Amarillo Sunday News* in 1938:

"First the ladies act suspicious of it, as if they thought there was something mean and ornery about it—because of the name, I suppose. Then they see everybody eating, and they get a whiff of how it smells, and they say, 'I believe I'll take just a small spoonful, please.' And in a few minutes their plates come back, and they don't say anything about a small spoonful."

COWBOY EATING "ROCKY MOUNTAIN
OYSTERS," QUARTER CIRCLE U RANCH
ROUNDUP, MONTANA. (PHOTOGRAPH
BY ARTHUR ROTHSTEIN)

Oklahoma Prairie Oysters

JOHN M. OKISON

*In 1938 John M. Okison published his biography of Tecum-
seh, the Indian leader.*

Mountain oysters, yes; this seasonal by-product of the sheep
business is well established in respectable circles as lamb
fries. But the prairie oyster, which is eaten by a more limited number

of initiates at fall branding time in the cattle country, is not yet to be spoken of freely as a delectable morsel in mixed company. Usually, it is cooked only at branding fires or in kitchens from which women are banished either voluntarily or by diplomatic hints that what is to take place there is wholly a man's affair.

By early November, at the ranches of Oklahoma, whitefaced calves are lusty, fat, and over-ripe for weaning from restive mothers. With these mothers, they are rounded up and driven to a corral; here the cows are separated from their 400-to-600-pound babies and, lamenting, driven back to pasture. To hold the suddenly bereft calves the corral must be stout, for the young ones are as strong, and nearly as agile, as overgrown wildcats; frantic, too, at being deprived of their doting female parents' attention and their, by now, rather skimpy portions of milk on demand.

With the cows driven far from the scene, three men climb the fence and descend among the milling, bawling mass of calves; the roper, flanker, and branding man. A flip of a three-eighths-inch rope noose over a bull calf's head, a sudden end-for-end reverse as the calf comes to the end of the rope, a rush by the flanker (by preference, let this one be the professional football tackle type) to wrestle the victim down, then the branding man's sharp, "Hot iron!" From a chunk fire just outside the corral is yanked the long-handled Lazy-J, or whatever hieroglyphic is required, and handed between the planks of the fence—usually by one of the two boys of fourteen or fifteen always on hand at a branding to tend the fire. The almost red-hot iron is pressed firmly to the young bull's hip, hair sizzles, a smell that only a cattleman loves fills the crisp autumn air, and the sound of agonized bawling that makes strong women shudder shatters the eardrums.

His branding iron withdrawn from quivering hide and handed outside for re-heating, the cruel branding man assumes the necessary role of destiny. With his big razor-sharp knife, he proceeds to turn a bull calf into a baby beef steer by the only successful process known to man.

As the oysters are removed they are tossed over the fence, to be placed in a tin bucket and kept until the last calf is branded and the last bull calf is "altered." By now the branding fire is a bed of coals, the irons are hanging on the fence and making their annual brown scar on the wood. There is silence among the outraged new young steers and the twitching, merely-branded heifers. The branding man climbs out of the corral, followed by roper and flanker, all sweat-streaked and grimy. The three stand over the oyster bucket, a hungry light in their eyes; one of the boys mutters, "Gee, they goin' to *eat* 'em?," and the other boy says, "Sure— wha'dya think!" One after the other, the three men lean to take two oysters from the bucket and toss them on the fire. The branding man suggests to one of the boys, "Bud, go on up to the house an' get us some salt."

The salt comes. With a sharpened stick the roasted tidbits are retrieved; they are split, and salted; when cool enough, they are eaten slowly, with the gusto of seasoned ranch epicures. One boy turns to the other, "Dare you to try one!" "Aw—" and the outcome of their dual of dares and double-dares is always a matter of doubt.

If, as is usually the case, the roper and flanker are from another ranch or from among the hardier of the town drugstore cowboys, the remaining oysters are divided among the three, who make up mental lists of other men to be invited to a feast on the evening when the missus remembers, or is reminded, that she really must go over and have supper with granma.

Oklahoma Kush

K ush," popular dish among pioneers: Take cornbread and crumble it up, cut up some onions, add black pepper, a pinch of salt, a little lard or butter, put it in a pan, pour boiling water over it (add eggs if desired), then put in the oven and bake.

FARM BOY EATING PIE, WHICH HE BOUGHT AT AUCTION AND
WHICH WAS MADE BY THE GIRL WITH WHOM HE IS EATING.
MUSKOGEE COUNTY, OKLAHOMA. (PHOTOGRAPH BY
RUSSELL LEE)

Oklahoma City's Famous Suzi-Q Potatoes

LILLIE DUNCAN

The famous Suzi-Q potatoes originated in Oklahoma City in 1938. The method was worked out by Ralph A. Stephens, owner of Dolores Restaurant and Drive-in. They are now being served in 700 different places, in practically every state in the Union, including the Stork Club in New York City.

Café and restaurant operators from San Francisco, from Miami to Boston, and from New Orleans to Montreal are serving these delicious Suzi-Q potatoes.

The cutting machine, made of stainless steel, cuts potatoes in a spiral shape; they are fried in deep fat to a golden brown.

AN INFORMAL
BIBLIOGRAPHY

Katherine Kellock's original plan for *America Eats* called for an "informal bibliography" to be created by each state's Writer's Project submitting a list of local cookbooks. Most states never sent one, but those that did included many obscure and out-of-print books. Ironically, with the availability of the Internet, today there is a better chance of finding these rare bits of culinary Americana than there would have been at the time of *America Eats*, had it been published in 1942.

Vermont Cookbooks

The majority of Vermont cookbooks, or cookbooks used by Vermont house-wives, are those brought out by different church societies of the State, supplemented by the innumerable ones offered free by the producers of various food brands.

For many years *Miss Parloa's Cook Book* was rated the aristocrat among the many. *The Successful Housekeeper, Lowney's, Housekeepers' Guide, The Guide to Good Cooking, Lend-a-Hand Cook Book, The Homekeeper's Friend*, are even now to be found in Vermont households. Also, *The Universal Common Sense.*

These all measure up to about the same standard with the same aim, namely, to quote from one of them: "to give the greatest amount of information possible, so arranged that any subject sought can be easily and quickly found and when found shall contain just the information sought."

The books also tended to emphasize the fact that bad cooking is waste and urged that the rising generation should be taught not to overlook it. Names of contributors were rarely given, as "most of them would be quite unknown and therefore add no authority."

Cook Books by Texans or Containing Recipes for Texas Foods

NOTE TO EDITOR: The six books here listed are the only notable ones in any list that we have been able to find. In great numbers of Texas communities church cook books have been published, locally and in limited quantities, usually sold at their first printing to members of the church and never available outside the community or listed in any catalogue or library. Such books usually give the favorite recipes of members of the group, but these recipes are not of peculiarly Texas foods except to a very limited extent; each housewife has her own inherited recipes, often brought by her parents from another State. So that even were we able to secure a list of such books, few of them would have any content of value for our purposes.

Title: The Argyle Cook Book.
Author: Alice O'Grady.
Publisher: Maylor Company, San Antonio.
Date: 1940.

Title: Mammy Lou's Cook Book.
Author: Betty Benton Patterson.
Publisher: Robert M. McBride and Company, New York.
Date: 1931.

Title: First Foods of America

Author: Blanche V. McNeil and Edna McNeil.

Publisher: Sutton House, Ltd., Los Angeles, San Francisco, New York.

Date: 1936.

> (Note: This book contains recipes for Texas-Mexican foods.)

Title: Home Cooking

Author: G. L. Nelson

Publisher: Nealen Sales Service, San Antonio.

Date: 1934.

Title: Menus and Recipes

Author: M. Gleason.

Publisher: Extension Department, College of Industrial Arts, Denton, Texas.

Date: 1928.

Title: Cooking Recipes of the Pioneers.

Author and Publisher: Under the auspices of the Bandera Library Association, printed by Frontier Times Magazine, Bandera, Texas.

> (Note: This book contains old-time Texas recipes, including son-of-a-gun and cowboy stew, crackling bread, and others.)

Partial Cook Books Edited and/or Published in Oregon

Web-Foot Cook Book
  W.B. Ayer, publisher, 1885. Recipes contributed by many Oregonians

Lewis and Clark Cook Book
  Woman's Guild, St. Matthews Mission, 1904

Portland Woman's Exchange Cook Book
  Published by Portland Woman's Exchange, 1913

All-Western Conservation Cook Book
  Telegram Publishing Co., 1917

Bio-Chemistry Cook Book
  Eunice M. Bothwell, 1924

Woman's Auxiliary to BPOE, 142, Cook Book
  Published by Woman's Auxiliary to BPOE, 142, 1926

Meier and Frank Cook Book
  Mabel Claire, 1932

Low Cost Menus for one month
  Oregon Agricultural College, 1933. Extension Bulletin No. 456

Good Foods for Better Health
  Compiled by Celia Bernards and Sibylla Hadwen, 1934

Neighborhood Cook Book
  Compiled by Council of Jewish Women, 1935

Mary Cullen's Cook Book
>   Compiled by Home Economics Staff, Oregon Journal, 1938

Mushrooms, How to prepare and cook them
>   Nina Lane Faubion, 1938

Cook Book of Many Lands
>   Portland Parent-Teacher Assn., Americanization Dept.

Camp Cookery
>   Oregon Agricultural College, Extension Bulletin No. 76

Recipes for Hot School Lunch dishes
>   Oregon Agricultural College, Extension Bulletin No. 455

Uses of Honey
>   Oregon Agricultural College, Extension Bulletin No. 472

The Bride's Cook Book
>   Pacific Coast Pub. Co., San Francisco, Compilers and Publishers

Given to Portland Brides by Portland merchants
    "   " Seattle   "   " Seattle   "   etc., etc., etc.
    "   " Spokane   "   " Spokane   "

Delaware Recipes
Bibliography

Bush, Mrs. *What and How. A Practical Cook Book for Every Day Living.* Published by Edna N. Taylor. Wilmington, Del., New Amstel Magazine Company, 1910. 336 p. $1.25.

From Delaware Cooks. Recipes contributed by Delaware homemakers. Delaware Home Economics Association, Kent County Branch, Dover, Del. Wilmington, Del., William N. Cann, Inc., 1941. ($1.20?) 300 pages lithographed, notebook form.

Del-Mar-Va Eastern Shore Association, Executive Offices, Saulsbury, Md. *Epicurean Gems for the Eastern Shore.* A rare collection of delectable dishes handed down from the earliest Colonial days. 25 recipes in folder form. 2 editions, no date. No price, on folder.

Fleck, Henrietta C. *A Recipe Primer.* School of Home Economics, Women's College, University of Delaware. Newark, Del., 1941. 150 p.

Haskell, Mrs. E.D. *A Modern Recipe Book.* Wilmington, Del., Charles H. Gray, 1926. 48 p.

Hynson, George B. "Sussex County Apple Jack." Board of Trade. *Journal.* 2: 16. April 1900.

Journal-Every Evening, Wilmington, Del. "Delaware Kitchens Reveal Old Family Cooking Recipes." 3–15–41: 12.

Tested Lewes Recipes. By the ladies of the Presbyterian Church, Lewes, Del. 1904–1916. (Apply to Mrs. George P. Tunnell or to Mrs. Wm. T. Atkins, Lewes, Del.)

Lathrop, Elise. *Historic Houses of Early America.* New York, Robert M. McBride & Co., 1927. 464 p. $3. P. 408: Delaware beverages quoted from Acrelius.

Manual of Soda Beverages. Published by Smith and Painter. Wilmington, Del., no date. 75 page pamphlet.

Milford New Century Club, Cook Book Committee. *The Blue Hen's Chickens' Cook Book*. Milford, Del., Caulk Press, 1904. 128 p.

News-Journal, Wilmington, Del. "Delaware Cuisine." April 23, 1936.

Parent-Teacher Association, Mt. Pleasant School Community, Wilmington, Del. *The Brandywine Cook Book*. May 1935. (No publisher given.) 133 p. No price quoted.

Scott Methodist Episcopal Church, Wilmington, Del., Standard Bearers Society. *Cook Book*. Wilmington, Del. 64 p. (No publisher or price given.)

Trinity Church, Ladies Parish Aid Society. *Trinity Parish Cook Book*. Wilmington, Del., The John M. Rogers Press, 1892. 200 p.

Wilmington Tested Recipes. Friends Society, Philanthropic Committee. Wilmington, Del., 1911. 92 p. 25¢.

Colorado Cook Books

1. R. Arnett, *Camp Cookery, Some Camping Experiences in Colorado in '81.*

2. Clara Goodell Mitchell (Mrs. John C.), *The Way to a Man's Heart,* (Denver: W. H. Kistler Stationary Co., 1897).

3. Norton, Caroline Trask, *The Rocky Mountain Cook Book for High Altitude Cooking,* (Denver: 1918).

4. Mrs. A. J. Rutherford, *Soup to Nuts,* (Denver: 1928).

5. Women of Central Presbyterian Church, *Favorite Recipes,* (Denver: 1896).

6. St. Marks Ladies Aid Society, *Our Kitchen Friend,* (Denver).

Arkansas Books

No bibliography of Arkansas cookbooks exists. The three books discovered by the Arkansas Writers' Project are:

Conant, Gertrude E.   *Preparation of Staple Foods for the Table.* Published as Extension Circular No. 370 by the Extension Service, College of Agriculture, University of Arkansas. P. 50. Fayetteville, June 1938 (reprint).

. . . .   A collection of indigenous recipes gathered and recommended by the Extension Service nutritionist.

. . . .   *Using Arkansas Apples.* Published as Extension Circular No. 411 by the Extension Service, College of Agriculture, University of Arkansas. P. 13. Fayetteville, June 1938. Contains recipes for apples as desserts, sauces, entrees, garnishes, relishes, salad ingredients, and preserves.

Y. W. C. A. Cook Book.   Norton Printing Co. Pine Bluff, 1924. P. 262. Recipes of a general nature contributed by members of the Pine Bluff Y. W. C. A. and their friends.

Mississippi Cook Books

The P. T. A. Cook Book

By the Parent Teachers Association, Shubuta, Mississippi, 1925. Printed by The Clark County Tribune, Commercial Printing Dept., Quitman, Mississippi. (Not available.)

Home Cook Book

1912 and 1913. Tested. Compiled and Published by Jackson Auxiliary of Old Ladies' Home Association. Tucker Printing Co., Jackson, Mississippi. (Not available.)

Cook Book From Ole Miss

By Bettie Jane Wilkins, 1924. The Issue Pub. Co., Jackson, Mississippi. (Not available.)

Floral Club Cook Book

250 Tested Recipes. Compiled by The Floral Club from Recipes of Vicksburg Housekeepers, 1914. (Not available.)

Ladies Aid Society Cook Book

Presbyterian Church, Port Gibson, Mississippi, 1906.
Mrs. Joseph Turpin Drake. (Not available.)

The Laurel Cook book

Edited by the Woman's Guild of St. John's Episcopal Church and Mrs. George S. Gardiner.

First printing 1900; second printing 1910; third printing 1914; fourth printing 1933. Printed by Dement Printing Company, Meridian, Mississippi, Price $1.25. (Available.)

Georgia Cookbooks

Owner: Mrs. Jouett Davenport,
        410 - 3rd St., Augusta, Georgia.

Title: Cook Book by Elizabeth Chapter, Eastern Star

Publisher: Not given. 44 pages.

> This book has forty-four pages of delicious and practical recipes that were contributed by the members of the Eastern Star. There are very good menus, recipes and table decorations for breakfast, luncheon, afternoon tea, dinner, buffet suppers and sandwiches. Proportions to use when serving large groups of people are also given.
>
> Especially good are the unusual recipes for Mexican, Swedish, Bohemian and Jewish dishes.

Owner: Mr. T. J. North
        824 - 11th St., Augusta, Georgia.

Title: Prize Recipes of Herald Readers

Published by: The Augusta Herald, Augusta, Georgia.

Date of Publication: 1940

> This is a book of general recipes published by the Herald in celebration of their Golden Jubilee in 1940. All of the recipes were contributed by people of Augusta and vicinity.
>
> Among the prize winning recipes are barbecue chicken, angel pie, and pumpkin pie.

Owner: Mrs. Rose Curry
        Walton Printing Company

Title: Choice Recipes of Georgia Housekeepers

Author: The Ladies of the Greene Street
          Presbyterian Church. Augusta, Ga.
          Third Edition.

Printed by: Ridgley-Wing-Tidwell Co.,
              7th & Ellis Sts.,
              Augusta, Ga. 1916

Copyright by: Trows Printing & Bookbinding Co. 1880.

Dates when printed: 1880, 1883, 1892, 1916.

This book has 180 pages of quaint and everyday recipes that are famous throughout the South. These recipes, contributed by the housewives of Augusta and vicinity, were published to raise money for the Greene Street Presbyterian Church. It is in use in many homes in Augusta.

There is a recipe for soft ginger bread, a dish that is very popular among the children of today.

A rather amusing recipe for Brandy Peaches is given. At the end of the recipe it is stated that, "they will keep as long as locked up."

Owner: Mrs. Walcott
         940 Murphy Street, Augusta, Ga.

Title: Famous Augusta Recipes
         Collected and presented by:
         Monte Sano Parent-Teachers Association,
         Augusta, Georgia. 1926–27.

Printed by: Walton Printing Co. 96 Pages.

This book has ninety-six pages of delicious Southern recipes. Contributed by Augusta people, many are over a hundred years old. Included also are printed advertisements of the different business concerns of Augusta.

Water melon rind preserves, Creo gumbo, and chow chow are only a few of the tasty recipes.

Owner: Mrs. Helen Brooks
         619 Bohler Ave., Augusta, Ga.

Title: "Recipes From Southern Kitchens."

Compiled by: The Junior-League of Augusta, Ga., Inc.

Published: 1940.

This book was presented by the Junior League in an attempt to preserve the tradition of Southern cooking. It contains many famous Southern recipes, both old and new. A large variety of them were contributed by people who are famous as good cooks. Each recipe has the name of the person who contributed it and many of them are in print for the first time.

Included in the section devoted to old recipes is an excellent one for that strictly Southern dish, "'Possum and 'Taters."

Wine Jelly is another old and popular recipe that is given.

There is also a very good recipe for Georgia Mint Julip, a famous Southern drink.

. . . .

Owner: Mrs. T. R. Perry
920 - 5th St., Augusta, Ga.

Title: Popular Dishes

Published by: Music Study Club
Americus, Ga.

No date given.

This little book, hardly more than a pamphlet in size, was compiled by the Music Study Club of Americus, Ga. It has many choice and delicious recipes, most of which are simple and inexpensive. Among the most tempting recipes are cocoanut cake and cheese delights.

. . . .

Owner: Mrs. Mary Garlington
624 Greene St., Augusta, Ga.

Title: Rare Recipes From Washington-Wilkes

Author: None

Publisher: Last Cabinet Chapter U.D.C.
Sponsored by: Washington Woman's Club.

Place of Publication: Washington, Ga.

Date of Publication: 1929.

Price: $1.00

Still in print?   No.

This book has many delicious and famous Southern recipes contributed by people of Wilkes county and vicinity. A number of these recipes are very rare, having been secured from people who regarded them as old family secrets.

Included are recipes for meats, vegetables, cakes and salads for the famous Southern dinners.

Bacon muffins, glorified rice pudding, Southern relish and Hard Times fruit cake are only a few of the tempting recipes given.

. . . .

Owner: Mrs. LeRoy Wright
             416 - 4th St., Augusta, Ga.

Title: Favorite Recipes

Author: Compiled by North Augusta Chapter of
             Winthrop Daughters, Augusta, Ga.

Publisher: Ridgley-Tidwell Company

Place of Publication: Augusta, Ga.

Date of Publication: 1929.

Price: 75 cents.

These recipes, contributed by the housewives of North Augusta and vicinity, include dishes for everyday meals and festive occasions. Some of the most unusual ones have been handed down for generations. Among the most popular recipes are pineapple salad, a favorite recipe of Mrs. Calvin Coolidge, and Heavenly Hash, which isn't a hash at all.

A very good recipe for Blackberry Wine is only one of the old and valuable wine recipes given.

. . . .

Owner: Mrs. LeRoy Wright
             416 - 4th St., Augusta, Ga.

Title: Digest of the Day

Author: Compiled by Central School P.T.A.

Date and place of publication not given.

Price: 25 cents.

This is a book of carefully selected and unusually fine menus and valuable recipes. There are many highly prized frozen recipes; among these are two very good ones for cherry almond parfait and caramel mousse. Included also are calorie charts, diet menus, time tables for cooking, health exercise, yearly budget charts and attractive illustrations of correct table service.

. . . .

Owner: Mrs. Ada Radford

        425 Milledge Rd., Augusta, Ga.

Title: Parent-Teachers Association Cook Book.

Author: Compiled by P.T.A. of Canton, Ga.

Publisher: Rudasill Printing Company, Canton, Ga.

Place of Publication: Canton, Georgia.

Date of Publication: 1925.

This book has 86 pages of delicious recipes contributed by people of Canton, Georgia. All the recipes are practical and were published in hopes of making menu planning and good cooking easier for the busy housewives of today. There are sixteen chapters in the book, each on different types of dishes such as vegetables, meats, cakes, pies and beverages.

Cranberry snow, salmon rice loaf, creamed chicken hash and Southern punch are only a few of the many tasty recipes in this book.

. . . .

Owner: Mrs. Luna A. Doolittle

        1021 D'Antignac St., Augusta, Ga.

Title: Spartanburg Housekeepers Cook Book

Presented by: Red Cross Flour Company, 1907.

This book has 132 pages of delicious and practical recipes. Although the recipes are written primarily for every day use, it has many helpful suggestions for dinners for festive occasions.

A very interesting recipe gives instructions on the curing of a 200 pound hog.

It tells how every part, from head to toe should be prepared.

Among the recipes for desserts is a very appetizing one for Bachelor Pudding.

. . . .

Owner: Mrs. Luna A. Doolittle

        1021 D'Antignac St., Augusta, Ga.

Title: Dr. Chase's Third, Last and Complete Receipt Book and Household Physician or Practical Knowledge for the People.

Author: A. W. Chase, M.D.

Publisher: Rowland Publishing Co., Atlanta, Ga. 1888.

This book has the choicest, most valuable and entirely new receipts and useful information on medicine, mechanics and household economy. Tasty recipes that will appeal to the sick person are wine jelly, arrowroot, pap, egg toast and graham pudding.

Delicious fruit or berry fritters and Prince of Wales cake are among the recipes for well people.

. . . .

Owner: Mrs. Fennell
          129 Broad St., Augusta, Ga.

Title: Fifty-two Sunday Dinners

Author: Elizabeth O. Hiller

Published by: The H. K. Fairbanks Co.,
                Chicago, Ill.

Copyright 1913 by H. K. Fairbanks Co.

Price: $1.00

This little book about 5 × 10 inches and 1 inch thick, has menus and recipes for fifty-two complete dinners, a dinner for every Sunday in the year. There are quotations and illustrated pictures for decorations and table services for each of these dinners. Included also are many interesting facts on the selection of meats and vegetables. The recipes for cherry pie in the spring and maced yams in the fall are two of the most tempting recipes given.

. . . .

Owner: Mrs. A. H. Nichols
          408 - 3rd St., Augusta, Ga.

Title: The White House Cook Book

Authors: Hugo Zieman and Mrs. F. L. Gillette

Publisher: The Saalfield Publishing Company, N. Y.,
              Akron, Ohio, Chicago, 1908.

Price: $2.00 - 590 Pages.

This book has much valuable information for the housewife. There are chapters on cooking, menus, dinner giving, table etiquette and health suggestions. Facts concerning the White House such as the menus served on special occasions, pictures of the dining rooms and portraits of all the first ladies share a prominent place in this book.

Menus for one week in each month of the year provides for the serving of all seasonable vegetables. Among the many delicious recipes given are ones for baked turkey, cranberry sauce and cream gravy.

. . . .

Owner: Mrs. Jack Rountree
          257 Telfair St., Augusta, Ga.

Title: The "Dixie" Cook Book

Front cover and imprint leaf missing. 688 Pages.

> This book has many practical recipes for everyday use that are of real value to all. Testimonials dated in 1880, praise the trustworthiness of the recipes for cakes, pies, vegetables, salads, ice cream, soups, bread, meat, meat curing, pickling. In the canning section there are some very good recipes for pickled peaches and sour Kraut. Also has useful information on household hints and management of servants.

. . . .

Owner: Young Men's Library, Augusta, Ga.

Title: Catering for Two

Author: Alice L. James

Publisher: G. P. Putnam's Sons

Place of Publication: New York

Date of Publication: 1907

Copyright: 1898

Price: No price listed.

Still in print?   Don't know.

> This book contains recipes for two people and although they sound delicious, they were written at a time when a woman had little to do but cook. Some of the recipes that are especially good, as well as practical, are oyster pie, hot potato salad and Princess cream. Others such as green tomato chili sauce, oxtail soup and steamed cherry pudding are listed as every day dishes, but the busy woman of today would not have time to prepare them.
>
>   "Throw a few sticks of kindling on the fire and then set meat in oven;" "put in cold water to chill;" and "bake in a quick, but not fierce oven" are only a few of the quaint and out-of-date instructions given.

. . . .

Owner: Mrs. Ruby Johnson
          805 - 13th St., Augusta, Ga.

Title: Recipes of all Nations

Author: Countess Morphy

Publisher: Wise & Co.

Place of Publication: New York

Date of Publication: 1935

Price: $2.00

Still in Print? Yes.

This book contains over eight hundred pages of recipes from twenty-nine different countries. Many have never been in print before but all are typical from the country from which they came. A few of the tasty dishes for which this book gives the recipes are:

Bleeny, a Russian pancake made of buckwheat flour, which is served with sour cream and caviar.

"Intoxicated Pig," an Italian dish, received its name from the red wine in which it is cooked.

Spanish Beefsteak, which is prepared by stewing the steak in an earthenware dish and serving with stuffed eggplant.

Shepherd's Pie, an English dish prepared from left-overs.

Many varieties of French pastry.

. . . .

Owner: Junior College, Augusta, Ga.

Title: The Settlement Cook Book

Author: Compiled by Mrs. Simon Kander

Publisher: The Settlement Cook Book Co.

Place of Publication: Milwaukee, Wis.

Date of Publication: 1940.

Price: $2.50

Still in Print? Yes.

This book contains over 3,000 recipes of which hundreds are in no other cook book. Simple directions cover entire field of cookery. It not only tells you how to cook, but tells you what to cook. Menus for daily use, informal and formal dinners, holiday dinners and all festive occasions are given. Liver loaf, chicken (Creole style), and Swedish layer cake are only a few of the tempting recipes given.

Bibliography

Offering Further Sources for Menus, Receipts,
and Eating Habits of Southern California.

America Cooks, Brown, C. L. Norton, New York, cir. 1940

American Cookery from California, (Good Housekeeping, New York, 1919, v. 69,
Sept., p. 61

As California Cooks, Conklin, Hester M. & Partridge, Pauline D. (Good Housekeeping, New York, 1921, v. 72, Feb., p. 67.)

Bohemian San Francisco, Edwords, C. E. Elder, San Francisco, cir. 1914.

California Cook Book, Belle, F. P. Regan, Chicago, 1925.

California Orange Cook Book, Barton, F. G. San Bernardino, cir. 1928.

Chef Wyman's Daily Health Menus, Wyman, A. L. Los Angeles, cir. 1927.

Chow, Liu, Dolly. Suttonhouse, San Francisco, 1939.

Clew Cook Book, Weiskirch, L. E. American, Los Angeles, cir. 1930.

Conservation Recipes, Mobilized Women's Organizations of Berkeley. *Courier,*
Berkeley, 1917.

Cook Book of Home Tried Recipes by Women of Carpinteria Valley, California,
Compilation.

Culinary Arts Western Cookery, Morrow, Kay. Culinary Arts Reading, Pennsylvania, cir. 1936.

Early California Hospitality, Packman, A. B. Clark, Glendale, 1936.

Eating Around San Francisco, Thompson, Ruth. Suttonhouse, San Francisco,
cir. 1937.

Famous Stars' Famous Foods, Sniff, Fannie. Hollywood, cir. 1938.

Fashions in Food in Beverly Hills, Beverly Hills Woman's Club. Beverly Hills
Citizen, Beverly Hills, 1931.

Favorite Recipes of the Famous Movie Stars, Schulman, B. Donald Milwaukee,
Wisconsin, 1934.

First Foods of America, McNeil, Blanche. Suttonhouse, Los Angeles, cir. 1936.

Five Hundred Ways to Cook California Sea Food, California State Fish
   Exchange, Sacramento, 1927.

Hollywood's Famous Recipes of the Movie Stars, Knight, Midge. Los Angeles,
   1932.

I'd Like the Recipe, Yeates, L. L. Compiler, Pasadena, 1938.

Landmarks Club Cook Book, Compilation. Out West, Los Angeles, 1905.

Los Angeles Times Prize Cook Book. Times-Mirror, Los Angeles, 1923.

Acknowledgments

I want to first of all thank Patrick Kerwin, a manuscript reference librarian at the Library of Congress, for his patience and invaluable assistance. I also want to thank Susan Birnbaum for her help. And my sister Ellen Kurlansky for her hospitality and friendship in Washington. Also my wonderful agent, Charlotte Sheedy, for standing by me, Geoffrey Kloske for his faith in me, and my great editor, Nancy Miller, with whom I have had such a good time doing a dozen books. And a special thanks to Marian, whom I love even more than all the good clams we've eaten.

Suggested Reading

Algren, Nelson. *America Eats*. Iowa City: University of Iowa Press, 1992.

Baron, Robert C., ed. *The Garden and Farm Books of Thomas Jefferson*. Golden, CO: Fulcrum, 1987.

Bordelon, Pamela. *Go Gator and Muddy the Water: Writings by Zora Neale Hurston from the Federal Writers' Project*. New York: W.W. Norton, 1999.

Davidson, Alan. *The Oxford Companion to Food*. New York: Oxford University Press, 1999.

Digges, Jeremiah. *Cape Cod Pilot: A Loquacious Guide*. Provincetown: Modern Pilgrim Press, 1937.

Donohue, H.E.F. *Conversations with Nelson Algren*. New York: Hill and Wang, 1964.

Drew, Bettina. *Nelson Algren: A Life on the Wild Side*. New York: G. P. Putnam and Sons, 1989.

Drury, John. *Rare and Well Done: Some Historical Notes on Meat and Meatmen*. Chicago: Quadrangle Books, 1966.

Edge, John T. *A Gracious Plenty: Recipes and Recollections from the American South*. New York: G. P. Putnam's Sons, 1999.

Fussell, Betty. *The Story of Corn: The Myths and History, the Culture and Agriculture, the Art and Science of America's Quintessential Crop*. New York: Alfred A Knopf, 1992.

Harvey, Chance. *The Life and Selected Letters of Lyle Saxon*. Gretna, LA: Pelican Publishing Company, 2003.

Kiple, Kenneth F. and Kriemhild Coneè Ornelas, eds. *The Cambridge World History of Food*, 2 volumes. Cambridge: Cambridge University Press, 2000.

MacDougall, Allan Ross. *The Gourmets' Almanac*. New York: Covici-Friede, 1930.

Mangione, Jerre. *The Dream and The Deal: The Federal Writers' Project 1935–1943.* New York: Avon Books, 1972.

Mariani, John F. *The Dictionary of American Food & Drink.* New York: Ticknor & Fields, 1983.

McClane, A. J. *The Encyclopedia of Fish Cookery.* New York: Henry Holt and Company, 1977.

Nabhan, Gary Paul. *Renewing America's Food Traditions: Saving and Savoring the Continent's Most Endangered Foods.* White River Junction, VT: Chelsea Green Publishing, 2008.

Oliver, Sandra L. *Saltwater Foodways: New Englanders and their food at sea and ashore in the nineteenth century.* Mystic, CT: Mystic Seaport Museum, 1995.

Penkower, Monty Noam. *The Federal Writers' Project: A Study in Government Patronage of the Arts.* Urbana: University of Illinois Press, 1977.

Rawlings, Marjorie Kinnan. *Cross Creek.* New York: Charles Scribner's Sons, 1942.

Root, Waverley. *Food.* New York: Simon and Schuster, 1980.

Root, Waverley, and Richard de Rochemont. *Eating in America: A History.* New York: William Morrow & Co., 1976.

Wormser, Michael. *"Collecting the WPA State Guides." Firsts: The Book Collector's Magazine.* Volume 12, Number 6, June 2002.

Index

Mark Kurlansky is the *New York Times*–bestselling and James A. Beard Award–winning author of many books, including *Cod: A Biography of the Fish That Changed the World*; *Salt: A World History*; *1968: The Year That Rocked the World*; *The Big Oyster: History on the Half Shell*; *The Last Fish Tale: The Fate of the Atlantic and Survival in Gloucester, America's Oldest Fishing Port and Most Original Town*; and *Nonviolence: The History of a Dangerous Idea*, as well as the novel *Boogaloo on 2nd Avenue*. He is the winner of a *Bon Appétit* American Food and Entertaining Award for Food Writer of the Year, and the Glenfiddich Food and Drink Award for Food Book of the Year, as well as a finalist for the *Los Angeles Times* Book Prize. He lives in New York City.